China's Aid to Africa

Although China has rapidly increased foreign aid to Africa and is now a relatively major player in the developmental assistance regime, little is still known regarding how China delivers its foreign aid, and even less about how this foreign aid actually works in the recipient countries.

This book, extensively utilising Chinese sources, many of which have not been available before, examines the effectiveness and sustainability of China's foreign aid in Africa, as well as the political, economic and diplomatic factors that influence Chinese aid disbursement policies. The book argues that a nebulous notion of "friendship", however ill-defined, is a key factor in Chinese aid, something which is often overlooked by Western scholars. Through a detailed examination of both the decision-making process in Chinese aid disbursements, as well as an examination of specific case studies in West Africa, this book improves our understanding of China's foreign aid policies towards Africa. It finds that there are profound shortcomings in China's foreign aid at present which, despite the protestations of "friendship" and solidarity, undermine Beijing's effectiveness as an actor in the developmental assistance enterprise in Africa.

This text will be of key interest to scholars and students of development studies, African studies, China-Africa relations and more broadly to international relations.

Zhangxi Cheng is Research Fellow at the School of International Relations, University of St Andrews, UK.

Ian Taylor is Professor in International Relations and African Political Economy at the University of St. Andrews (UK); Chair Professor at Renmin University of China (China); Professor Extraordinary at the University of Stellenbosch (South Africa) and Professor at the Centre of African Studies, Federal University of Rio Grande do Sul (Brazil).

Routledge Studies in African Politics and International Relations

Edited by Daniel C. Bach

Emile Durkheim Centre for Comparative Politics and Sociology, Sciences Po Bordeaux

3 **The Politics of Elite Corruption in Africa**
Roger Tangri and Andrew M. Mwenda

4 **Reconstructing the Authoritarian State in Africa**
George Klay Kieh, Jr. and Pita Ogaba Agbese

5 **Critical Perspectives on African Politics**
Liberal interventions, state-building and civil society
Edited by Clive Gabay and Carl Death

6 **Homegrown Development in Africa**
Reality or illusion?
Chukwumerije Okereke and Patricia Agupusi

7 **Real Governance and Practical Norms in Sub-Saharan Africa**
The game of the rules
Edited by Tom de Herdt and Jean-Pierre Olivier de Sardan

8 **African Migrants and Europe**
Managing the ultimate frontier
Lorenzo Rinelli

9 **Africa in Global International Relations**
Emerging approaches to theory and practice
Edited by Paul-Henri Bischoff, Kwesi Aning and Amitav Acharya

10 **Regionalism in Africa**
Genealogies, institutions and trans-state networks
Daniel C. Bach

11 **China's Aid to Africa**
Does Friendship Really Matter?
Zhangxi Cheng and Ian Taylor

China's Aid to Africa

Does Friendship Really Matter?

Zhangxi Cheng and Ian Taylor

LONDON AND NEW YORK

First published 2017
by Routledge
2 Park Square, Milton Park, Abingdon, Oxon OX14 4RN

and by Routledge
711 Third Avenue, New York, NY 10017

Routledge is an imprint of the Taylor & Francis Group, an informa business

© 2017 Zhangxi Cheng and Ian Taylor

The right of Zhangxi Cheng and Ian Taylor to be identified as authors of this work has been asserted by them in accordance with sections 77 and 78 of the Copyright, Designs and Patents Act 1988.

All rights reserved. No part of this book may be reprinted or reproduced or utilised in any form or by any electronic, mechanical, or other means, now known or hereafter invented, including photocopying and recording, or in any information storage or retrieval system, without permission in writing from the publishers.

Trademark notice: Product or corporate names may be trademarks or registered trademarks, and are used only for identification and explanation without intent to infringe.

British Library Cataloguing-in-Publication Data
A catalogue record for this book is available from the British Library

Library of Congress Cataloging-in-Publication Data
Names: Cheng, Zhangxi, author. | Taylor, Ian, 1969– author.
Title: China's aid to Africa : does friendship really matter? / Zhangxi Cheng and Ian Taylor.
Description: Abingdon, Oxon ; New York, NY : Routledge, 2017. | Series: Routledge studies in African politics and international relations ; 11 | Includes bibliographical references and index.
Identifiers: LCCN 2016053636 | ISBN 9781138630390 (hardback) | ISBN 9781315209432 (ebook)
Subjects: LCSH: Economic assistance, Chinese—Africa. | China—Foreign economic relations—Africa. | Africa—Foreign economic relations—China. | China—Foreign relations—Africa. | Africa—Foreign relations—China.
Classification: LCC HC800 .C43 2017 | DDC 338.91/5106—dc23
LC record available at https://lccn.loc.gov/2016053636

ISBN: 978-1-138-63039-0 (hbk)
ISBN: 978-1-315-20943-2 (ebk)

Typeset in Times New Roman
by Apex CoVantage, LLC

Printed and bound in Great Britain by
TJ International Ltd, Padstow, Cornwall

This book is dedicated to the memory of Cheng Yucheng (1956–2013)

Contents

Author's note

Unless otherwise specified, the term *China's foreign aid* in this study refers to *China's Official Bilateral Development Assistance*. It therefore differs from China's other foreign aid activities such as Military Aid, Humanitarian Aid, Peacekeeping and participation in International Multilateral Aid.

Whilst this study adopts official translations for titles and policies that were originally introduced in Chinese, not all of these have an official English translation. Whilst some of the interviewees spoke English as their first or second language, the majority of the interviews in this study were conducted in Chinese. In these situations, the information obtained in Chinese has been translated into English by Zhangxi Cheng. Important titles, events, documents and quotations are accordingly noted in the body of the text and endnotes in their original language for further clarification.

Acknowledgements

The authors gratefully acknowledge the help given to this study by Liu Liyun at Renmin University; Li Xiaoyun at China Agricultural University; Liu Hongwu, Xiao Yuhua, Niu Changsong and Hu Mei at Zhejiang Normal University; He Wenping at the Chinese Academy of Social Sciences; and Mao Xiaojing at the Chinese Academy of International Trade and Economic Cooperation of MOFCOM. The numerous interviewees in both China and Africa are also deeply thanked. Family and friends are of course thanked for their support.

Acronyms

AIBO	Academy for International Business Officials
APC	All People's Congress
CAITEC	Chinese Academy of International Trade and Economic Cooperation
CCCPC	Central Committee of the Communist Party of China
CCP	Chinese Communist Party
CDB	China Development Bank
CECEP	China Energy Conservation and Environment Protection Group
CGC	China GEO-Engineering Corporation
CICETE	China International Centre for Economic and Technical Exchanges
CIRR	Commercial Interest Reference Rates
COMPLANT	Complete Plant Import and Export Cooperation Group
CPC	Communist Party of China
CRTV	China Radio and TV
CSSD	Central Sterile Supply Department
CT	Computed Tomography
DAC	Development Assistance Committee
FDI	Foreign Direct Investment
FOCAC	Forum of China-Africa Cooperation
GIETC	China Guangzhou International Economic Technical Cooperation Co.
HRDC	Human Resources Development Cooperation
IMF	International Monetary Fund
LDG	Least Developed Country
LIC	Low-income Country
MFA	Ministry of Foreign Affairs
MOF	Ministry of Finance
MOFCOM	Ministry of Commerce
MOFTEC	Ministry of Foreign Trade and Economic Cooperation
ODA	Official Development Assistance
OECD	Organisation for Economic Co-operation and Development
OOF	Other Official Flows

SLPP	Sierra Leone People's Party
SOE	State Owned Enterprise
UN	United Nations
UNDP	United Nations Development Programme
UNIDO	United Nations Industrial Development Organization
WB	World Bank
Xinhua	Xinhua News Agency

Introduction

When asked why China gave aid to African countries, the then–Vice Minister of the Ministry of Commerce Fu Ziying, replied that China was in Africa 'for friendship' (*Xinhua*, 2011). The context was that journalists were insinuating that China was scrambling for natural resources on the continent. The question was raised during the media conference on the release of China's first official foreign aid publication, *The White Paper on China's Foreign Aid*.

Over the past two decades, the rapid development of China-Africa relationship has attracted tremendous attention worldwide. In view of China's continuously growing foreign aid budget, increasing investments, and its steadily deepening cooperation with African countries, every move that China has taken on the continent is under intense scrutiny. Particularly after the launch of the Forum on China-Africa Cooperation (FOCAC) in 2000, along with the wider global theme that emphasised African development, the relationship between China and Africa has made headlines. What has been interesting is that whilst all African recipient countries welcome China's foreign aid, many external voices have been tirelessly criticising China's alleged "real motivations" on the continent. Not only has China been accused of scrambling for African natural resources, but it has also been blamed for worsening corruption, hampering alleged Western efforts in establishing African democracies, as well as causing serious environmental problems (Brautigam, 2009).

Particular Western media sources and reports, regardless of the repeated clarifications and explanations made in academic research (see Woods, 2008; Cotula et al., 2009; Dreher and Fuchs, 2012; Yan and Sautman, 2013), continuously publishes articles that condemn China for violating human rights in African recipient countries (see Dasgupta, 2015), allow African presidents to use Chinese foreign aid for patronage politics (see Anderson, 2014), and argue that, 'China often gives aid directly to state leaders and regimes', and as a result, receiving African government become more violent towards its citizens (see Kishi and Raleigh, 2015). Further, by completely ignoring the non-interference principle, one of the most symbolic and well-discussed features of China's foreign aid (see Taylor, 2008; Hess and Aidoo, 2010; Condon, 2012; Grimm, 2014, and many others), one recent report from the *Financial Times* even went as far as suggesting that 'few policymakers in the developing world trust China's advice' (see Donnan, 2015). This is curious given that another critique of China in Africa is that the Chinese do not give any development advice at all.

In fact, despite recent interest in China's foreign aid in Africa, Beijing has a long foreign aid history that is no less than other so-called traditional foreign aid donor countries. To provide some historical context, from the 1950s onwards, China has extended its foreign aid to 51 African countries, and improved its foreign aid approaches to include three main funding methods and six implementation methods. However, regardless of these valuable experiences as a foreign aid donor country, detailed accounts of China's foreign aid exercises in Africa are still largely absent from existing studies. In the light of this situation, apart from continuously looking for China's ostensible "real" motivations in Africa or adopting estimated figures which are then deployed to criticise China's involvements on the African continent, this study seeks to improve our understanding of how China delivers its foreign aid in Africa. It is from this query that this study seeks to discuss how China delivers its foreign aid to Africa, how China's foreign aid has impacted upon Africa's development, and how the performance of China's foreign aid in Africa can be further improved.

Previous studies on Chinese aid to Africa

There is a developing literature on contemporary China's foreign aid to Africa. A few scholars such as Brautigam (2008) and Kragelund (2008) as well as the recently released work by the AidData project (see http://aiddata.org), have attempted estimates of China's foreign aid to Africa, bearing in the mind the absence and lack of transparency within this sector. Both Kragelund and Brautigam concur that, even though China is one of Africa's major aid donors, aid flows from China are relatively small when compared to the flows from Organisation for Economic Co-operation and Development (OECD) Development Assistance Committee (DAC) countries. Especially in her 2009 book, *The Dragon's Gift*, Brautigam discusses the differences between Official Development Assistance (ODA) and Other Official Flows (OOF), stating that most Western foreign aid is ODA, while most China's foreign aid is OOF. A critique of Brautigam's work, however, might be that it seems strongly influenced by her extensive cooperation with Chinese officials and is in some ways too optimistic about the efficacy of China's foreign aid.

Obviously, some scholars (see Youde, 2010; Jiang, 2014) have questioned the motivation of China's foreign aid to Africa. For them, China gains both economic and political benefits and obtains more opportunities for trade and access to natural resources through giving aid; and China's image in the African continent is enhanced and friendship and goodwill are improved at the same time (see Askouri, 2007; Marks, 2007; Naim, 2007; Rotberg, 2008). Scholars such as Pehnelt (2007) have been very critical of Chinese policies with regards to the nature, modalities and composition of Beijing's foreign aid. Pehnelt is particularly concerned about China's non-interference policy which allegedly prompts China not to take into consideration at all the quality of governance in the recipient countries. This is a familiar criticism, usually implying that China is willing to provide foreign aid to unstable, problematic and rogue countries without taking into consideration issues such as human rights. Kaplinsky and Morris (2006) have similarly pointed to several examples of China's significant involvement in "fragile states". It should be pointed out here however that thus far no one has attempted to provide a proven correlation to strengthen claims that China provides foreign aid with little or no regards on the recipient quality of governance (or that this is qualitatively different from Western aid regimes, which equally support non-democratic regimes if and when "national interest" dictates).

Interestingly, Shinn (2009) compares US and Chinese interests in Africa and concludes that they are similar. Shinn suggested that the similarities between US and Chinese interests in Africa created a base for broader cooperation. As an ex-US ambassador, Shinn served in numerous African posts (including as US Ambassador to Ethiopia). Thus his viewpoint is important and cannot be discounted.

Scholars such as Davies et al. (2008), whilst acknowledging some of the controversial aspects of China's foreign aid to Africa, conclude that China's ongoing relations with both Angola and Sudan are mutually beneficial. To further support this position, Nour (2010) argues that even though there are some lapses within the parameters of China's foreign aid to Sudan, China's funding and implementation of project aid in Sudan had a positive impact, for instance in increasing the availability of services, increases in skill levels, increases in production levels, the transfer of knowledge and availability of machinery, equipment and employment opportunities. Guloba et al.'s (2010) research on China's foreign aid to Uganda further supported similar tentative positive impacts of China's foreign aid. Whilst acknowledging these possibilities, however, the study highlighted some major concerns surrounding China's foreign aid. These included the marginal employment of locals and the continuous utilisation of Chinese expatriates where projects are effectuated. Nonetheless, the findings indicated that China's foreign aid (which is mainly in the form of technical assistance through training in Chinese institutions, grants, interest-free loans, preferential loans, debt relief, etc.) have all gone towards reducing Uganda's external burden and, hence, have had a positive impact on the Ugandan peoples' welfare. Wang (2010) further delineates some positive impacts of China's foreign aid by making references to China's substantial funding of multipurpose development projects in sectors such as power supply (hydropower) and transportation (railways and motorways), which are sectors within recipient countries that attracts relatively small assistance from the traditional (Western) donors.

Within this context, this study aims to improve our understanding of China's foreign aid in Africa. It builds on the findings of earlier studies and shares in part with 'the "mainstream" assumptions that underdevelopment and poverty are objective, measureable phenomena, and that foreign aid, when designed and implemented appropriately in a supportive policy and institutional environment in recipient countries, can further development' (Lancaster, 1999: 10). In addition to this, on the basis of noting Brautigam's caveat that 'politics in the receiving country determine much of the sustainability of aid once it is received' (1998: 3), this study was carried out on the assumption that whilst the recipient countries' conditions are pre-existing (institutional deficiencies or a lack of human resources), the donor country, as a foreign aid provider, is responsible for adjusting its foreign aid accordingly to these conditions in order for its foreign aid to perform effectively and sustainably in these recipient countries.

Based on this assumption, this study draws particular attention to China's traditional foreign aid, which is the part of China's foreign aid that is solely funded by the foreign aid budget of the Chinese government, and is 'provided primarily to serve China's political interests'.[1] By definition, in accordance with the DAC, this is the part of foreign aid that is administered with the promotion of the economic development and welfare of developing countries as its main objective. In the words of Chinese foreign aid officials, this is the part of foreign aid that is implemented 'with a view of building friendly foreign relationships'.[2] In line with these claims, this is the part of China's foreign aid that uses the funding methods of Grant and Interest-free Loans (and Low-interest Loans). Low-interest Loans were a former funding method for China's foreign aid, terminated at the end of the 1980s. Although rather identical to China's contemporary Concessional Loans, Low-interest Loans were established solely relying on China's government foreign aid budget, and were only utilised with the intention to sustain China's foreign aid while China's economic capacity was extremely limited. Either way, Chinese aid to Africa is delivered via the implementation methods of Complete Project Aid, Technical Aid, Goods and Materials Aid, Human Resource Development Cooperation, Medical Teams and Overseas Volunteer Programs.

This aspect of China's foreign aid has been chosen as the focus of this study because China's traditional foreign aid conforms to the general understanding of the 'aid-for-development' norm (Lancaster, 2006: 7) and, albeit not in great detail, its amount can be easily identified via China's official publications. Unlike China's contemporary foreign aid, the amount of China's traditional foreign aid can be easily found either in *The White Paper of China's Foreign Aid*, or *China Statistical Yearbook*. Whereas regarding the other part of China's foreign aid, Concessional Loans, including Preferential Buyer's Credits and all other China EXIM Bank operated funding methods (termed 'contemporary foreign aid' in this study), it to some extent deviates from the foreign aid norm given that it is provided only if the proposed project is profitable. According to the loan regulations for Concessional Loans, concessional loan funded foreign aid projects must meet the requirement of "具有还本付息能力", i.e., the ability to repay capital and interests. Concessional loans "不再投向社会福利性项目, 有经济效益的除外" are no longer applicable to social charitable projects unless they have economic benefits.[3] This causes controversy in calculations (see Lum et al., 2009; Paulo and Reisen, 2010). In addition, focusing on China's "traditional" foreign aid is also appropriate considering that it has 'a broad range of flexibility'.[4]

It is built on this practical foundation that this study attaches specific importance to China's traditional foreign aid. Whilst improving our understanding of China's foreign aid in Africa, it attempts to find the ways in which this particular part of China's foreign aid could possibly further benefit African countries' development. In order to achieve this, this study now proposes three objectives to set out the understanding of China's foreign aid in Africa: understanding the development of China's foreign aid in Africa, assessing the performance of China's foreign aid in Africa and investigating the successes and failures of China's foreign aid in approaching the factors that affect its outcomes in Africa. To elaborate on this sequence, the first objective is particularly aimed at providing an overview of China's foreign aid in Africa. In the interests of establishing a foundation for the following assessment and investigation of China's foreign aid, this objective explores the foreign aid objectives that China has implemented in Africa, as well as the foreign aid planning and implementation approaches it accordingly has developed over decades to secure these objectives.

After grasping the development of China's foreign aid on paper, the second objective is then followed to take our understanding of China's foreign aid in Africa to the practical level. With the view of learning the effectiveness and sustainability of China's foreign aid in Africa, this objective observes and assesses three foreign aid packages that China delivered in West Africa according to its foreign aid objectives, and attempts to find out the factors that affected their outcomes. Moving to the third objective, this study investigates the successes and failures of China's foreign aid in approaching the factors that affected its outcomes. In order to bring our understanding of China's foreign aid in Africa further to its substance, this objective leads this study back to the development of China's foreign aid in Africa and identifies the hidden problems that have resulted. In addition to this, whilst going into details regarding the decision-making processes of China's foreign aid objectives, as well as the planning and implementation approaches of China's foreign aid projects and programs, it also searches for possible solutions that may improve the outcomes of China's foreign aid in Africa.

In short, improving our understanding of China's foreign aid in Africa is achieved in six steps: understanding the development of China's foreign aid in Africa; exploring China's foreign aid objectives and planning and implementation approaches; assessing the performance of China's foreign aid in Africa; finding out the factors that affect China's foreign aid effectiveness and sustainability; investigating how China's foreign aid approached the factors that affect its outcomes; and identifying the shortcomings of China's foreign aid at present.

"Friendship" as an analytical approach

As a donor country–centred foreign aid study, the above outlined scope of China's foreign aid, one that is driven by political interests, has seemingly made the theoretical approach of this study straightforward. After all, it almost completely reflects the Realist argument that foreign aid is an instrument of the donor countries for pursuing their national interests; however, there are two points that need to be addressed. First, as Liu Liyun of Renmin University has asserted, 'Albeit national interest is consistently underpinning the motivation of providing foreign aid in the real world, it is never the only consideration that determines foreign aid'.[5] Undoubtedly, being one of the most important diplomatic instruments, foreign aid is driven by complex motivations (Brautigam, 2009). Not only does this vary from donor to donor, it also evolves over time. As Lancaster pointed out in her study of five donor countries, 'No one theory can adequately explain this twentieth-century innovation in relations between states' (2006: 212).

Particularly in the research on China's foreign aid in Africa, apart from the obvious political and economic interests (such as fulfilling the obligations of proletarian internationalism during the 1950s and 1970s, seeking mutually beneficial economic cooperation during the 1980s and early 2000s, and promoting China-Africa strategic partnership more recently), considering the repeated mentioning of building 'friendly' foreign relationships, the question whether these claims are only rhetoric that hides China's real national interests in providing foreign aid is pertinent. Alternatively, given that China *is* actually building hospitals and other social facilities across Africa, does the concept of *friendship,* which is a typical moral value of Chinese philosophy, have any purchase in analysing China's political considerations vis-a-vis China's foreign aid in Africa?

Although the concept of friendship thus far has not been sufficiently discussed in Western studies on China's foreign aid, there is a developing literature on friendship in the broader context of International Relations. Whilst there are no fundamental differences between the friendship *per se* discussed in the Western international relations studies and Confucianism (they both share the emphasis on consideration for others), a significant difference is that studies tend to make distinctions between friendship between states and friendship between peoples (see Keller, 2009; Lu, C., 2009). Interestingly, Chinese political thought tends to regard state and people as integral: "国之本在家, 家之本在身" or, the state has its basis in the family, and the family has its basis in oneself (see De Bary, 2008). Of note, in the Chinese language, a state is called "国家", which directly translates as country-family.

As one of the core essences of Chinese philosophy, Confucianism (founded by Confucius, 孔子, 551–479 BC), emphasises friendship. In the modern-day interpretation of Confucian conceptions of harmony (和), this 'should be the highest pursuit of inter-state relations' (Zhang, 2012b: 56). Instead of solely emphasising power, security and self-interest (私利), Confucianism believes that a stable international status is achieved through the emphases on both self-interest and consideration for others and further asserts that even in disagreement, consideration for others should be given the utmost priority (Zhang and Qin, 2012). On the basis of stressing the balance between self-interest and consideration for others, not only has Confucianism suggested that a government should be 'embarrassed if their way of governing would involve naked self-interest' (Lengauer, 2011: 43), but also explicitly stresses that self-interest often leads to instability.

In light of this philosophy, whilst it completely differs from traditional Western concepts such as alliances in the eyes of the Realists (Lebow, 2007: 55–60), or, as Poncet attempted to make it, 'charity' (although she did point out that China's foreign aid tends to focus on countries with 'long-established relationships') (2012: 7), it is Lancaster's interpretation of 'creating warm relations with developing countries' (2007: 1) and Li's reading of 'the substance of a *win-win* situation is not only a simple share of benefits, but requires caring for and supporting poor and developing countries' (2010: 26) that most aptly grasp the essence of this friendship in China's foreign aid. Yet what needs to be clarified here is that although this study regards friendship as an integral part of China's national interests, in order to incorporate this concept with traditional Western understandings, friendship should be considered as a moral pursuit that is rooted in Chinese culture rather than a national interest that is built on Western values.[6] As an aside, this is reflected in a growing range of research specifically studying the influences of Confucianism in China's development and how adapted Confucianism helps understand the decision-making process of China's foreign policy (see Feng, 2007; Chen and Lee, 2008).

Thus this study takes up Bobiash's proposal that 'it is essential to analyse aid as it is . . . aid is intertwined with the activities of states, institutions, and diverse processes of development; its analysis is enriched when researchers draw upon diverse strands of the social sciences' (1992: 1–2). In addition to observing and assessing the performance of China's foreign aid in Africa with the conventionally considered political and economic factors in mind, so as to maximise our understanding of China's foreign aid in Africa, this study takes into account other subjects concerned with social, institutional and technological factors that likewise influence China's foreign aid performance in Africa. In all, this study understands China's foreign aid in Africa with two further integrated elements: first, friendship is introduced as an aspect of China's political considerations to its aid, and second, observation is applied to explain how China's foreign aid influenced the recipient countries' development.

Method

In view of Brautigam's earlier warning that 'the Chinese do not publish any official reports, figures, or evaluation of their aid' (2009: 20), and the limited and vague information stated in the published *White Paper* (MOFCOM 2011), this study has utilised various methods to piece together the information required for the above-proposed objectives. To be specific, in the understanding of the development of China's foreign aid in Africa, research was first conducted utilising both English and Chinese language sources. In order to get as close as possible to the original thoughts of Beijing in putting forward foreign aid objectives and adjusting foreign aid planning and implementation approaches, this study then consulted with well-established personal connections that Zhangxi Cheng (whose father and grandfather were Chinese diplomats in Africa for decades) has within the Chinese government. Cheng's connections resulted in access to documents, elite statements and files that are not in the public domain and to detailed records of the evolvement of China's foreign aid. Particularly in the interpretation of China's current foreign aid development, the majority of information included in this study is based on internally circulated government documents that have not previously been released to the public.

The practical assessment of China's foreign aid performance in Africa is based on fieldwork carried out in Sierra Leone and Ghana. Research was conducted onsite through the observation of eight of China's foreign aid projects. In Sierra Leone, research was conducted on the Magbass Sugar Complex, the Friendship Hospital, the National Stadium and the Youyi Building. In Ghana, research was carried out on the National Theatre, the Lekma Hospital, the Bui Dam and the Asogli Power Plant. Whilst in Africa, 26 Chinese and local foreign aid workers were interviewed, as well as large groups of Chinese and local employees working on the projects that were still in operation. In addition, one medical team in each of the two recipient countries was interviewed, alongside 21 foreign aid officials (including 2 African development planning officials, 2 African foreign affairs officials, and 12 Chinese diplomats). Interviewing local African informants complemented the information collected.

In China, interviews and discussions with scholars were held in the Chinese Academy of Social Sciences, Renmin University, Zhejiang Normal University and China Agricultural University. Additionally, some 20 Chinese foreign aid officials and researchers in all main departments involved in the planning and implementation of China's foreign aid were interviewed (namely, the Department of Aid to Foreign Countries of Ministry of Commerce [MOFCOM], the Department of Western Asian and African Affairs of MOFCOM, the Chinese Academy of International Trade and Economic Cooperation [CAITEC], the Executive Bureau of International Economic Cooperation, the China International Centre for Economic and Technical Exchanges [CICETE] and the Academy for International Business Officials [AIBO]). In addition, supplementary interviews and follow-ups with Chinese officials were conducted via the telephone and email. Of course, even though this study benefits from exclusive access to China's foreign aid officials, participants, projects and programs in Africa, it has its limitations.

Structural layout

The following chapters begin to pursue the objectives set out to improve our understanding of China's foreign in Africa. Purposed to identify China's foreign aid objectives in Africa, and the foreign aid planning and implementation approaches it accordingly developed, the first objective in understanding China's foreign aid development in Africa is carried out chronologically, with focuses on the emergence and the early development of China's foreign aid in Africa. Beginning with 1955, when the Bandung Conference promoted the first modern contact between China and Africa, and ending with 1993, when China's planned economic system was exploited to the limit, the development of China's foreign aid is broken down into four periods: The Beginning (1955–1963), The Development (1963–1970), The Outrageous (1971–1978), and The Initial Reform (1979–1993). This helps us investigates how China's foreign aid objectives evolved.

After grasping the initial development of China's foreign aid in Africa, with the same purpose of identifying China's foreign aid objectives in Africa and its accordingly developed foreign aid planning and implementation approaches, the study focuses on the contemporary development of China's foreign aid in Africa. Beginning with 1994, when the new market economic system brought along the funding method of Concessional Loans, and ending with 2012, when the latest FOCAC meeting held in Beijing proposed to open up new prospects for a new type of China-Africa strategic partnership, the study examines the development of China's foreign aid in two periods: The Further Reform (1994–2004) and The Return (2005–present). Whilst exploring how China's traditional foreign aid worked with its contemporary foreign aid, the study investigates China's current foreign aid objective in improving people's livelihoods. In addition to surveying the contemporary development of China's foreign aid in Africa, a detailed breakdown of China's current foreign aid set-up is presented.

Upon identifying the objectives of China's foreign aid in Africa, and the foreign aid planning and implementation approaches Beijing has accordingly developed to secure these objectives, the study looks at the implementation sites of China's foreign aid in Africa with a view to assessing the performance of China's foreign aid in Africa. Purposed to demonstrate the effectiveness and sustainability of China's foreign aid in assisting African recipient countries' development, and finding the factors that affect these outcomes, the study visits three foreign aid packages that China delivered to Africa: the Magbass Sugar Complex (Sierra Leone, 1982), the National Theatre (Ghana, 1992), and the Lekma Hospital (Ghana, 2010). Apart from bringing forth a practical view to the development of China's foreign aid in Africa, this examination compares and searches for the factors that affect the outcomes of China's foreign aid in Africa.

Subsequent to revealing the rather disappointing outcomes and finding factors that affect performance, the study then turns the focus back to the development of China's foreign aid in Africa with the aim of investigating the successes and failures of China's foreign aid in approaching the factors that affect its outcomes in Africa. Purposed to identify the hidden factors within the development of China's foreign aid itself that undermine its outcomes in Africa, and therefore shed light on the development of China's foreign aid, this work individually surveys the decision-making processes of China's foreign aid objectives, the allocation and packaging of China's foreign aid projects and programs, and the handling and supervision arrangements of China's foreign aid implementation. Not only does it offer an in-depth study of the current operation and arrangement of China's foreign aid, but upon understanding the underlying aspects of China's foreign aid, the study explores practical solutions that may improve the outcomes of China's foreign aid in Africa.

Subsequently, the study is concluded by a recapping of the development of China's foreign aid in Africa, centred around the intention to build friendly foreign relationships. In addition to highlighting China's largely unimproved foreign aid outcomes in assisting African recipient countries' development, and the shortcomings that China's foreign aid must overcome, it summarises the ways in which China's foreign aid may make more contributions to African recipient countries' development.

On the whole, this study in understanding China's foreign aid in Africa finds China's foreign aid in Africa as simple yet complicated. It is simple because for most of the time there is only one goal that the Chinese government is aimed to pursue – friendship. It is complicated because this 'friendship' has been secured through miscellaneous projects and programs that are planned and implemented according to various foreign aid objectives. In essence, this study suggests that whilst aimed at helping African recipient countries achieve self-reliance, China's foreign aid is driven by the underlying political consideration of building friendly foreign relationships. On the one hand, this friendship is bringing China's foreign aid both the uniqueness that is welcomed by many African recipient countries and the largely unconstrained planning framework; on the other hand, it is also undermining China's foreign aid outcomes in Africa. In the end, as this study points out, if China could attach as much importance to the improvement of its foreign aid capacity as it is now emphasising on friendship, China's foreign aid may make a greater and better impact on Africa's development.

Notes

1 Interview with senior Chinese official, Freetown, Sierra Leone, 2 September 2011.
2 Interviews with Chinese officials, Freetown, Sierra Leone; Accra, Ghana; Beijing, China, 2011 and 2012.
3 Unpublished document, *The Loan Regulations of the EXIM Bank.*
4 Discussion with senior Chinese officials, Beijing, China, 19 November 2011.
5 Interview with Prof. Liu Liyun, Renmin University, Beijing, China, 27 November 2011.
6 Ibid.

1 Foreign aid

Measurements and studies

As an initial step towards improving our understanding of China's foreign aid in Africa, this chapter looks into the terminology of "foreign aid" and the existing literature on the subject. In the interests of establishing a framework for the study, as well as integrating it with prior knowledge, this chapter is arranged in two sections discussing standard definitions of foreign aid and how China's foreign aid in Africa has been previously researched.

Even amongst international organisations such as the DAC, the World Bank and the International Monetary Fund (IMF), different criteria summarises different scopes of foreign aid (also known as development assistance). Given this situation, relying on the donor country's description of foreign aid can be problematic. For instance, in the Chinese *White Paper* on aid, it is stated that 'Concessional Loans are mainly used to help recipient countries to undertake productive projects generating both economic and social benefits and large and medium-sized infrastructure projects' (2011: 8). Yet two pages over, it is written in the 'Forms of Foreign Aid' section, that 'Complete projects refer to productive or civil projects constructed in recipient countries with the help of financial resources provided by China as Grants or Interest-free Loans' (2011: 10). Notably, the second release of *The White Paper on China's Foreign Aid* in 2014 did not manage to clarify this issue. In light of these official definitions, what is then the *form of foreign aid* employed that happens to be delivering a productive project financed by Concessional Loans?

What *is* foreign aid?

In the understanding of this most widespread yet confusing international behaviour, foreign aid is recognised in many different ways. Whilst generally speaking, according to the *Oxford Dictionary*, 'Foreign Aid' is plainly defined as 'money, food, or other resources given or lent by one country to another'; within the discipline of International Relations, the understanding of foreign aid is noticeably more complicated. With particular concerns to ODA, in spite of the fact that foreign aid is clearly defined by the DAC as the official and concessional part of resource flows to developing countries that is administered with the promotion of the economic development and welfare of developing countries as its main objective, considering the substance of resource flows, it is more complicated. Not only based on varied criteria, the scope of these parts of resource flows are individually outlined by different foreign aid research and participating parties, but, depending on the various perspectives adopted by these parties, they are also frequently put into different categories. Even considering the research that is aimed at helping explain this behaviour, diversified approaches also lead to different interpretations. In view of this situation, for the purpose of providing an overview of the theme of this study, this section first delves into the broadly accepted criteria, perspectives and approaches to find out where China's foreign aid resides in these miscellaneous understandings.

On the basis of the above-stated ODA definition, given by the DAC, there are two internationally accepted criteria: the DAC's criteria (for recognising the scope of foreign aid to ODA recipients and ODA eligible organisations), and the World Bank's and IMF's criteria (for recognising the scope of foreign aid to Low-income Countries [LICs]). In accordance with the Development Assistance Committee of the Organisation for Economic Co-operation and Development, foreign aid (ODA) is the part of resource flows to developing countries that is provided by official agencies, including state and local governments, or by their executive agencies, and is concessional in character and conveys a grant element of at least 25 per cent (calculated at a rate of discount of 10 per cent). Based on revisions implemented in October 2013, the World Bank and the IMF currently adopt a single, fixed and unified rate of discount to calculate the grant element of the resource flows (foreign aid) to LICs. In contrast to the previous rate of discount based on currency-specific Commercial Interest Reference Rates (CIRRs), the new rate of discount is set at 5 per cent and will be calculated based only on the US dollar value of the resource flows.

Apart from the earlier introduced greater categories, which were determined by the nature of the foreign aid, with regards to development assistance in particular, there also are four broadly adopted perspectives used for classifying its conduct: the participants of the foreign aid, the financial resources of the foreign aid, the packaging of the foreign aid and the focusing area of the foreign aid. With regard to the participants of foreign aid, the exercise of this is usually divided into two main categories: Bilateral Aid and Multilateral Aid. Bilateral Aid (双边援助) refers to the aid that the donor country directly transfers to its recipient countries. Although in recent years, there has been an increase in participation in International Multilateral Aid, 'around 70% of ODA from the DAC participating countries are Bilateral Aid at any given time' (Zhang, 2012b: 27). Bilateral Aid certainly remains the primary practice in development assistance. As far as implementation is concerned, Bilateral Aid is considerably easier to process than International Multilateral Aid. More importantly, whilst Bilateral Aid only involves the donor and the recipient country as the participants, it also 'grants the donor country much greater flexibility in terms of integrating particular aims to its foreign aid so that the donor country can achieve its national interests and establish its national image' (Ding, 2010: 19).

On the basis that participation in International Multilateral Aid is generally not regarded as development assistance, in the study of China's foreign aid, the term Multilateral Aid (多边援助) is recognised differently from English language usage. Instead of referring to donations to International Multilateral Aid agencies, Multilateral Aid in Chinese literature refers *only* to 'China's foreign aid to multiple recipient countries'.[1] For example, one training program that China organised might enrol participants from several recipient countries. This would be classified by the Chinese as Multilateral Aid. With a view to separating China's Multilateral Aid from its participation in International Multilateral Aid, one senior Chinese researcher has suggested that 'All of China's participations in International Multilateral Aid are detailed and stated as it is in Chinese language based literatures, including official publications'.[2]

On the ground, the majority of foreign aid can be classified into two main categories: Grant Aid and Loan Aid. Grant Aid (无偿援助) is the type of foreign aid in which the donor country transfers resources to its recipient countries without any financial reservations. With Grant Aid, the recipient country is not held responsible for compensating the resources received, meaning that it can use the resources free of charge and need not repay the principal or interest. As for the recipient country, this is one of the most favoured types of foreign aid. Since Grant Aid is practically organised on a donation basis, the scale of Grant Aid is generally small in comparison to Loan Aid. In contrast to Grant Aid, Loan Aid (贷款援助) refers to the foreign aid which the recipient country is held responsible for compensating resources received. Although this is the most challenging type of foreign aid to determine and is based on varied criteria, one could be regarded as foreign aid and the other is not. Loan Aid is the preferred practice by most donor countries, including China.

Depending on the ways foreign aid is utilised, foreign aid is primarily broken in two categories: Project Aid and Programme Aid. Project Aid (项目援助) concerns aid in which the donor country applies its aid budget directly in the assistance of particular development projects in recipient countries. Other than constructing development facilities such as factories, roads and hospitals, programs organised for training human resources, medical assistances and so on are also regarded as Project Aid. At present, Project Aid is the most common type of foreign aid utilised by both emerging and traditional donor countries. Programme Aid (方案援助) refers to aid that supports particular development plans in recipient countries. Instead of building or organising specific foreign aid projects, it is utilised for import allocations, budget subsidies, allowances for balance of payments, debt repayment and regional development planning. Besides being frequently employed by the UN as part of International Multilateral Aid, Programme Aid is especially favoured by traditional foreign aid donors.

With reference to the development areas that the foreign aid is intended to assist, aid is often put into several different categories. Of these, the most common categories are Industrial Aid and Agricultural Aid. Industrial Aid (工业援助) involves aid that is aimed at promoting recipient country's industrial development. Provided the scale and complexities of most industrial projects, this particular type of foreign aid is usually financed by Loan Aid, and it is delivered through Project Aid including a combination of the construction of the project and training programs.

Where the recipient country requires, Industrial Aid may at times also include the marketing of the final product. Agricultural Aid (农业援助) refers to the foreign aid that is aimed at assisting the recipient country's agricultural development. Owing to the relatively longer period of investment, Agricultural Aid is also commonly financed by Loan Aid and is delivered via Project Aid (generally involving the dispatch of agricultural experts, the building of irrigation stations, agricultural technology demonstration centres and experimental farms).

China's foreign aid

All in all, based on the above identified definitions of foreign aid, with the exceptions of government foreign aid budgets utilised for Military Aid, Humanitarian Aid, Peacekeeping and participation in International Multilateral Aid, it can be found that based on the information given by *The White Paper* (2011), China's foreign aid is primarily arranged as bilateral development assistance following the aim of helping recipient countries achieve self-reliance. Whilst China's Grant Aid and Loan Aid (Interest-free Loans; Concessional Loans) measure up to both the DAC and the United Nations' and IMF's criteria, it is comprehensively focused on improving the recipient countries' development capacities in industry, agriculture, economic infrastructure, public facilities, education, medicine and public health. In the delivery of these development assistance packages to developing countries, China's foreign aid is overall packaged as Project Aid using six implementation methods i.e. Complete Project Aid, Technical Aid, Goods and Materials Aid, Human Resource Development Cooperation, Medical Teams and Overseas Volunteer Programs.

Ever since the swift take-off of modern China-Africa relationship in the late-1990s, the interest in this subject has grown dramatically. However, in spite of this great interest, whilst the studies on foreign aid and, indeed, China-Africa relations are fast expanding, studies thus far that have particularly focused on China's foreign aid in Africa are still noticeably limited. Besides, only some efforts have been made to understand the development and the practices of China's foreign aid in Africa. Before reviewing the existing literature, there is one point and two books that need to be first mentioned.

There are two arguably comprehensive books that underpin current understandings of Chinese aid to Africa. These are namely 对外经济合作 (*Economic Cooperation with Foreign Countries*), by Shi Lin (1989), and *The Dragon's Gift: The Real Story of China in Africa,* by Deborah Brautigam (2009). Having essentially founded the Chinese academic study of China's foreign aid, Shi extensively recorded the development of China's aid before the 1990s. Albeit not specifically aimed at understanding China's foreign aid *in Africa*, Shi's research benefited from him being one of the primary decision-makers of China's foreign aid. Shi Lin joined the works of China's foreign aid in 1964 as the Chief of the Executive Bureau of International Economic Affairs (国际经济事务局) of the Foreign Economic Liaison Commission. He was then promoted to the position of Vice Minister of the Ministry of Foreign Economic Liaison in 1973 and stayed in office until his retirement in 1982. Not only did Shi observe and assess the performance of China's foreign aid with exclusive access to official figures, field reports and government documents, but he also criticised China's foreign aid and proposed practical development suggestions. Unique to the study of China's foreign aid during the Cultural Revolution period (1966–1976), Shi's book is arguably the only Chinese resource commonly available to the public.

Concerning Deborah Brautigam's book, which was completed after extensive fieldwork carried in both China and Africa, *The Dragon's Gift* has brought the understanding of China' foreign aid in Africa to the West, and clarified a number of prevalent myths (Marks, 2010). Whilst aimed at revealing China's real foreign aid activities, it also aptly extended to the greater scope of the whole of China's involvement on the continent, the investments, immigration and other various by-products that China's relations with the continent has brought. In an attempt to figure out China's foreign aid expenditure, Brautigam made notable efforts in distinguishing China's foreign aid input and its government investment. Additionally, she also placed particular focus on China's industrial and agricultural aid. In all, as Brautigam suggests, China's foreign aid serves its national interests like any other foreign aid and is based on the development experience of itself: the investments, trades and technologies that this foreign aid along brings 'may be the dragon's ultimate, ambiguous gift' to Africa (2009: 312).

Still, even though these two important works build a solid foundation for understanding China's foreign aid in Africa, Shi's study is now completely out of date and Brautigam's study remains a Western approach, i.e., it only to some extent understood China's foreign aid from the *Chinese perspective*. In particular, the driver of China's foreign aid in Africa is seen as 'strategic diplomacy, commercial benefit, and as a reflection of society's ideologies and values' (2009: 15). Friendship, which is one of the primary interests of Beijing, is deemed a 'rosy picture', not worthy of study (2009: 3). However, it can be said that the book is certainly the best in studying Chinese aid to Africa, at least in English.

With reference to Chinese studies of China's foreign aid, one recent publication needs to be first mentioned, i.e., Zhang Yuhui's 2012 book 中国对外援助研究 1950–2010 (*Research on China's Foreign Aid 1950–2010*). Based on her PhD thesis, Zhang thoroughly investigates the evolution of the motivations, objectives and practices of China's foreign aid over the past six decades, and introduces a great amount of first-hand data regarding the scale and distribution of China's foreign aid in different development periods. Although similar to Shi's *Economic Cooperation with Foreign Countries*, Zhang's study is not specifically focused on China's foreign aid *in Africa* but is built on a theoretical foundation which integrates Chinese ideologies and Western understandings. Zhang has successfully brought our understanding to an academic audience and has carried out work to the present day. However, a lack of empirical evidence to practically examine the development of China's foreign aid and to support her arguments is the main shortcoming of this otherwise inclusive study.

Apart from dedicated literature on China's foreign aid development, the development of China's aid in Africa has been surveyed with various intentions in mind. Whilst a small number of Chinese studies have delved into the development of China's foreign aid in Africa for the purpose of grasping China's economic cooperation with foreign countries (see Li, 2003; Liu, 2009) and enhancing an understanding on China-Africa relations (see Li, 2006a; Zhang, 2006), the majority of these studies are carried out for two objectives, namely exploring China's motivations for providing aid and investigating how China delivers its aid. With regard to the studies that read China's motivations, most of these have come to the conclusion that China's foreign aid is driven by national interests, whether political or economic, or both, depending on the development period (see Sun, 2007; Davies et al., 2008; Wang and Zhu, 2008; Brautigam, 2009; Li, 2010; Zhang, 2010). In addition to some Chinese studies (see Bin, 2008; Zhang, 2012b), Lengauer's *China's Foreign Aid Policy: Motive and Methods* (2011) is one of the rare English studies which also surveyed the development of China's foreign aid in Africa taking into account cultural influences.

Concerning studies that surveyed how China delivers its foreign aid, *Economic Cooperation with Foreign Countries* by Shi remains the only work that demonstrates the development of all the aspects of China's foreign aid arrangements (including institutions, operating mechanisms, planning and implementation approaches). Albeit dated, whilst recent studies have attempted to update our understanding, the majority of these have only captured the evolvement of *some* aspects of China's foreign aid arrangement (see Chaponniere, 2009; He, 2011). Amongst the scholars who have focused on China's foreign aid arrangements, Huang Meibo is one of the most noteworthy, given that she has consistently followed the development of China's foreign aid institutions, operating mechanisms, and implementation approaches (see Huang, 2007; Huang and Hu, 2009; Huang and Lang, 2010). Besides these studies which survey the development of China's foreign aid arrangements, there also are studies that look into its current setup (see Mao, 2012), and provide diagrams illustrating its administrating and funding processes (see Chin and Frolic, 2007; Davies et al., 2008; Zhou, 2008b; Brautigam, 2009).

Whilst most of these studies are limited in explaining the development of all the aspects of China's foreign aid arrangement, to some extent they complement each other. Two studies however need to be specifically pointed out given that they have provided inaccurate information. First, *How China Delivers Development Assistance to Africa* (Davies et al., 2008) examined 'grant aid and technical assistance' together, yet the former is a funding method and the latter is an implementation method of China's foreign aid. Within the same section, Davies' inaccurately suggested that because technical assistance is mainly carried out as onsite training courses, 'technical assistance from China is often in the form of turnkey joint ventures' (Davies et al., 2008: 11). Secondly, on the basis of again improperly grouping concessional finance and interest-free loans (the former draws mostly commercial funding from China EXIM Bank and the latter is entirely reliant on China's government foreign aid budget), it is incorrect to assert that 'these are medium to long-term loans with an emphasis on the profitability of projects' whilst the latter is emphasised *only* on promoting development (Davies et al., 2008: 12).

The other problematic study that has given inaccurate understandings regarding China's foreign aid arrangement is *Emerging Donors in International Development Assistance: The China Case* (Chin and Frolic, 2007). The legitimate information in this study is indeed scarce. To give some examples, the study was based on misleading grounds by claiming that the grant portion of China's foreign aid is managed by four organisations, namely the 'Ministry of Commerce (known as MOFCOM in this study), Ministry of Foreign Affairs, select line ministries,[3] and the International Liaison Office of the CCP Central Committee' (Chin and Frolic, 2007: 6), when in fact, its management should be *led* by the Ministry of Commerce, Ministry of Foreign Affairs and Ministry of Finance, and *jointly participated* by 19 other government institutions. While placing a specific emphasis on China's 'Support for Research for Development' (Chin and Frolic, 2007: 9), the study goes as far as claiming that 'MOFCOM administers 90 percent of all grant aid, while MOST [Ministry of Science and Technology] controls 10 percent' (Chin and Frolic, 2007: 8). This is neither referenced nor has it been remotely true at any given point in the history of China's foreign aid. The participating government institutions *altogether* share less than 10 per cent of China's foreign aid budget planned for grants.[4]

Nevertheless, despite the contributions that existing studies have made to improve our understanding of China's foreign aid in Africa, on the basis that only a small number of them were especially concerned about explaining the development of China's foreign aid in Africa with the impact of Chinese characteristics in mind, and most of them insufficiently illustrated the development of China's foreign aid arrangements, the main gap amongst these studies is a lack of empirical evidence to practically examine the development of China's foreign aid in Africa. Regardless of whether they were aimed at exploring China's motivations for providing foreign aid or investigating how Beijing delivers foreign aid, the majority of these studies only managed to survey the development of China's foreign aid in Africa through theoretical approaches and policy analyses. Apart from a few studies integrated with recent case studies (see Davies et al., 2008) and brief case studies (see Liu, 1998; Zhang, 2012b), it is again the two comprehensive works of Shi and Brautigam that provide a practical view on the development of China's foreign aid in Africa.

With regard to studies that have assessed the performance of China's foreign aid, the majority of these studies are based on specific projects or programs, or an individual focusing area. Besides some studies such as Grimm et al.'s *Coordinating China and DAC Development Partners: Challenges to the Aid Architecture in Rwanda* (2010), which assessed the performance of China's aid with a view to finding out the possibilities of cooperation between China and traditional foreign aid donor countries, most of these studies have emphasised two objectives: assessing how China's foreign aid influences the recipient countries' development, and investigating how the outcomes of China's aid are affected. Studies that assessed the effectiveness and sustainability of China's aid in Africa have been primarily carried out by academics. Whilst specific projects or programs are plenty (see Li, 2009; Yu and Yuan, 2010; Niu, 2011), there are studies that have looked into the focus areas of agriculture, education, medicine and public health (see Brautigam, 1998; Zhang et al., 2013; Tang et al., 2014; Cheng et al., 2015).

Amongst the studies that have focused on specific projects or programs, one of the most chosen case study is the Tanzam railway. While remaining the single largest foreign aid project ever undertaken by China, the Tanzam railway has been studied since the 1970s (see Yu, 1971) when it was still under construction to today (see Chen, 2012). Not only do studies survey the decision-making process (see Lu, 2006; Wu, 2008), the implementation of the project (see Bailey, 1976; Jin, 1996), and the operation of the project (see Jin, 1987; Anon., 1988c), there also are studies assessing its prospective development (see Hu, 2000; Zhang, 2006c). Of these, Jamie Monson's *Africa's Freedom Railway: How a Chinese Development Project Changed Lives and Livelihoods in Tanzania* (2009) is arguably the most noteworthy study which specifically investigated the influences of the Tanzam railway. On the basis of observing that the Eight Principles were fully realised in the implementation of the project, Monson pointed out that China's foreign aid has been aimed at promoting African self-reliance rather than making Africa dependent.

Whereas in reference to studies that investigated how the outcomes of China's foreign aid are affected, these studies have been primarily conducted by Chinese aid practitioners and engineering specialists reporting on their working projects. These studies are often published in the journal of *International Economic Cooperation* (国际经济合作). This particular journal is edited by CAITEC, which is a subsidiary academy of the MOFCOM. Apart from a few studies that were positive about the outcomes and prospects of China's foreign aid in Africa (mainly the studies carried out prior to the 1990s) (see Guo, 1965; Feng, 1987; Anon., 1988a; Anon., 1988b), the majority of these studies have raised concerns about the African recipient countries' diverse domestic conditions, and how Chinese aid projects continue under the impact of such processes (see Lai, 1995; Li, 2000; Li et al., 2010; He, 2013). However, whilst most of these studies are critical, the most evident limitation amongst these studies is the limitation of case study selection approaches.

To be specific, in addition to a particular focus on specific projects and programs, these studies have only reached some focus areas of China's foreign aid such as agriculture, industry, economic infrastructure, education, medicine and public health and have left aside one of the most important focus areas of China's foreign aid in Africa: social infrastructure (which includes both landmark projects and people's livelihoods related projects). This is curious given that social infrastructure projects (known as public facilities in *The White Paper on China's Foreign Aid*) accounted for 670 of a total 2,025 Complete Project Aid projects that China delivered by the end of 2009. Within the same period, China delivered 635 industrial projects and 215 agricultural projects (see Government of China, 2011).

Whilst some of these studies were able to compare the performance of specific projects and programs in an individual focus area, owing to a lack of a comprehensive basis which would enable assessment across these focus areas, these studies have also been limited in providing a comparative view of how China's foreign aid performs in different focus areas (e.g., is China's industrial aid more appropriate to African recipient countries than social infrastructure aid?). As a consequence of these limitations, in spite of the outcomes and the contributing factors that these studies have assessed, they do not paint an overall picture of how China's foreign aid has performed in Africa.

Concerning studies that investigated the shortcomings of China's foreign aid, instead of assessing the performance of China's foreign aid in Africa, these studies have been mainly focused on the practices of China's foreign aid itself. Whilst a great number of these studies are found to be urban myths (collectively investigated and made clear by Brautigam, 2009), certain tropes have emerged and have tended not to go away. These might include, inter alia, claims that China hurts efforts to strengthen democracy and human rights in Africa by 'providing aid to other countries, the Chinese government . . . never attaches any conditions' (see Manning, 2006; McGreal, 2007); or 'China is making corruption worse' (see Naim, 2007; Malone, 2008).

Of those studies which have attempted to read China's foreign aid expenditures in Africa, Grimm et al.'s *Transparency of Chinese Aid: An Analysis of the Published Information on Chinese External Financial Flows* (2011) is amongst one of the most thorough studies which both pointed out that the sensitivity of China in publicising its foreign aid figures owes to its 'cultural traditions and philosophy' and 'persisting high demands for development finances "at home"' (2011: 4). The study suggested how China can take steps to improve its transparency. Whilst paying specific attention to published data, not only did this study put forward a considerably more accurate way of understanding China's foreign aid inputs (it looked into the currently available information rather than estimated figures and also investigated and grouped different figures made available by different foreign aid participants), the study suggested that the Chinese government, overall, publishes less data than the 'traditional donors', but provides material that can be more usually believed (2011: 23).

In contrast to Western studies, which placed a specific stress on best practice, the Chinese studies that have investigated the shortcomings of China's foreign aid are mainly focused on building China's foreign aid capacity. Whilst some studies looked into the developing implementation methods of China's aid at given periods and provided suggestions for adjustment, such as boosting the efficiency of Management Cooperation (Lu, 1988) and completing Overseas Volunteer Programs (Cao, 2013), more studies have had an eye on the underdeveloped administration of China's foreign aid. In particular, the incompetent foreign aid implementation management, the insufficient coordination between foreign aid institutions and the need for establishing a dedicated foreign aid institution (see Zhao and Xue, 2010; Hu and Huang, 2012; Huang and Xie, 2013; Lu et al., 2014). In addition to these, there has also been a recent increase in discussing the much lagged legal development of China's aid, and these studies suggest that China should promptly transform its current, primarily ministerial codes of practices to relevant legislation (see Cao, 2014; Guo, 2014; Li, 2014; Wang, 2014).

Nevertheless, in spite of the understandings contributed by these existing studies, while the shortcomings highlighted by Western studies are for the greater part built on Western values, the shortcomings pointed out in most Chinese studies are a lack of empirical evidence. More to the point, with a glance to the solutions brought forward by these studies, on the basis that the majority of these studies did not go into details exploring the practical situation of the Chinese government (indeed, the real capacities of China's aid), as a result of this negligence, as constructive as these solutions may conceptually be to the improvement of China's foreign aid, they are generally unrealistic to China's immediate development agenda, and only to some extent beneficial to China's long-term foreign aid development planning.

Under-researched areas in China's foreign aid in Africa

On the whole, despite the diverse and multi-dimensional nature of existing studies, there remain several gaps and confusing areas in the current understanding of the development, performance and shortcomings of China's foreign aid in Africa. First, on the basis of some understandings in regard to China's evolving motivations for providing foreign aid, and its developing practices and arrangements for delivery, existing studies do not include sufficient empirical examination of China's foreign aid development. As a result of the lack of practical demonstrations, not only is it difficult to grasp why, in the development of China's foreign aid in Africa, one aid objective is particularly emphasised and implemented over another, but it is also a challenge to find the practical reasons that drive the development of China's aid planning and implementation approaches.

Secondly, while a number of assessments have been offered regarding specific projects, programs, and particular focus areas of China's foreign aid in Africa, existing studies do not supply an overall understanding of how China's foreign aid has performed. Owing to the limitation of existing case study selection approaches, some focus areas of China's foreign aid remain unexamined. This is a limitation that becomes apparent when it comes to finding the particular focus areas in which China's aid has worked more effectively and sustainably. Thirdly, although there are studies that have investigated the shortcomings of China's aid from both a Western and a Chinese point of view, these studies are only minimally beneficial to those seeking to improve China's foreign aid. In addition to a general lack of empirical evidence supporting the identified shortcomings, there is also a common failure to take into account the real capacities of China's aid; thus, neither are the shortcomings that these studies identified straightforward to understand, nor are their proposed solutions realistic.

Last and most importantly, given that so far the majority of the studies on China's foreign aid development and China's foreign aid performance are carried out separately (the former only focused on grasping the evolution of objectives, planning and implementation approaches of China's foreign aid and the latter only focused on assessing the effectiveness and sustainability of China's aid in Africa), the current understandings do not explain how the development of China's aid is related to its foreign aid outcomes in Africa. Not only is such an explanation vital to the identification of factors that affect China's outcomes in Africa but also are important when proposing suggestions to China's next foreign aid development.

Notes

1. Interview with senior Chinese official, Beijing, China, 16 November 2011.
2. Interview with senior Chinese researcher, Beijing, China, 22 November 2011.
3. 'Including MOST (Ministry of Science and Technology), the Ministry of Agriculture (MOA), the Ministry of Education (MOE), the Ministry of Health (MOH), and the Ministry of Communications (MOC)'. See Chin and Frolic (2007: 6).
4. Online interview with senior Chinese official, 10 November 2012.

2 The history of China's foreign aid in Africa

The next two chapters aim to fulfil a key objective of this study, namely to understand the development of China's foreign aid. Arranged in chronological order, the historical and present-day conditions of China's foreign aid in Africa are examined. With the view of identifying China's foreign aid objectives in Africa, and the foreign aid planning and implementation approaches China developed accordingly, this chapter focuses on the emergence and early development of China's foreign aid. It addresses two primary questions: How has China's foreign aid objectives in Africa progressed? How have China's foreign aid practices developed? Along with these queries, this chapter surveys the development of China's foreign aid between 1955 and 1993, when foreign aid was primarily influenced by China's political pursuits (up to 1976, strongly influenced by Maoism). It is divided into two sections, split by the reform policy inaugurated in 1978.

In the first section, China's foreign aid development prior to the reform period is looked at. It is inclusive of three distinct development periods: The Beginning (1955–1963), The Development (1963–1970) and The Outrageous (1971–1978). On the basis of finding that the aims of China's foreign aid in Africa evolved from liberating the oppressed peoples in the so-called Third World to strengthening global forces against imperialism, colonialism and hegemonism and to helping African countries achieve self-reliance, this section reveals that in line with its duly determined foreign aid objectives, China not only established practical foreign aid planning and implementation approaches, but to some extent, successfully delivered development assistance to Africa; however, this rather positive outcome was eventually torn apart when China's political and economic systems were paralysed by the Cultural Revolution. China was henceforth forced to reconsider the continuation of its foreign aid.

In the second section, a substantial historical turning point in China's development, the implementation of the reform policy and the carrying through of China's foreign aid into a fourth period (The Initial Reform [1979–1993] surveys the dramatic shift in China's aid objectives in Africa as it moved towards reducing expenditure while consolidating outcomes. In this phase, China placed considerably greater emphasis on the economic aspects of its foreign aid programs while attempting to relieve its financial burdens. Regardless of such changes however, Beijing did little to benefit the development of Africa in comparison to the previous period. By the early 1990s, China's planned economic system had been stretched to the limit whilst the Tiananmen Square events of 1989 provoked a major crisis in Chinese foreign policy. These are the cornerstones leading to the contemporary era of China's foreign aid, which is discussed in the subsequent chapter.

From the Bandung Conference to the end of Cultural Revolution, 1955–1978

As pointed out by Mao Zedong early on in the history of the People's Republic of China, 'Considering the fact that China is a country that has 9.6 million square kilometres of land and 600 million people, it has an obligation to contribute to the whole of mankind' (*Xinhua*, 1956b). Mao also made specific his belief that 'those who have already emerged victorious from revolutions should help those who are still striving for independence. This is our obligation to proletarian internationalism' (*Xinhua*, 1963). This combination of internationalism and patriotism was based on two ideas. Firstly, as a country that had just emerged from external domination, China needed to support the other oppressed peoples struggling for national independence. Secondly, as an economically underdeveloped country, China's request for a fair political and economic international environment was consistent with the interests of the mass of underdeveloped countries. Therefore, helping other countries meant improving China's own external situation (Zhou, 2008a).

Derivative of this internationalist responsibility, China began to deliver Foreign Economic and Technical Assistance (对外经济技术援助) shortly after 1949 (Li, 2010). Specifically regarding China's foreign aid in Africa, this began with the Asian-African Conference held in 1955. At that time, China's priority was to reverse the extremely negative situation left by the Guomindang and the Japanese occupiers, as well as seek to break out of the United States–led blockades. Meanwhile in Africa, rising nationalism pushed liberation movements to their final stages in confronting colonialism (Luo and Liu, 2007). In view of this situation, and regardless of the immediate needs of domestic recovery, China adopted a foreign policy in response to its urgent situation and promptly developed diplomatic relationships with the Soviet Union and other socialist countries (Zhang, 2011).

China at this stage was, on the one hand, highly concerned about the situation in Korea and Indo-China. On the other hand, it was keen to establish relationships with other underdeveloped countries and to assist in the liberation movements in the colonial world (CCCPC Party Literature Research Office, 1990). Against this background, the newly established People's Republic of China and Africa moved closer together.

The beginning

From 18 April to 24 April 1955, the seminal event of the Asian-African Conference (万隆会议) was staged in Bandung, Indonesia. This provided the very first modern opportunity for China to make a tentative approach to Africa (Taylor,

2006). Based on the diplomacy developed by a Chinese delegation led by Prime Minister Zhou Enlai, Bandung helped establish optimal conditions for China to cooperate with Asian and African countries. As a prelude to China's foreign aid, in regards to the principles of cooperation among Asian and African countries, *The Final Communiqué of the Asian-African Conference* stated: 'The Asian-African Conference recognises the immediacy of promoting economic development of the Asian-African region, and the common aspiration among the participating countries to mutual beneficial and respected economic cooperation' (1955). Regarding these approaches, it further stated that 'all the participating countries agree to provide technical assistance to the best of their ability, in the methods of overseas experts, training programs, engineering equipment, technology exchanges, and so on'.

Concerned with realising this economic and technical cooperation agreement so as to break out of China's diplomatic isolation, Zhou delivered his opinions on initialising China's foreign aid at the 3rd Session of the First National People's Congress:

> On the basis that China is a newly liberated country, with an as of yet underdeveloped and dependent economy, we are primarily seeking trade based economic cooperation. However, since we also are aware of the significance of economic development in consolidating political independence, China is willing to maximise its contributions in assisting other countries' economic development within its capacity.
>
> (*Xinhua*, 1956a)

Zhou further stressed the principles in conducting foreign economic and technical assistance, in that 'China upholds the principle of equality and mutual respect for sovereignty. Therefore it will never intervene or impose political, economic and military disadvantages on other countries in the name of economic cooperation' (*Xinhua*, 1956a).

Meanwhile in Africa, and echoing China's eagerness to establish diplomatic relationships based on mutual respect and cooperation, Africa's liberation movements were further encouraged by China's support for Egypt during the Suez Crisis. This officially marked the outset of China's foreign aid involvement in Africa, when Beijing sent 20 million Swiss francs in cash and also dispatched medical teams to Egypt. This made Egypt the first African recipient country of China's aid (Li and Wu, 2009: 47).

Subsequent to this historical episode, in October 1958, with consideration to advancing the importance of foreign aid, the Central Committee (中共中央) approved for the first time an official paper regarding China's foreign aid (关于加强对外经济、技术援助工作领导的请示报告 or *Report on Strengthening Foreign Economic and Technical Cooperation*). This stated: 'Foreign economic and technical assistance is both a serious political mission, and the Chinese people's internationalist obligation to brotherhood and nationalist countries'. In light of this confirmation, Zhou immediately gathered the corresponding ministries and introduced the very first objective of China's foreign aid:

> In accordance with the growth of China's economic and technological capacities, China's foreign aid will become an increasingly onerous task. We should uphold the spirit of internationalism, assist those socialist countries that are in the need, earnestly carry out existing assistance to North Korea, Vietnam, Mongolia and Albania, and arrange foreign aid with the priorities and appropriateness in economic development focused aspects. In the meantime, within our allowance, we also should assist those economically underdeveloped Asian and African nationalist countries, to help them build their own industrial foundations on a small to medium project basis.
>
> (Shi, 1989)

The period 1955 to 1963 was the emerging era in China's foreign aid in Africa. At this stage, while political interests in proletarian internationalism were dominating China's development, foreign aid decisions were made primarily to assist the communist battle against imperialism and colonialism. There was during this initial period only secondary awareness placed on the liberation movements of Africa, primarily in French-held North Africa. Otherwise, the priorities of China's foreign aid in this period were given to North Vietnam and North Korea (Li et al., 2009). To evidence this, of the 20 countries that signed the Economic and Technical Cooperation Agreement (经济技术合作协定), also known as the Comprehensive Loan Aid Agreement with China, only 6 were African countries, namely Egypt, Algeria, Guinea, Ghana, Mali and Somalia.

With regards to China's foreign aid administration, owing to the limited number of recipient countries, China's aid was directly governed by the Central People's Government (中央人民政府) and coordinated by the State Planning Commission (国家计划委员会). In August 1952, the Ministry of Foreign Trade [of the Central People's Government] (中央人民政府对外贸易部) was established to take over the management of Goods and Materials Aid, as well as subsidiary institutions responsible for project implementation. The management of Cash Aid, meanwhile, was devolved to the Ministry of Finance (MOF). Two years later in 1954, the Ministry of Foreign Trade was renamed the Ministry of Foreign Trade [of the PRC] (中华人民共合国对外贸易部), a designation that lasted until 1982. This body was assigned the management of the newly introduced Complete Project Aid program. As for the implementation of Complete Project Aid, the State Planning Commission was charged with coordinating such projects with relevant government institutions.

As a result of the growing number of independent countries and the subsequent foreign aid demand that this led to, in the late 1950s the 12th Session of the Standing Committee of the Second National People's Congress approved the establishment of the Bureau of Foreign Economic Liaison (对外经济联络总局). As a government institution that took direct instruction (归口管理) from the State Council, this body was appointed to unify the divided management of foreign aid and to house China's foreign aid under the same administrative roof (Huang and Hu, 2009). Anticipating this merger, China also introduced the Delivery Ministry In-chief Mechanism (总交货人部制) to organise aid implementation. Largely based on the Soviet Union's management of Complete Project Aid, this mechanism was operated as follows. First the State Planning Commission appointed a delivery ministry according to the specialty of the foreign aid projects. Then this delivery ministry organised project implementation. The project would either be commissioned within the ministry or assigned to subordinate institutions or provincial bureaus (Zhang, 2012b).

Because the majority of China's foreign aid was directed to cope with its immediate national security threats and the regional sphere, China's aid during this period was largely organised in the military and humanitarian aspects, and Beijing provided only a limited amount of assistance to African countries. Nevertheless, although China's foreign aid in Africa at that stage had yet to progress to development assistance, it proposed the objective of building African industrial foundations on a small to medium project basis and in pursuit of this objective, China founded its basic foreign aid institutions, operating mechanisms and three foreign aid implementation methods .

The development

Struggling in the battle against imperialism and hegemonism, the widening gap between China and the Soviet Union worsened China's external situation at the beginning of the 1960s. Rooted in ideological divergence, China's objection to the Soviet Union's revisionism and the continuing blockade led by the United States almost completely immobilised China's diplomatic relations (Zhou, 2007: 14). In order to escape these difficult circumstances, rather than relentlessly confront both superpowers, China shifted its primary interests from the few developing socialist countries to the considerably larger number of new Asian and African countries. The progression of African independence in particular allowed China to escape certain constraints and China began to balance its foreign aid priorities towards Asian and African countries, placing particular emphasis on the latter.

On 13 December 1963, in the interests of further deepening China's relationship with Asian and African countries, Zhou embarked on his Fourteen Countries Tour, visiting the United Arab Republic, Algeria, Morocco, Tunisia, Ghana, Mali, Guinea, Sudan, Ethiopia, Somalia, Myanmar, Pakistan and Ceylon between 13 December 1963 and 1 March 1964. This was China's first ministerial-level visit to Africa. During Zhou's stop in Accra, and in response to Kwame Nkrumah's proposal to work on 'seeking the best way to achieve peaceful co-existence' (Chen, 2007: 207), Zhou promptly offered a framework that he sketched for conducting China's foreign aid. These became known as the Eight Principles for Economic Aid and Technical Assistance to Other Countries (中国政府对外经济技术援助八项原则). The Principles were as follows:

1 The Chinese government always bases itself on the principle of equality and mutual benefit in providing aid to other countries. It never regards such aid as a kind of unilateral alms but as something mutual.

2 In providing aid to other countries, the Chinese government strictly respects the sovereignty of recipient countries, and never attaches any conditions or asks for any privileges.
3 China provides economic aid in the form of interest-free or low-interest loans, and extends the time limit for the repayment when necessary so as to lighten the burden on recipient countries as far as possible.
4 In providing aid to other countries, the purpose of the Chinese government is not to make recipient countries dependent on China but to help them embark step by step on the road of self-reliance and independent economic development.
5 The Chinese government does its best to help recipient countries complete projects which require less investment but yield quicker results, so that the latter may increase their income and accumulate capital.
6 The Chinese government provides the best-quality equipment and materials manufactured by China at international market prices. If the equipment and materials provided by the Chinese government are not up to the agreed specifications and quality, the Chinese government undertakes to replace them or refund the payment.
7 In giving any particular technical assistance, the Chinese government will see to it that the personnel of the recipient country fully master the technology.
8 The experts dispatched by China to help in construction in recipient countries will have the same standard of living as the experts of the recipient country. The Chinese experts are not allowed to make any special demands or enjoy any special amenities.

By placing emphasis on the Eight Principles, China clearly stated that when it provided foreign aid to other countries it acted on the principles of unity and friendship, respect for the recipient country's sovereignty, non-interference in another country's internal affairs, freedom from political conditions attached to their aid and never asking for any privileges. These principles not only significantly improved China's diplomatic relations with African countries, but also took China's foreign aid to a whole new level.

At the same time in China, however, the Three Years of Natural Disasters between 1959 and 1961 and the sudden loss of major support from the Soviet Union caused great domestic difficulties. In view of the continuously expanding foreign aid input, this brought a number of opposing voices against Zhou's aid diplomacy. Zhou argued in return at the 1st Session of the Third National People's Congress that:

> The foundation of China's foreign aid is the persistence of proletarian internationalism, that is to support brotherhood countries to establish socialist regimes; to support global liberation movements; and to support the newly independent countries to achieve self-reliance, and to strengthen their anti-imperialist capabilities. And that is also beneficial to us. In the past it was suggested that we should reduce our assistance to other countries, and that

> is completely wrong. In pace with China's growing economy, we should provide more foreign aid, and make greater contribution to the cause of internationalism.
>
> (*Xinhua*, 1964)

From 1964 to 1970, China's foreign aid in Africa rapidly developed and the Eight Principles were used as the basis of significantly improving the relationship between China and Africa. Not only did this guidance serve to standardise China's foreign aid approaches, it consequently became the most influential tool in the development of bilateral relations between China and Africa (Shi, 1989). From this point, in the pursuit of supporting liberation movements and helping newly independent countries achieve self-reliance, the Eight Principles led to China's aid being disseminated to 11 more countries, bringing the total number of its foreign aid recipient countries at the time to 31, of which 14 were African countries.

Subsequent to this success in putting forward aid principles and in the interest of improving the administration of China's foreign aid, the Central Committee revoked the Bureau of Foreign Economic Liaison and established the Foreign Economic Liaison Commission (对外经济联络委员会) in June 1964 to further upgrade China's foreign aid capacity (a body which lasted until 1970). Arranged as four bureaus and one office, the Foreign Economic Liaison Commission allocated three bureaus to individually manage foreign aid to the then major recipient groups which were grouped as Socialist Countries, Asian Countries and African Countries. The other bureau and the office were tasked with the coordination of technical support and managing foreign aid equipment and materials. Along with this institutional advancement, the funding methods of China's foreign aid were confirmed as the Grant, the Interest-free Loan and the Low-interest Loan (which was is restricted to a maximum interest rate of 2 per cent) (Shi, 1989).

As Africa became a priority recipient of China's foreign aid, a delegation led by the Vice Director of the State Planning Commission Fang Yi[1] was dispatched to Algeria, Mali and Guinea in 1964 in order to explore the most appropriate measures to be taken for planning practical and effective aid packages to these countries. Based on observations of the colonial legacy in Africa, it was decided that the immediate foreign aid objective in Africa should be the delivery of basic necessities such as food and clothes. Long-term foreign aid objectives were deemed as helping African countries make use of their natural resources, master new technologies and ultimately achieve self-reliance. This support for African industry and agriculture was to be through a combined approach of Complete Project Aid and Technical Aid (Xue, 2013a).

In addition to these efforts, what was also found to be noticeable was that along with the increase in foreign aid demands, the lasting effects of colonialism were still impacting Africa's development and thus China's foreign aid implementations. As Shi (1989) pointed out:

> While a number of African countries agreed on China's foreign aid, some of them hesitated due to the influences from the capitalist countries, certainly

> their former colonies. However, demonstrated by the completion of the first lot of foreign aid projects, China has evidently proved its commitments to The Eight Principles. Aside from this reassuring the existing foreign aid recipient countries' confidence, the uncertain minds of the hesitating African countries were also removed, and thereafter motivated further African countries to request foreign aid from China.

Summarising the developing period of China's foreign aid in Africa, since the inauguration of the Eight Principles, the influence of China on the African continent expanded notably alongside other important developments in Chinese foreign policy. It was during this time that the Chinese government realised the potential of aid in strengthening diplomatic relations. Following Fang Yi's investigation, the objectives of China's foreign aid in Africa was confirmed as building up industrial and agricultural foundations on the continent. In pursuit of this objective, besides the streamlined aid administration and approval of foreign aid funding methods, according to Shi, 'China in total delivered 313 Complete Project Aid projects in 20 countries during this period, an increase of 210% in comparison to the period of 1950 to 1963' (Shi, 1989). The introduction of Technical Aid and the sharp increase in Complete Project Aid schemes clearly demonstrated this rapid development. It was now that China's foreign aid evidently began to evolve into development assistance.

The outrageous

With China's external situation continuing to improve, the 26th Session of the UN General Assembly Resolution took place on 25 October 1971 and introduced a completely new paradigm for China's foreign relationships. Passed with a two-thirds majority vote, including those of 26 African countries, UN General Assembly Resolution 2758 recognised the People's Republic of China as 'the only legitimate representative of China to the United Nations' (1971).[2] As a consequence of this diplomatic victory over the Republic of China, the majority of developing countries among the 76 endorsing countries quickly established diplomatic relationship with China and expectations that they would soon become the recipients of China's foreign aid was high. Those African countries needing replacements for the now-vacated Taiwan agricultural aid projects were particularly keen in this regard. However, given the state of China's economy at the time and the political chaos that existed as a result of the Cultural Revolution, China found itself in great financial difficulties and struggled to fulfil such anticipations. Nonetheless, between 1970 and 1976, China made more aid commitments to Africa than the Soviets did; China committed 1,815 million US dollar to Africa whilst Moscow committed 1,019 million US dollar (for figures, see Yu, 1978: 42).

In the case of Africa, China planned its aid with three aims in mind: to support African liberation movements, to unite African countries against imperialism and to assist African countries in achieving self-reliance (Li, 2006a). To achieve these aims, besides the Eight Principles, China made substantial efforts in developing its aid. For instance, along with the increase in recipient countries, China's multiple institutions involved into an aid administration which was gradually unified under the sole authority of the Ministry of Foreign Economic Liaison. Subsequently, this ministry was successively accommodated by the Delivery Ministry In-chief Mechanism and the Contract Department In-chief Mechanism to regulate capacity. In addition to participating in International Multilateral Aid, China adopted three funding methods to make best use of its limited foreign aid budget. Of these, the Interest-free Loan was utilised as the primary method while Low-interest Loans were arranged for recipient countries with relatively sufficient economic resources. Grants were delivered to those recipient countries that were still striving for independence or facing particular financial difficulties.

To realise China's aid objectives in Africa meant assisting recipients in building their own economic foundations. China practised four implementation methods, namely Complete Project Aid, Technical Aid, Goods and Materials Aid (aid which provides livelihoods supplies, technical products and individual equipment), and Cash Aid (mainly involving direct transfers of funds). First Introduced in 1954, Complete Project Aid was initially inaugurated to assist North Korea and Vietnam. As a result of the development of China-Africa relationships in the 1960s, Complete Project Aid was brought to the repertoire of China's aid in Africa so as to demonstrate China's aim to support African liberation movements. It was then utilised in building African economies. Through the implementations of Complete Project Aid, China not only provided project construction, but also took on the responsibility for field surveys, project design etc.

Coordinated in conjunction with Complete Project Aid, Technical Aid was introduced to improve the effectiveness of technology and management transfers. At the early stage of China's foreign aid development, along with other Individual Programs (单项援助), both Medical Teams and overseas training programs were classed as Technical Aid. Whereas the former evolved into a permanent feature of China's foreign aid in 1963, the latter became individualised only in the 1970s. As an exploratory attempt at Human Resource Development Cooperation (HRDC), China-based training courses were offered as Foreign Internships and Overseas Student Programs. While the internships were arranged to train technicians to run delivered projects, the Overseas Student Programs were specifically implemented to meet the employment demands of the Tanzam Railway. These were later developed into the Overseas Scholarship Programs.

With regards to the collaboration of these implementation methods, Complete Project Aid and Technical Aid were utilised as the primary methods in assisting Africa's development, and both have seen continuous expansion since their introduction. Goods and Materials Aid only accounted for a minor contribution, since it was mainly organised through military and humanitarian efforts. While it was primarily offered to neighbouring communist countries, Goods and Materials Aid was only applied to African countries to supply their immediate needs. Owing to China's extremely limited foreign exchange reserves, Cash Aid was rarely delivered at all and only in urgent situations. During this period, African countries had gradually become the largest recipient group of China's foreign aid; as Li et al.

pointed out, 'from the 1950s when China's delivered its first lot of foreign aid to Africa to the end of Cultural Revolution in 1978, 56.96% of China's total foreign aid budget was delivered to 43 African countries' (2009: 336).

However, given the significant efforts that the Chinese government made in assisting Africa's development, a number of drawbacks also appeared which damaged both China's economic development and its aid outcomes in Africa (despite the fact that China's political interests *were* achieved as evidenced by its substantially improved international status). Grounded in ideology when projected abroad, the Cultural Revolution steered China's foreign aid away from what promised to be cooperation based on mutual development and turned into a political instrument dedicated to China's ideological concerns. As Zhang noted, 'China was trading Africa's diplomatic recognition and ideological support with its continuous development assistance' (2006: 44).

China's proletarian internationalism had shortcomings in four major instances during this period. In regards to the aid decision-making process, the fact that China's foreign aid served ideological objectives not only restricted its foreign aid diplomacy to socialist and Third World countries, but also the amount of foreign aid to a particular recipient country was heavily influenced by their ideological stance. According to this logic, depending on the recipient country's relationships with the United States and the Soviet Union (or both), China's aid was endlessly involved in a dilemma. China either missed the opportunity to obtain *non-politically* considered development interests, or suddenly turned against its recipient countries due to changes in political strategies (as seen with Albania and Vietnam, see below). The net result was aid wastage (Xue, 2013a).

Whilst China delivered its aid to the countries that it trusted politically, this substantial political emphasis overshadowed economic considerations aid (Liu, 2008b). It also oversimplified the planning of such aid and therefore led to failed outcomes. As a senior Chinese official noted:

> China's foreign aid at this stage was mostly agreed during the visits between principal decision-makers and considered only in terms of political interests. Unsurprisingly, given the lack of financial assessments, feasibility studies, and other necessary processes of foreign aid planning, a number of China's foreign aid projects were unable to meet the recipient countries' demand.[3]

As a consequence, this tendency sometimes resulted in unsustainable foreign aid dependency (Zhang, 2001: 44).

In addition to these concerns, given that the aid operating mechanisms were built on China's planned economic system, its implementations were also open to doubt. In spite of the Delivery Ministry In-chief Mechanism and Contract Department In-chief Mechanism, these mechanisms managing China's aid were grounded on an administrative basis rather than on an economic basis. Together with China's aid expenditures which were at the same time reimbursed upon invoice (实报实销), the investment, construction period, as well as the quality of the aid was essentially disconnected from economic considerations. This inevitably resulted in the excessive reimbursement of costs and worked to the disadvantage of implementation. As confirmed by Shi, 'The drawbacks of these administrative means based operating mechanisms become increasingly problematic in the late 1970s' (1989).

Furthermore, while government budgets remained the only resource for aid, the funding methods were questionable in channelling China's limited aid budget. Not only were two-thirds of these methods (the Grant and the Interest-free Loan) established on an unidirectional financial basis, as one senior Chinese official put it, 'The chances of receiving repayments of both these loans were [also] extremely low, as they are no different financially to Grants to a large extent'.[4] Therefore, all of China's aid funding methods during this period were in essence based on a donation approach.

Concerned with meeting foreign aid requests though, Beijing convened five National Conferences on Foreign Aid (全国援外工作会议), of which the first three conferences were directly addressed by the Central Committee. Aside from repeatedly emphasising the diplomatic importance of China's aid, the Chinese government brought in provincial departments to take part in aid implementation and furthermore, outlined a number of instructions to be followed in order to maintain foreign aid outcomes. These instructions included: 'Upholding proletarian internationalism and the Eight Principles', 'Preventing and overcoming great power poses, focusing on recipient countries' conditions and striving for practical results', 'Preventing unrealistic planning and prodigal practices, to ensure a steady and reliable progress' etc. (Zhang, 2012b: 138).

Yet despite the domestic conditions in China, aid from Beijing remained relatively high. As Fang notes, 'The percentage of China's national budget earmarked for foreign aid was only a cut above 1% during the first and second Five-Year Plan periods (1953–1957; 1958–1962), but in fiscal years 1972, 1973 and 1974, this amount had risen to 6.7%, 7.2% and 6.3%, respectively' (1984: 544). As a result of its victory at the UN, Beijing approved aid requests from an additional 35 developing countries, sharply increasing the total number of its aid recipient countries to 66. Amongst these, 27 were from the African continent.[5] This decision was primarily made in line with Mao's appreciation that 'It was our African friends who brought us back to the UN, we shouldn't forget the helping hand lent by the Third World countries in any way' (Weng, 1995: 9 cited in Li, 2006a: 18). Further in line with this determination, in June 1970, the Central Committee and the State Council promoted the Foreign Economic Liaison Commission to the Ministry of Foreign Economic Liaison (对外经济联络部). In this upgrading process, two additional bureaus were introduced to deal with budget planning and foreign economic cooperation with the intention to further complete China's aid administration. In addition to this, with considerations to improving Complete Project Aid implementation, a dedicated subsidiary public institution to the newly upgraded ministry, that is, the Complete Plant Export Company (成套设备出口公司) was established. Moreover, 26 provincial foreign aid departments were also set up.

Subsequent to this institutional change, and on the basis of recognising the incompetence of the existing aid operating mechanism, the Ministry of Foreign

Economic Liaison replaced the Delivery Ministry In-chief Mechanism with the Contract Ministry In-Chief Mechanism (承建部负责制). Particularly concerned with the ability to cope with dramatically increased foreign aid demands, this new operating mechanism required the appointed implementation (contract) ministry to monitor foreign aid expenses and project quality, whereas elements of the implementation process such as the design and construction of foreign aid packages were allocated to provincial departments. In this way, the new operating mechanism both relieved the stress on the Ministry of Foreign Economic Liaison and mobilised additional support and productivity from the provincial foreign aid departments (Huang and Hu, 2009).

Yet, with the interference of the Cultural Revolution and the active pursuit of proletarian internationalism, aid objectives were implemented with 'enormous investment, gigantic planning and technical complexity' (Shi, 1989). As a result of a failure to abide by the aid objectives and practices, a number of the most demanding Complete Project Aid projects were constructed in the 1970s, including the Guinea Tinkisso Hydroelectric Power Station, the Mali Sugar Complex, the Sudan Hasahaisa Textile Plant and, of course, the Tanzam Railway. All of these rapidly propelled the financial burden of China's aid (Li et al., 2009).

This high foreign aid expenditure eventually exceeded China's capacity and forced the government to amend its foreign aid strategy. As the Central Committee and the State Council's resolution delivered at the 4th National Conference on Foreign Aid stated:

> Considering China's limited financial resources, further foreign aid agreements should be approached with extreme caution. While earnestly implementing the already agreed terms, the subsequent annual foreign aid budget, indeed the quota of new agreements, must be restricted within China's financial allowance; the structure of foreign aid in the meanwhile, also needs to be further adjusted towards Complete Project Aid. In addition to these, the allocation of foreign aid projects and programs to each recipient countries should be planned comprehensively, with particular attention drawn to match the local conditions.
>
> (Shi, 1989)

One year after these adjustments, the end of the Cultural Revolution finally put an end to one of the most chaotic periods in China's modern history and also led to a reappraisal of Chinese aid and a search for scapegoats as to why Chinese aid had got out of hand.

During the 5th National Conference on Foreign Aid convened in June 1977, the "Jiang Qing led Anti-Party Clique" (四人帮 or Gang of Four) was squarely blamed for causing the exponential increase in aid spending during a period of chaotic governance where ideology trumped practical limitations. After summarising China's two decades of foreign aid experiences, the conference concluded with the new instruction that China's aid in the future should 'uphold proletarian internationalism, uphold the Eight Principles, actively and steadily focus on clearly and comprehensively bringing up the recipient countries' economic capacity and help them achieve self-reliance' (Shi, 1989).

Following the conference, the Central Committee approved and distributed the Ministry of Foreign Economic Liaison's *Report on Further Improving the Work of Foreign Aid* (对外经济联络部的"关于进一步做好援外工作的报告") which for the first time officially restricted the budgetary allowance of China's foreign aid. As it stated:

> Along with the rapid development of China's foreign relations, the foreign aid requests from the developing countries are becoming increasingly demanding. While China's own economic and industrial resources are still limited, it is suggested that other than exceptional circumstances, further foreign aid expenditures should not exceed the ratio of 4% of total annual governmental budget.
>
> (Fang, 1984: 586, cited in Shi, 1989)

This new approach was clearly an attempt to rein in the excessive amount of approved aid requests that China had approved in the previous decade. This was facilitated in part by the break from China by both Vietnam and Albania (hitherto key foreign aid recipients).[6] It was this development that might be said to have ended China's proletarian internationalist aid, forcing China to reconsider its interests in delivering further aid.

Thus by 1978, China's aid to Africa might be said to have had both positive and negative outcomes. On the one hand, it had helped significantly improve China's external situation and provided African recipient countries with noticeable assistance, securing a solid foundation for cooperation between China and Africa. On the other hand, the proletarian internationalist obligations underpinning foreign aid led to extremes, as 'the leader [Mao] normally planned foreign aid according to his personal ideological considerations. Although arguably he was making decisions at the strategic level, the negligence to China's financial situation caused great difficulties to China's domestic development' (Yuan and Yang, 2003: 576 cited in Zhang, 2012b: 136). Furthermore, when this situation was accompanied by China's incompetent aid practices, limited outcomes were achieved. In view of this, as the emphasis begins shifting towards economic reform, China initiated its own aid reform measures.

From initial reform to the end of the Cold War, 1979–1993

With the Socialist Modernisation project evolving once Deng Xiaoping consolidated his rule, revolutionary causes and ideological conflict was no longer relevant for China in Africa. Rather, the economy and technology were leading concerns. From the post-Mao leadership's standpoint, seeing the drawbacks of ideologically determined policies, it was vital to realise immediate domestic recovery. Thus the importance of economic development became central. In the meantime, on the basis that most African countries had achieved political independence, economic development was also pushed to the front of the agendas. On the ground, provided with the opportunity granted by the switch of leadership, China promptly replaced its foreign policy with a non-aligned diplomatic approach, with an emphasis on mutually beneficial economic cooperation (Liu, 2008b).

In December 1978, based on summarising the previous foreign aid experience, the 3rd Plenary Session of the Eleventh Central Committee of the CPC (中国共产党第十一届中央委员会第三次全体会议) brought China's development assistance into a completely new era:

> On the basis of achieving self-reliance, China should actively develop equal and mutually beneficial relationships with all foreign countries, and effectively take advantage of world leading technologies and equipment . . . In order to realise China's Socialist Modernisation, we should utilise both domestic and international resources, open up both domestic and international markets, and acquire the ability to both realise domestic constructions as well as develop foreign economic relations.
>
> (CCCPC Party Literature Research Office, 1982a: 5)

In light of this, China began to accept international multilateral development assistance in the following year. While fully concentrating on domestic development, in July 1979, Deng Xiaoping pointed out in the Central Meeting on the Works of Foreign Affairs (中央外事工作会议) that:

> We should acknowledge that the decision to assist the Third World countries was correct. Although our economy is still having difficulties, we have to come up with the necessary budget for foreign aid. From a strategic standpoint, when we are developed, we need to provide more assistance to other countries. China should always keep this in mind. In providing foreign aid, we should continue to comply with The Eight Principles, but it is the specifics that we have to adjust in order to really benefit the recipient countries.
>
> (Wang, 1998, cited in Liu, 2009: 51)

China continued to deliver development assistance to such countries while also gradually recovering domestic productivity and subsequent economic capacity. It was then that China launched a complete reform of its foreign aid.

In line with the newly determined diplomatic objectives of expanding foreign economic relations, in March 1980, the Ministry of Foreign Economic Liaison put forward guidelines for conducting further aid during the National Conference on Foreign Economics (全国外经工作会议). The guidelines confirmed that China's aid should 'uphold proletarian internationalism, stand by the Eight Principles, expand foreign economic and technological cooperation, to provide and to receive equally and to mutual benefit, make due contributions to friendly countries and accelerate China's Four Modernisations (四个现代化)' (Shi, 1989). Later, in May of 1980, with the formal approval of these guidelines from the State Council, not only did the Chinese government affirm that its aid would be an integral part of foreign economic cooperation, but it also plainly implied that economic interests were no longer secondary to political concerns. Instead, economic interests became a decisive factor for China providing aid.

However, due to Vietnam and Albania's continuing problematic relations with China, both the Chinese public and officials hesitated with regard to China's aid, questioning whether it was necessary to provide foreign aid at all. Despite the revised guidelines, the implementation of China's aid encountered a number of difficulties in the early 1980s. In order to cope with this situation, the Central Committee and the State Council delivered in November 1980 *The Comments on Conscientiously Providing Foreign Aid* (关于认真做好对外援助工作的意见). This document stated:

> Since the establishment of China, foreign aid has directly coordinated with China's foreign conflicts, improved China's foreign diplomatic relations and consolidated the international alliance against imperialism, colonialism and hegemonism. Concerning China's current international status, it is aided by the support of Third World countries. Although problems and issues have surfaced, some of them have been sorted out and the rest are being resolved.
>
> (CCCPC Party Literature Research Office, 1982b: 727)

Added to these comments, the General Secretary of the CPC Hu Yaobang again stressed the meaning of China's foreign aid:

> To assist people in the Third World defend their national independence, and to help them develop their economy is our compelling obligation. In the past 30 years, we have devoted ourselves to this mission. Although there have been some mistakes, generally speaking, our work has played an important role in international affairs . . . Our comrades should know that delivering foreign aid to Third World countries is a strategic matter; it is too serious to be taken lightly.
>
> (CCCPC Party Literature Research Office, 1982b: 1127)

Subsequent to these efforts in reinstating confidence in providing foreign aid, the 12th National Congress of the CPC further commented on China's foreign policy. It suggested that when China approaches another country, it should abide by the principles of mutual trust, mutual respect and non-interference in each other's internal affairs whilst striving for mutually economic benefits and achieving common development (Li, 2006b: 17).

In December 1982, to further promote confidence in the effectiveness of China's foreign aid, the Prime Minister, Zhao Ziyang, conducted China's second ministerial tour of Africa.[7] Upon completion, Zhao announced in Dar es Salaam on 13 January 1983 that:

> On the basis of continuingly providing available foreign aid, the Chinese government is seeking to expand economic and technical relations with African

> countries, to advance the essentially donated, unidirectional assistance to effect mutually beneficial economic and technical cooperation; therefore promoting Sino-African relations as the power to achieve our individual economic development and modernisation.
>
> (*Xinhua*, 1983)

Such an aim was summarised on Zhao's return as the intention by China to uphold equality and mutual benefits, place emphasis on practical results, bring forward diverse methods and achieve common progress. These words later became the specific guideline for China's foreign aid in Africa, i.e., the Four Principles of Economic and Technical Cooperation between China and African Countries (中非经济技术合作四项原则). These were:

1. In carrying out economic and technological cooperation with African countries, China abides by the principles of unity and friendship, equality and mutual benefit, respects their sovereignty, does not interfere in their internal affairs, attaches no political conditions and asks for no privileges whatsoever.
2. In China's economic and technological cooperation with African countries, full play will be given to the strong points and potentials of both sides on the basis of their actual needs and possibilities, and efforts will be made to achieve good economic results with less investment, shorter construction cycles and quicker returns.
3. China's economic and technological cooperation with African countries takes a variety of forms suited to the specific conditions, such as offering technical services, training technical and management personnel, engaging in scientific and technological exchanges, undertaking construction projects and entering into cooperative production and joint ventures. With regard to the cooperative projects it undertakes, the Chinese side will see to it that the signed contracts are observed, the quality of work guaranteed and stress laid on friendship. The experts and technical personnel dispatched by the Chinese side do not ask for special treatment.
4. The purpose of China's economic and technological cooperation with African countries is to contribute to the enhancement of the self-reliant capabilities of both sides and promote the growth of the respective national economies by complementing and helping each other.

If one examines Beijing's economic and developmental connections with Africa in this period it is apparent that China's concern for its own economic evolvement was paramount. Instead of granting spectacular aid as in the past, China insisted that it would suit 'the task to one's capacity in giving economic and technical aid' (*Jingji Ribao*, 9 June 1986). As China's preoccupation was with improving the economic situation of the country, undertakings of overseas aid necessarily experienced a decline. This obviously influenced the amount of aid given to African states, and it became even more apparent that China's foreign aid budget was limited. Aid which was granted was largely small scale with only short periods of Chinese commitment necessary. Capital investment in such projects was minimal, and the need for trained technical assistance after the project was completed and spare-part requirements was relatively small (although as will be shown, this later led to problems). In an attempt to continue to boost China's prestige, Beijing ingeniously suggested what it termed "triangular co-operation" whereby financial assistance from developed countries would be used to fund Chinese aid projects in Africa (*Xinhua,* 17 May 1986). Unsurprisingly, this particular Chinese plan was not greeted with any enthusiasm by the West.

Chinese policy was now committed to cultivating as many allies as possible in Africa and to maintaining those friendships already in existence through low-level aid projects and limited grants of capital. The focus now was on unassuming diplomatic endeavours designed to maintain existing Sino-African linkages and to carry on providing practical developmental economic assistance to those states that needed it. Promotional propaganda advancing Beijing's version of Marxist-Leninism and seemingly routine agitational threats against China's perceived enemies – notably the Superpowers – had now been discarded. In its place were projects aimed at assisting Africa's agriculture and health.

To implement the new principles, carry on further research and devise measures for the future of foreign aid, the 6th National Conference on Foreign Aid was convened in September 1983. In addition to re-stressing the importance of consolidation and cooperation with Third World countries, it placed particular emphasis on the cost-effectiveness of aid. As this conference concluded:

> In order to conduct further foreign aid, China needs to arrange projects and programs in accordance with the available resources, to explore varied methods and therefore to utilise the limited funds available to achieve maximum practical results. While keeping foreign aid expenditure within China's financial capacity, the distribution of foreign aid must also be optimised in order to strictly avoid past mistakes where certain countries were allocated significantly more foreign aid than others.
>
> (Li, 2010: 22)

As a result of this conference, not only was China's foreign aid given a new framework, but the confidence in providing foreign aid was resumed, thus guaranteeing the ensuing foreign aid implementations. Further, in accordance with these instructions, Zhao subsequently outlined in 1984 the specific emphases on aid in a government report:

> For the existing foreign aid with Third World countries, we will continue to provide services to realise their economic potentials. For the agreed foreign aid projects and programs, we will continue to fulfil them to the highest standard. As for the Third World countries that are suffering particular difficulties, we will keep on providing available foreign aid, with the focus on

> less financially demanding, more effective projects and programs that directly benefits the local people.
>
> (1986: 504)

Adhering to these emphases, China began to request that the recipient countries share some of the foreign aid costs, and officially adjusted its aid objective in Africa from building African industrial and agricultural foundations to reducing expenditure while consolidating outcomes. Moreover, on the basis that China instructed its future foreign aid planning to be downsized in order to reduce expenditures, less financially demanding and less technical projects replaced industrial and agricultural foundation projects (Yang and Chen, 2010). Aid which was granted was largely small scale with only short periods of Chinese commitment necessary. Capital investment in such projects was minimal, and the need for trained technical assistance after the project was completed and spare-part requirements was relatively small.

To coordinate with China's emphasis on domestic development, aside from introducing the Four Principles as an Africa-centred, economic interests–emphasised addition to the Eight Principles, China's aid administration was restructured along with major reforms to accommodate the new objectives of reducing expenditure while consolidating outcomes. In March 1982, with approval from the Standing Committee of the 5th National People's Congress, the Ministry of Foreign Trade, Ministry of Foreign Economic Liaison, State Planning Committee and Foreign Investment Managing Committee (外国投资管理委员会) merged into the Ministry of Foreign Economic and Trade (对外经济贸易部). In this process, the Ministry of Foreign Economic Liaison was transformed into a single department, the Department of Aid to Foreign Countries (援外司) within the new ministry. This took charge of aid planning and budget management, while the management of implementation was entirely delegated to the Complete Plant Export Company, at this stage also known as the Foreign Aid Implementation Bureau (援外项目执行局).

Ensuing this institutional merger, China's aid was improved with the Investment Responsibility Mechanism (投资包干制) and the Contract Responsibility Mechanism (承包责任制). Of these operating mechanisms, the former was implemented to replace the Delivery Department In-chief Mechanism, which was found to be unable to adequately control expenditure. It assigned the responsibility of overseeing the entire implementation process to the given ministerial or provincial departments, therefore granting autonomy. Following three years of piloting, in December 1983, the Contract Responsibility Mechanism was then implemented, based on a policy of creating separate enterprises from government administrations. Instead of ministerial and provincial institutions, the newly established subsidiary enterprises of these institutions (i.e., State Owned Enterprises [SOE]) became the main parties of aid implementation. They were made to work to the advantage of realising financial autonomy (Huang and Hu, 2009).

To overcome difficulties, China trialled a number of tailored methods based on the existing Technical Aid packages, including Management Participating, Management Cooperation, Mandatory Administration, Joint Investment Cooperation and Contract by Lease (Lu, 1988). In order to move these individual trials to standard practice, and with the aim of fundamentally revising the situation, in January 1984 the Ministry of Foreign Economic and Trade delivered additional instructions in the work of *Opinions Regarding the Consolidation of Constructed Complete Projects* (关于巩固建成经援成套项目成果的意见). On the basis of integrating Management Cooperation (管理合作) into Technical Aid, this reform enabled Chinese experts to be directly involved in project management and operation.

The search for methods of delivering effective and sustainable foreign aid continued. In 1987, owing to the lack of technical and managerial capacities of the recipient country, a team of Chinese experts was dispatched to lease the Togo Anie Sugar Refinery, which had been delivered by Chinese aid in January 1987. In view of the improved production subsequent to the lease, this approach quickly became a new implementation method of China's foreign aid, which became known as Foreign Aid Joint Ventures and Cooperative Projects (援外项目合资合作). In support of this method, the State Council approved the Fund of Multiple Foreign Aid Forms (多种形式援外专项资金) and allocated this to the management of MOFTEC and the MOF. Regardless of it being relatively limited in scale (a maximum 200 million Chinese Yuan from China's foreign aid budget per annum), it was nevertheless the first attempt by the Chinese in the promotion of what was regarded as a mutually beneficial, cooperation-based foreign aid approach (Liu, 1998).

What was a decade of continuing aid reform ended with the collapse of the Soviet Union in the early 1990s and the events of Tiananmen Square. Post-1989, China underwent a re-evaluation of its foreign policy vis-à-vis the Superpowers and towards Africa and the developing world as the Tiananmen crackdown resulted in a severe crisis in China's relations with the West. The Chinese leadership had been surprised by the depth of Western condemnation of Tiananmen Square and responded by an assiduous courting of the Third World. The anti-imperialist and anti-hegemonist rhetoric was revived.

Whilst the events in Tiananmen Square provoked a serious rupture in relations with the West, the Third World's reaction was far more muted. As one observer noted 'the events of June 1989 . . . did not affect the PRC's relations with the Third World as it did with the Western world . . .What changed [was] the PRC's attitude towards the Third World countries, which . . . turned from one of benign neglect to one of renewed emphasis' (Gu, 1995: 125).

Tiananmen in many respects revealed the place of Africa in China's thinking. As one source revealed:

> In the past, China's relations with Western countries have been overheated, giving a cold-shoulder to the Third World countries and old friends (meaning Africa). Judging from the events in this turmoil, it seems that at a critical moment it was still those Third World countries and old friends who gave China the necessary sympathy and support. Therefore from now on China will put more efforts in resuming and developing relations with these old friends.
>
> (*Cheng Ming*, 10 October 1989)

Isolated by the West, the PRC became introspective for a period and condemned foreign criticism of its domestic policy as "hegemonic" interference in its affairs. Indeed, the Chinese response to post-Tiananmen criticism was largely defiant and uncompromising. As a self-perceived "great power" and with historical baggage continually in mind, Beijing deeply resented the West's critique of China's human rights record and the meddling in China's affairs – resonant of the historical imperialist in Chinese eyes. As one Chinese commentator put it, 'hostile forces in other countries in the world today are not willing to see the socialist PRC moving towards prosperity and strength and are also determined to overthrow it . . . this [bears] a striking similarity to . . . past events' (*Liaowang*, 23 October 1989). Deng Xiaoping also melodramatically commented, 'I am Chinese and familiar with the history of foreign aggression against China. When I heard . . . Western countries . . . had decided to impose sanctions on China, my immediate association was [of] 1900 when the allied forces of eight foreign powers invaded China' (Deng, 1994: 344).

As a result, China embarked on a campaign to widen its contacts in the developing world as an attempt to counter and resist the isolation endured at the hands of the West. Since the events of June 1989, a shift in PRC foreign policy orientation and interaction occurred (Yu, 1991: 34). Thus between June 1989 and June 1992, Qian Qichen visited 14 African countries. In addition, numerous developing world dignitaries paid visits to China, with Africa second only to Asia in the number of dignitaries visiting China in the post-Tiananmen era. Such a fact highlights the importance Beijing held Africa as a constituency in garnering potential political support. Mindful of the fact that the West is in fact a minority in international organisations such as the United Nations, courting of developing world nations such as in Africa would enable the PRC to successfully resist Western "hegemonism", which now took on the role of interfering in China's domestic affairs. Premier Li Peng's comments at the Asian-African Law Consultative Committee meeting in Beijing in March 1990 are illuminating on this point and worthy of quoting:

> [The] new order of international politics means that all countries are equal, and must mutually respect each other . . . regardless of their differences in political systems and ideology. No country is allowed to impose its will on other countries, seek hegemony in any regions, or pursue power politics to deal with other countries. They are not allowed to interfere in the internal affairs of the developing countries, or pursue power politics in the name of 'human rights, freedom and democracy'.
>
> (*Xinhua*, 12 March 1990)

Whilst it was unclear from exactly whence Li Peng derived these new "rules" of the international system, it was transparent that anti-hegemonism became a major theme of China's foreign policy once again and drove to a certain extent the PRC's policies in Africa. Whilst the Soviet bloc collapsed, China still conceptualised the world as being threatened by hegemony. As Deng asserted (1994: 318), 'the world used to be dominated by the Superpowers. Now things have changed. Nonetheless, power politics is escalating, and a few Western developed countries wish to monopolise the world. This is something of which we are very aware'.

During this period, China changed its foreign aid approaches. As Minister of Foreign Economic and Trade Li Lanqing put it, 'Where possible, China's foreign aid in the future should be further integrated with economic and technical cooperation, to develop across financial and human resources sectors and comprehensively establish cooperation based relationship with the recipient countries' (1993, cited in Zhang, 2009).

Underscoring the new approach to China's foreign aid, the 1st Session of the Eighth National People's Congress changed the Ministry of Foreign Economic and Trade to the Ministry of Foreign Trade and Economic Cooperation (对外贸易经济合作部). It also reorganised the Complete Plant Export Company to the Complete Plant Import and Export Cooperation Group, generally known as COMPLANT (成套设备进出口集团公司), by making it a SOE instead of a subsidiary public institution. While completely centralising aid administration to MOFTEC, COMPLANT was made responsible for aid implementation, which substantially improved planning integration and maximised the financial autonomy of implementation. In addition, the operating mechanism of China's foreign aid, was upgraded to the Enterprise Contract Responsibility Mechanism (企业总承包责任制) to further accommodate institutional reforms.

Concluding remarks

To sum up this period of China's foreign aid in Africa, following the inauguration of the reform policy and additional foreign aid principles, China's aid focus was further adjusted to Africa, and the newly stressed economic interests significantly improved the efficiency of China's aid. Not only did the initial reform of aid relieve China's financial burdens but it also introduced China's foreign aid to an emphasis on both political and economic benefits. China's aid regime successfully broke away from its earlier situation dominated by political interests. It began to take shape in a relatively balanced agenda that encompassed both economic and political interests. Not only was China at this stage enabled with international assistance to promote domestic development, but its own aid programs transformed from being predominately instruments of political ideology to an approach for promoting bilateral economic development. Consistent with the principal aim of helping African countries achieve self-reliance, this dimension of economic interests replaced the objectives of building African industrial and agricultural foundations. There was clearly a new emphasis on reducing expenditure while consolidating outcomes.

In line with this revised objective, The Four Principles were subsequently put forward to lead China's foreign aid through this period. As an inheritance from and development of The Eight Principles, this new guidance was established upon China's claimed principles of internal affairs non-interference and mutual respect. The Chinese government centralised the administration of its foreign aid and also allowed SOEs to take over implementation to maximise the economic interests of its aid. Moreover, determined to reduce expenditure, with regards to the progression of aid implementation, this transitional period witnessed the creation of a number of cooperative methods. Not only were explorations carried out in the implementations of aid projects but Beijing also attempted to direct its aid towards mutual cooperation by initiating particular funds. Whilst Goods and Materials Aid and Cash Aid continuously decreased, Complete Project Aid and the Management Cooperation integrated Technical Aid again led China's development assistance to Africa, with the proportion of Complete Project Aid and Technical Aid rising to 74 per cent by the mid-1980s (see Shi, 1989).

Nevertheless, the shortage of financial capacity forced China to opt for the less financially demanding and less technical landmark projects. One Chinese official commented: 'Albeit such an alteration seemingly catered for both China's contemporary economic situation and African countries' divergent local conditions, the nature of these projects determined their limitations in delivering a similar degree of development assistance compared to the industrial and agricultural projects'.[8] As a result of the inadequately delivered Complete Projects Aid and Technical Aid, the shortage of human resources led to insufficiencies, regardless of the Management Cooperation scheme that was arranged to resolve this issue. As noted by Zheng, 'Even with the switch to landmark projects, most of the African recipient countries have still failed to maintain their functionality, and eventually became dependent on China's foreign aid' (2000: 98).

To conclude, during the initial reform of China's foreign aid, other than some improvements made in accordance with China's development concerns, the outcomes of China's aid in Africa by and large remained the same. From the Chinese standpoint, it put forward the objective of reducing expenditure while consolidating outcomes, and China's aid began to transform from a donation-based approach to ostensible mutually beneficial cooperation. From the African side, given the general incompetency of China's aid, some of the recipient countries raised concerns and felt that 'the Chinese [were] keen on securing foreign exchanges rather than providing development assistance' (Yan, 1987: 53). As pointed out by Li, 'Despite China's new funding method and Management Cooperation, the majority of its foreign aid have stayed in non-profit forms' (2010: 24). With both donor and recipient countries struggling with the initial reforms of China's aid, the opportunity arose to develop another series of reforms. Thus, by the end of 1993, China began to further reform its foreign aid.

Notes

1 Fang Yi was appointed Vice Director of the State Planning Commission in between 1961 and 1963, and he was subsequently appointed Head of the Foreign Economic Liaison Commission in between 1964 and 1970 and Minister of the Ministry of Foreign Economic Liaison in between 1970 and 1976.

2 Among the total of 23 proposing countries, 11 were African: Algeria, Sierra Leone, Equatorial Guinea, Guinea, Mali, Mauritania, Congo, Somalia, Sudan, Tanzania and Zambia. The 26 African countries among the total of 76 endorsing countries were: Algeria,

Burundi, Botswana, Cameroon, Congo, Egypt, Equatorial Guinea, Ethiopia, Ghana, Guinea, Kenya, Libya, Mali, Mauritania, Morocco, Nigeria, Rwanda, Senegal, Sierra Leone, Somalia, Sudan, Togo, Tunisia, Uganda, Tanzania and Zambia.

3 Interview with senior Chinese official, Freetown, Sierra Leone, 2 September 2011.

4 Interview with senior Chinese official, Freetown, Sierra Leone, 29 August 2011.

5 There were 27 additional African countries signed the Agreement on Economic and Technical Cooperation with China between 1971 and 1978. These were Equatorial Guinea, Sierra Leone, Ethiopia, Rwanda, Mauritius, Tunisia, Togo, Burundi, Madagascar, Benin, Zaire (DRC), Cameroon, Chad, Senegal, Upper Volta (Burkina Faso), Niger, Gabon, Mozambique, Morocco, Gambia, Guinea-Bissau, Cape Verde, São Tomé and Príncipe, Comoros, Botswana, Seychelles and Liberia.

6 China terminated its foreign aid to Vietnam and Albania on 3 and 7 July 1978, respectively.

7 Duration: 20 December 1982 to 17 January 1983. The visited countries were Egypt, Algeria, Morocco, Guinea, Gabon, Zaire, Congo, Zambia, Zimbabwe, Tanzania and Kenya.

8 Interview with senior Chinese official, Freetown, Sierra Leone, 29 August 2011.

3 Contemporary China's foreign aid in Africa

This chapter examines the development of China's foreign aid in Africa since 1994. It focuses on two primary questions: What are China's current foreign aid objectives in Africa? How does China currently deliver its aid to Africa? With these questions in mind, the chapter is arranged into two sections exploring, first, the contemporary aims of China's aid to Africa and, second, the practices it has developed in pursuit of these aims.

In the first section, the development of China's aid from the early 1990s is examined. This covers two effective periods: The Further Reform (1994–2004) and The Return (2005–present). On the basis of finding that the development of China's aid to Africa was further pushed to explore mutually beneficial economic cooperation, this section first brings out the profit-seeking nature of China's aid funding method through the Concessional Loan. Having established that this commercial approach to aid overshadowed China's "traditional" foreign aid practices for almost an entire decade, the chapter surveys China's current aid objectives of improving people's livelihoods.

Subsequent to identifying China's current foreign aid objectives in Africa, the second section focuses on China's duly developed aid planning and implementation approaches. On the basis of elaborating on the framework introduced by *The White Paper* of 2011, this chapter's sections are then composed of three parts that detail the current practices of China's foreign aid. To be specific, the first part summarises the institutions involved in planning and managing China's aid, setting out China's current aid operating mechanisms. In the second part, methods of funding and aid statistical regulations are discussed. Finally, based on reviewing China's foreign aid implementation methods, the third part links each of these methods to the management institutions. It is aimed that this chapter completes our understanding of how China's foreign aid has developed. What needs to be stressed is that China's foreign aid has split into two paths since the inauguration of the Concessional Loan in 1994. In accordance with the specifics pointed out by the Chinese officials put forth in the introduction chapter, this study is concentrated only on the foreign aid funded by Chinese government budgets and used for the promotion of recipient countries' economic development and welfare (this is "traditional foreign aid"). This is distinguished from the Concessional Loan as a new, integrated type of foreign aid. In terms of the Concessional Loan, as identified earlier, it conflicts to some extent with the general understanding of recognised aid norms, and as such it is not considered as China's foreign aid in this study, but rather as a *competitively rated* commercial funding method.

From the Grand Economic Strategy to the 5th FOCAC Meeting, 1994–2012

In pace with the evolving global development trend and China's deepening domestic reforms, both the internal and external situations for China's foreign aid underwent profound changes. With the ending of the Cold War and the stabilising of the international situation, political rivalry and military confrontations declined between states. Traditional foreign aid donor countries have shifted their priorities away from the Least Developed Countries (LDGs) and have begun focusing instead on China, India, and other developing countries that possess greater capabilities of repayment (and also the development of markets). Since the mid-1990s, this current has gradually pushed grant-based foreign aid out of the focus of international development assistance. Now, business-orientated cooperation is the dominant theme in modern-day donor-recipient relations (Yuan and Yang, 2003). China is really no exception in this regard.

Regarding China's foreign aid specifically, realising that inter-governmental cooperation-based foreign aid was no longer satisfactory, China has speeded up its transformation of foreign aid towards one in which the economic interests of China are embedded. Following the institutional adjustments at the end of 1993, which established a more marketised foreign aid arrangement (MOFTEC for aid administration and COMPLANT for implementation), the Chinese government introduced development guidance for its current foreign aid, known as the Grand Economic Strategy (大经贸战略). In line with this strategy, pushing forward aid restructuring and promoting direct cooperation between Chinese and recipient countries' enterprises thereafter became the new goals (Lin, 1995).

The further reform

On 11 May 1994, following the conclusion of China's foreign aid institutional reform and market economic system conversion, the Minister of MOFTEC, Wu Yi, addressed The 1990s China's International Business Strategy Seminar (吴仪在90年代中国外经贸战略国际研讨会上的主旨报告), stating that:

> Considering the next step of Reform and Opening Up, the increasing demand for further development and the current circumstances of foreign trade, China's foreign economic relations in the 1990s must proceed in accordance with import and export trade based goods, capital, technology, labour cooperation and exchange in foreign trade, manufacturing, technology and finance. All jointly as the Grand Economic Strategy.
>
> (1994: 4)

In light of this, not only was China's aid continuously asked to uphold friendship-building, but it was also intended to stimulate China's foreign trade, to assist Chinese enterprises to open up the markets of recipient countries and to carry out various funding methods based on comprehensively focused cooperation (Zhang, 2012b).

Apparently, grant-based, non-profit driven traditional foreign aid was unable to achieve this advanced and economically based objective. To break out of such a restrained framework and interact with China's market economy, the next step in China's aid reform was twofold. On the one hand, it focused on diversifying aid implementation participants in order to truly pass on the financial autonomy of implementation to enterprises, as well as to improve budget coordination amongst financial institutions. On the other hand, it stressed expanding the current implementation approaches in order to explore economic cooperation, one grounded in business-orientated development assistance (Li, 2010). Abiding by this thinking, after a year of research and preparation, the State Council brought forward in May 1995 a paper entitled *On the Issues Related to the Foreign Aid Reform Approval* (关于改革援外工作有关问题的批复). This officially launched the sequence of China's aid reforms emphasising domestic economic development needs (Huang, 2010).

In accordance with this formal approval, whilst also reconfirming the Eight Principles and Four Principles relevance to China's aid in the subsequently convened National Conference on Foreign Aid (in October 1995), the State Council clearly expressed its encouragement for all aid projects that were going to be carried out on any kind of joint management, cooperative management and enterprises solely operated by China (Huang and Lang, 2010). Aimed at integrating China's reform experience with its aid and initiating a schema where foreign aid combined with overseas investments, the Vice Prime Minister Zhu Rongji pointed out that with regard to China's aid:

> We have to adopt incentive policies to support our outstanding enterprises in order to conduct various sector-specific cooperation programmes in Africa. The goal is to promote these viable resources, to make them marketable and profitable at both medium and small sized project level and to push forward direct cooperation between competitive Chinese and recipient countries' enterprises.
>
> (Qi, 1995: 4)

To put these words into practice, in the subsequent report entitled *Implementation of the State Council's Directives, Further Reform of Foreign Aid* (贯彻国务院指示, 进一步改革援外工作), the specifics for China's further foreign aid adjustments were discussed. With regards to the packaging of China's aid, it was suggested that China should promote the existing implementation methods of Foreign Aid Joint Ventures and Cooperative Projects, as well as the newly introduced funding methodology of the Government Subsidised Concessional Loan (政府贴息优惠贷款).[1] This Concessional Loan is a funding method that mobilises funds from commercial banks where the interest rate is subsidised by the government budget so that the loan interest rate is reduced for recipient countries and hence loan conditions become more favourable. Concerning the utilisation of these, it was added that the Chinese government should encourage and support enterprises to apply the former method to reinstate the operations of delivered projects and to employ the latter method to initiate viable, marketable and profitable medium to small sized projects. Considering the future budget planning of China's aid, it was confirmed that 'aside from continuingly fulfilling the already agreed Interest-free Loans, China hereafter terminates this funding method fully supports the promotion of Concessional Loan and Grant' (Zou, 1995).

Following these instructions, China made a number of efforts in Africa in promoting these new types of its foreign aid. In addition to the Vice Prime Ministers Zhu Rongji, Li Lanqing and Qian Qichen's 18 visits in 1995 (Li, 2012: 19), Chairman Jiang Zemin conducted China's first head of state African tour in 1996.[2] Subsequent to recognising that African countries' rich resources and vast potential markets were highly complementary to China's economic development, Jiang noted that 'Africa's immense territory and rich natural resources has provided it with great potentials for economic development . . . China should place particular attention on conducting variously sized, broadly focused mutual beneficial cooperation between capable Chinese and African enterprises' (quoted in Chen, 2008). On his return, not only were these words put forward as China's contemporary economic development guidance (the Going Out strategy [走出去战略]), but China's aid thereafter stepped up from a passive role in China-Africa relations to become the initiative that drove China's economic links to the continent.

After three years of successful aid reform, and in response to Africa's readily growing interests in China's business-orientated combination of cooperation and aid, China decided to advance this relationship to an institutional level. Thus it launched the Forum of China-Africa Cooperation (FOCAC) and convened its first ministerial meeting in Beijing on 10 October 2000 (Zhang, 2006). This conference was concluded with *The Beijing Declaration* (中非合作论坛北京宣言) and *The Program for China-Africa Cooperation in Economic and Social Development* (中非经济和社会发展合作纲领) as guides for the development of Sino-African relations. In the words of Minister of MOFTEC, Shi Guangsheng, China additionally promised:

> To gradually increase foreign aid to Africa to implement projects and programs across extensive sectors; to cancel the debt of 10 billion CNY to relieve the Heavily Indebted Poor Countries (HIPCs) and LDGs; to set up particular funds for joint ventures and cooperative projects; and to establish a Africa Human Resources Development Fund (非洲人力资源开发基金) to help African countries train professional talents.
>
> (2000)

As a result of the establishment of this multilateral liaising platform, FOCAC ensured a steady development of China-Africa relationships so that by the time the second ministerial meeting convened in Addis Ababa in 2003, China's compliance with the Beijing Declaration and its prompt efforts in realising its pledges had won much praise from African states.[3] These efforts included establishing 22 special committees to liaise with aid implementation, cancelling debt worth 10.9 billion Yuan, delivering 72 complete projects, introducing 1.2 billion US dollars worth of investments with 826 Chinese enterprises, training more than 7,000 professional personnel, achieving more than 20 bilateral ministerial visits, etc. Not only did this demonstrate that China had competently integrated its own economic interests with its aid, but that the progress of FOCAC had built a solid foundation for the implementation of the Going Out policy.

The mid-1990s and onwards saw a huge rise in China's foreign aid in Africa. Guided by the Grand Economic Strategy and the Going Out policy, further reforms advanced China's aid with government, enterprises and financial institutions working within a joint participation framework. China's aid funding and implementation methods were further diversified. At this stage, China determined Africa to be its main economic cooperation partner, thus Africa became the primary ground for China's foreign aid.

Along with this substantial shift, China carried out a number of adjustments to its aid approach. Of these, the most significant changes were the introduction of the Concessional Loan and the promotion of the Foreign Aid Joint Ventures and Cooperative Projects. A dedicated policy bank, the Export and Import Bank (EXIM Bank) was consequently established in 1994 to manage the former. By collecting repayments on China's early Interest-free Loans, Low-interest Loans, and the Fund of Multiple Foreign Aid Forms, the Fund of Foreign Aid Joint Ventures and Cooperative Projects (援外合资合作项目基金) were also set up four years on to support the latter. However, what needs to be pointed out here is that Foreign Aid Joint Ventures and Cooperative Projects were only a small part of China's foreign aid. It was more a supportive method owing to the particular focus of China's earlier delivered projects. Equally, it had a rather limited financial allowance (each loan generally did not exceed the amount of 1.53 million US dollar).[4]

In addition to these newly integrated implementation and funding methods, regarding the development of China's traditional aid approaches in this period, in spite of China's unimproved aid budget, it separated the Human Resource Development Cooperation (HRDC) from Technical Aid in 1998. Replacing the previous training programs and scholarships that were focused on Chinese aid projects, this improved HRDC was broadly organised in the subjects of Government Official Seminars, Technical Professional Training, Overseas Student Scholarships, Expert Going Out Programs and Exchange Programs (Li et al., 2009). It further pushed the emphasis of China's traditional foreign aid towards developing African human resource capacity. More to the point, according to the pledges that China made in the FOCAC meeting in 2000, and in addition to setting up the Africa Human Resources Development Fund to support the above-mentioned programs, China's foreign aid also welcomed a new implementation method of Debt Relief.[5]

Together with these improvements in China's aid approaches, the changes applied to China's institutions and mechanisms can be considered. Subsequent to the establishment of the MOFTEC and COMPLANT in 1993, China successively introduced the Project Tendering Mechanism (援外项目招投标机制), Project Supervision Mechanism (援外项目设计施工监理机制) and other integral mechanisms to encourage the involvement of SOEs (Xue, 2011), and to further expand the scope of participants in aid deliveries (Xiao and Zhang, 2002). Additionally, China also put forward a series of codes of practices to govern the amplified aid process.[6] In March 2003, with the purpose of further integrating China's domestic trade with its international economic cooperation, the 1st Plenary Session of the Tenth National People's Congress converted MOFTEC into the Ministry of Commerce (商务部) and appointed to it the complete administration of China's internal and external economic and trade affairs.

This further reform period led to an integrated aid approach in association with China's overseas economic and trade cooperation. It also strategically fixed China's partnership with Africa. Provided with the extensive promotion and wide acceptance of its new cooperative aid approaches, the earlier situation in which only the bare minimum of loan repayments were received was substantially altered. As implied by a senior Chinese official, 'By providing foreign aid loans through a commercially managed policy bank in essence changed the scenario from that of a friendly government loan to that of a business loan, and in doing so China has managed to recover more than 98% of its total loans due from Africa'.[7] As a result of this significantly improved financial situation, the Concessional Loan became the most prominent funding method of China's foreign aid.

In contrast, while China's commercial approach to aid created economic benefits for both China and Africa, the development of China's traditional aid has yet to make any substantial progress. Aside from the HRDC programs introduced in the late 1990s, China's traditional foreign aid remained focused on providing landmark projects.[8] Only in August 2004, subsequent to the change in principal leadership did China's traditional foreign aid catch the attention of its decision-makers once again. As indicated in China's first Conference on China's Economic Diplomacy in Developing Countries (全国对发展中国家经济外交的工作会议), 'For future foreign aid works, China has to make due improvements in both its political and economic influences in the international ground, adequately places foreign aid emphasis on people's livelihoods related projects, emergency humanitarian assistance, medical teams and human resources training' (Xinhua, 2004). Thus another change in the trajectory of China's aid to Africa began.

The return

A year after the above-mentioned conference, on the basis of continuing to promote its more commercialised aid approach, China's traditional foreign aid made a sharp return on 15 September 2005, when Chairman Hu Jintao delivered a speech entitled *Strive to Build A Harmonious World, Where There is Permanent Peace and Common Prosperity* (努力建设持久和平、共同繁荣的和谐世界) at the Summit on the 60th Anniversary of the Establishment of the United Nations. The key points of his speech focused on the need to 'uphold equality and realise harmonious cooperation, persist in mutual trust and realise common security, uphold mutual benefits and realise common development, uphold the spirit of inclusiveness and realise civilised dialogue' (*Xinhua*, 2005). This pointed to the fact that 'the substance of a win-win situation is not only a simple share of benefits, but requires caring for and supporting poor and developing countries' (Li, 2010: 26). China's foreign aid swiftly entered a new development phase in the aim of building a harmonious world.

To demonstrate China's commitment, Hu announced in the successive UN High-Level Meeting on Financing for Development, the Five Measures to Accelerate Development for Developing Countries (中国加强与发展中国家经济合作的五项举措). These were:

1 China has decided to accord zero tariff treatment to some products from all of the 39 least developed countries (LDCs) having diplomatic relations with China, which covers most of the China-bound exports from these countries.
2 China will further expand its aid programs to the heavily-indebted poor countries (HIPCs) and LDCs, and, through bilateral channels, write off or forgive in other ways, within the next two years, all the overdue parts as of the end of 2004 of the interest-free or low-interest governmental loans owed by all the HIPCs having diplomatic relations with China.
3 Within the next three years, China will provide 10 billion US dollar in concessional loans and preferential export buyer's credit to other developing countries to improve their infrastructure and cooperation between enterprises on both sides.
4 China will, in the next three years, increase its assistance to other developing countries, African countries in particular, by providing them with anti-malaria drugs and other medicines, helping them set up and improve medical facilities and training medical staff. Specific programs will be implemented through such mechanisms as the Forum on China-Africa Cooperation as well as bilateral channels.
5 China will train 30,000 personnel of various professions from other developing countries within the next three years so as to help them speed up their human resources development.

These pointers outlined the next phase of China's foreign aid. According to the announcement, besides continuing to support the recipient countries' economic development utilising Debt Relief, Concessional Loans (and Preferential Buyer's Credits, 优惠出口买方信贷) and Zero-tax Treatment, two of the five measures directly emphasised improving people's livelihoods. In addition to restating the importance of medical and health development, particularly with consideration to Africa's current development conditions, China's determination to advance developing countries' human resources capacities was for the first time elevated to a primary concern in its aid.

Subsequent to this UN meeting, and in view of further aligning China's Going Out policy towards Africa, the Chinese government quickly released the first issue of *China's African Policy Paper* (中国对非洲政策文件) in January 2006. This paper first suggested that China and Africa should establish politically mutual trust, economically mutual benefits and culturally mutual dialogues. Beyond this conventional rhetoric, new types of strategic partnerships to further expand the scope of China-Africa cooperation were advanced. The document elaborated additional plans for political dialogue, economic cooperation, medical and health support, humanitarian assistance and peace-building operations. Likewise, these plans were correspondingly stated in China's 11th Five-Year Development Guidelines (2006–2010), which was stressed by Hu in the next Central Meeting on the Works of Foreign Affairs in August 2006:

> We should accordingly increase our foreign aid as our economic capacity improves, particularly in consideration to support the developing countries to accelerate their economic development, and to improve their people's livelihoods standards.
>
> (*Xinhua*, 2006a)

In December 2006 in order to follow up commitments and Hu's instructions and in order to advance this cooperative relationship to a strategic partnership, 'deepening political relations of equality and mutual trust, expanding mutually beneficial economic cooperation, boosting mutual learning and cultural exchange, promoting balanced and harmonious global development, and strengthening mutually supported international cooperation' (*Xinhua*, 2006b), the FOCAC Beijing Summit quickly came to the agreements of a Declaration and an Action Plan. As a concluding remark, China also put forward an Eight-Point Plan (中国对非洲合作八项举措) to coordinate this newly established strategic partnership. This was, namely:

1 Increase assistance to African countries, and by 2009 double the size of its assistance to African countries in 2006.
2 Provide 3 billion US dollars in concessional loans and 2 billion US dollars in preferential export buyer's credit to African countries in the next three years.
3 Set up the China-Africa Development Fund, the total amount of which will gradually reach 5 billion US dollars, to give encouragement and support to Chinese companies investing in projects in Africa.
4 Help the African Union to build a convention center in order to support African countries in their efforts to strengthen themselves through unity and speed up African integration.
5 Cancel the repayment of interest-free government loans that had become due by the end of 2005 to China by Heavily Indebted Poor Countries (HIPCs) and Least Developed Countries (LDCs) in Africa that have diplomatic ties with China.

6 Further open the Chinese market to Africa, expand the scope of imports from African LDCs having diplomatic ties with China entitled to zero duty treatment from 190 tariff lines to over 440 tariff lines.
7 Set up three to five overseas economic and trade cooperation zones in African countries in the next three years.
8 Train 15,000 professionals for African countries in the next three years; send 100 senior agro-technology experts to Africa; set up in Africa 10 agro-technology demonstration centres with special features; assist African countries in building 30 hospitals and provide African countries with a grant of 300 million Yuan that is used to supply anti-malaria drugs like artemisinin and build 30 centres for prevention and treatment of malaria; dispatch 300 youth volunteers to African countries; help African countries set up 100 rural schools; increase the number of Chinese government scholarships for African students from the current 2,000 per year to 4,000 per year by the end of 2008.

Initiated with the intention to increase assistance to African countries, and by 2009 double the size of its assistance to African countries, this plan advanced the development of China's traditional aid by a number of specified projects and programs related to improving people's livelihoods. In addition, it also included the building of the African Union Headquarters in Addis Ababa.

From this point onwards, on the basis of setting the developing principles of the China-Africa strategic partnership, the desire to improve people's livelihoods officially evolved into a key objective of China traditional aid. In accordance with which, not only have the packages of China's traditional aid become increasingly complete (blending Complete Project Aid, Technical Aid, Goods and Materials Aid, Medical Teams and HRDC), the advantages of this friendship-building aid was also clearly exercised. By explicitly revolving around Africa's underlying needs of livelihood improvement and human resource capacity building, it has echoed China's principal aid aim of helping African countries achieve self-reliance. Considering the current landmark projects were no longer adequate for this revised objective, schools, hospitals, training programs and other related projects and programs in turn became the main theme of China's foreign aid in Africa.[9]

In the meantime, while attention was on HRDC, in July 2007 the Minister of MOFCOM Bo Xilai stressed at the 1st National Conference on Foreign Aid HRDC (全国援外培训工作会议) that 'since the progress of international development assistances gradually places emphasis on *social* development, in providing China's HRDC, we should follow this tendency, and meet the recipient countries' development concerns so as to create an optimised external environment for our enterprises *going out* and enhance China's international influence'.[10] To be specific about the promotion of HRDC in Africa, as Vice Prime Minister Wu Yi indicated during a specialised ministerial meeting entitled the Conference on Foreign Aid HRDC to Africa (对非援外培训工作会议) convened on the 25 February 2008, 'China's massive investments in African human resources is owed to the rising international importance of Africa and to the particularities of African human resources development in strengthening the China-Africa friendship'.[11] As a result of these instructions, in addition to revising HRDC programs to further accommodate the individual conditions of African countries, China's entire aid planning priorities began to shift from a focus on infrastructures to a focus on building African human resources capacity.[12]

Following two years realising its latest commitments, in September 2008 Prime Minister Wen Jiabao delivered China's future concerns for developing countries and additional foreign aid plans at the UN High-Level Meeting on the Millennium Development Goals (MDGs) (*Xinhua*, 2008). Beginning by demanding that developed countries create an accommodating environment in which developing countries could focus on improving their people's livelihoods instead of simply aiming for economic development, Wen insisted on adopting a 'selfless and non-conditional' approach in providing international development assistance.[13] Upon stressing 'China's commitments to honour its responsibility', Wen proposed the Six Measures for Foreign Aid (对外援助六项措施) for the promotion of the MDGs achievement. These were:

1. In the coming five years, China will double the number of agricultural technology demonstration centres it builds for other developing countries to 30, increase the number of agricultural experts and technicians it sends overseas by 1,000 to double the present figure, and provide agricultural training opportunities in China for 3,000 people from other developing countries.
2. China will contribute 30 million US dollars to the UN Food and Agriculture Organization to establish a trust fund for projects and activities designed to help other developing countries enhance agricultural productivity.
3. China will increase exports and aid to countries facing food shortages.
4. In the coming five years, China will give 10,000 more scholarships to other developing countries and offer training programs exclusively for 1,500 principals and teachers from African countries. China will ensure that the 30 hospitals it builds for African countries are properly staffed and equipped, and train 1,000 doctors, nurses and managers for the recipient countries.
5. China will cancel the outstanding interest-free loans extended to LDCs that mature before the end of 2008, and give zero-tariff treatment to 95 per cent of products from the relevant LDCs.
6. In the coming five years, China will develop 100 small-scale clean energy projects for other developing countries, including small hydropower, solar power and bio-gas projects.

However, by the end of 2008, the dramatic global economic crisis substantially impacted Africa's development once again. Many of the traditional foreign aid donor countries found great difficulties in realising their promised ODA targets and the result was an overall decrease in overall international development assistance. In this situation, China's aid became even more critical. With the aim of building Africa's confidence in China's foreign aid, in February 2009, Hu conducted his second African tour, visiting Mali, Senegal, Tanzania and Mauritius. He announced in Mali that 'although China is also suffering from this economic crisis, nonetheless China will insistently fulfil all the pledges made in the 2006 FOCAC meeting, continuously increase foreign aid to Africa wherever possible within its capacity allowance, and expand the scale of trade and investment so as to boost pragmatic cooperation between China and Africa' (*Xinhua*, 2009).

To prove commitment to honouring China's responsibility, in the immediate 2009 FOCAC Ministerial Conference held in Egypt, while noting that China already fulfilled more than 90 per cent of its 2006 FOCAC pledges, the participants promptly agreed on a Declaration and an Action Plan to proceed with China-Africa strategic cooperation in the next three years. Additionally, following Wen's speech entitled 'Deepening the New Type of China-Africa Strategic Partnership for Sustainable Development', China announced the New Eight-Point Plan (中国对非洲合作新八项举措) to further encourage strategic cooperation between China and Africa. Aside from broadening the scale of projects and programs used to drive international development, concerns regarding the environment and climate changes were also brought to bear on China's foreign aid in Africa. The eight measures were:

1 China proposes the establishment of a China-Africa partnership in addressing climate change and the holding of senior official consultations on a non-regular basis, and strengthening of cooperation in satellite weather monitoring, development and use of new energy, prevention and control of desertification, and urban environmental protection. The Chinese government decides to assist African countries with 100 clean energy projects in the fields of solar energy, bio-gas and small hydropower stations.
2 To intensify cooperation in science and technology, China proposes to launch the China-Africa Science and Technology Partnership Plan, carry out 100 joint research demonstration projects, invite 100 African post-doctoral students to conduct scientific research in China and subsidize them when they return to their home countries to work.
3 In order to improve African countries' capacity in financing, the Chinese government will provide 10 billion US dollars in concessional loans to African countries. China supports the establishment by Chinese financial institutions of a special loan of 1 billion US dollars for the development of small and medium enterprises (SMEs) in Africa. The Chinese government will cancel debts of interest-free government loans that mature by the end of 2009 owed by all HIPCs and the LDCs in Africa having diplomatic relations with China.
4 China will further open its market to African countries. It will gradually give zero-tariff treatment to 95 per cent of exports from the LDCs in Africa having diplomatic relations with China. As the first step, China grants zero-tariff treatment to 60 per cent of the exported commodities from those countries in 2010.
5 In order to further strengthen agricultural cooperation and improve African countries' capacity for food security, China will increase to 20 the total number of agro-technology demonstration centres built for African countries,

send 50 agro-technology teams to Africa and help train 2,000 agro-technicians for African countries.

6 China will continue to deepen China-African cooperation in medical care and public health service. It will provide 500 million Yuan worth of medical equipment and malaria-fighting materials to 30 hospitals and 30 malaria prevention and treatment centres which have been built with China's assistance, and help African countries train a total of 3,000 doctors and nurses.
7 In order to further enhance cooperation in human resource development and education, China will help African countries to build 50 China-Africa friendship schools and train 1,500 school principals and teachers; increase the number of Chinese government scholarships for African students to 5,500 by 2012; and train a total of 20,000 professionals in various sectors for African countries in the next three years.
8 To enlarge people-to-people exchanges, China proposes to implement a China-Africa Joint Research and Exchange Plan to strengthen cooperation and exchanges between scholars and think tanks, which will also provide intellectual support for better policy-making regarding cooperation between the two sides.

Subsequent to putting forward these agreements and pledges, and in line with the focus on improving people's livelihoods and the newly added aim of providing developing countries with an accommodative developing environment, the Minister of MOFCOM, Chen Deming, explained in regards to the next phase of China's foreign aid implementation:

> The New Eight-Point Plan is primarily aimed at improving Africa's self-development capacities. That is in practice, we should keep on building up our HRDC capacity, train more technical and management professionals to accelerate African countries' infrastructure development, improve African people's livelihoods, take further effective measures to reduce poverty and upgrade education and medical standards, support more Chinese enterprises to invest in the cause of African people's livelihoods and create more employment opportunities to deliver the benefits directly to the hands of African people.
> (MOFCAM, 2009b)

Not only did the New Eight-Point Plan continue the principles of China's previous pledges, but in accordance with this new promise, the implementations of China's foreign aid became increasingly versatile.

With these continuingly adjusted aid aims and objectives, in the interest of upgrading China's aid capacity to accommodate change, in the 9th National Conference on Foreign Aid in August 2010, Wen addressed the key points to improve the performance of China's foreign aid:

> Further foreign aid has to be alert to the aspects of foreign aid distribution: pushing the balance further towards LDGs, inland and island countries,

> increasing the proportion of projects that favour local people. It must also be aware of foreign aid quality: upholding scientific appraisal, adequately plan foreign aid projects and improve feasibility research. Additionally, besides focusing on bringing up recipient countries' development capacities, attention also needs to be placed on upgrading foreign aid mechanisms: speed up the process of building an active, effective and flexible foreign aid processing mechanism.
>
> (*Xinhua*, 2010)

Explicitly pointing out the existing issue of the unbalanced development of China's aid and the growing requirements of international development assistance, not only were Wen's instructions highlighting the immediate need to improve China's aid capacity but the methods to further adapt China's aid to African conditions were raised.

Shortly after this conference, Wen attended the UN High-Level Meeting on the MDGs for a second time. With the experiences attained in implementing China's previous Six Measures for Foreign Aid, Wen pointed out the difficulties caused in recent years by natural disasters and the global economic crisis. Whilst calling attention to China's present concerns for developing countries' livelihoods and economic development, Wen put forward new Six Measures for Foreign Aid (对外援助六项新措施) to assist developing countries to achieve the MDGs. These were:

1 Helping improve the people's livelihood in developing countries is the primary objective of China's foreign aid. To date, China has built over 150 schools, nearly 100 hospitals, more than 70 drinking water facilities and 60-plus stadiums for other developing countries. China has sent more than 20,000 medical personnel to nearly 70 countries, offering treatment to hundreds of millions of patients. In the coming five years, China will take the following steps in support of a better livelihood for people in other developing countries: building 200 schools; dispatching 3,000 medical experts, training 5,000 local medical personnel, and providing medical equipment and medicines to 100 hospitals, with priority being given to women's and children's health, and the prevention and treatment of malaria, tuberculosis and AIDS; building 200 clean energy and environmental protection projects; and increasing assistance to small-island developing states in the fields of disaster prevention and mitigation to help build their capacity for countering climate change. China will, within the next three years, donate 14 million US dollars to the Global Fund to Fight AIDS, Tuberculosis and Malaria.
2 Reducing and cancelling the debts of the LDCs. By the end of 2009, the Chinese government had cancelled debts worth 25.6 billion Yuan owed to it by 50 HIPCs and LDCs. Moreover, China will cancel their debts associated with the outstanding governmental interest-free loans that mature in 2010.
3 Deepening financial cooperation with developing countries. To help other developing countries counter the adverse effects of the international financial

crisis, China has provided 10 billion US dollars in concessional loans to African countries and 15 billion US dollars in credit support to ASEAN countries, including Vietnam, Cambodia, Laos and Indonesia. China has contributed an additional $50 billion to the IMF, with an explicit request that the fund should be used, first and foremost, to help LDCs. China will continue to extend financial support of a certain scale to developing countries in the form of concessional loans and preferential export buyer's credit.

4 Broadening economic and trade ties with developing countries. China has worked consistently to create conditions for developing countries to increase their exports to China through tariff relief and other measures. China has made a commitment to phasing in zero-tariff treatment to 95 per cent of products from relevant LDCs. Since July 2010, China has given zero-tariff treatment to imported products from 33 LDCs covering more than 4,700 tariff lines, accounting for the overwhelming majority of the products from these countries. In the future, the Chinese government will give zero-tariff treatment to more products and let more countries benefit from this arrangement, while continuing to encourage Chinese companies to expand investment in developing countries.
5 Strengthening agricultural cooperation with developing countries. China has completed more than 200 agricultural cooperation projects in developing countries, and sent a large number of agro-technology experts to those countries, giving a strong boost to their agricultural development. In the next five years, China will dispatch 3,000 agricultural experts and technical staff abroad, provide 5,000 agriculture-related training opportunities in China, and give priority to cooperation with other developing countries in agricultural planning, hybrid rice cultivation, aquaculture, farmland water conservancy and agricultural machinery development.
6 Helping developing countries enhance their human resources. China has held over 4,000 training courses and trained 120,000 managerial and technical personnel in various professions for developing countries, helping recipient countries build human resources, which are their most valuable assets. In the next five years, China will train another 80,000 professionals in various fields for developing countries. It will also increase the number of scholarships and on-the-job master's degree programs for people from developing countries, and provide training opportunities in China to 3,000 school principals and teachers.

Largely planned in reference to the previous Six Measures, these measures expanded the list of qualifying countries and products exempt from import duties as well as extending debt relief terms. In addition to these items, China also pledged a number of projects and programs in agricultural, educational and human resources development.

In order to realise Wen's instructions and China's promises, the Central Committee designated the following year (2011) as the Year of Foreign Aid Quality (援外质量年). The Minister of MOFCOM named five objectives to the annual foreign aid development agenda: 'Steadily increase foreign aid scale, promote foreign aid legal construction, improve the quality of foreign aid works, boost foreign aid capacity building, and carry out foreign aid research'.[14] Guided by these objectives, as well as releasing 12 codes of practices and initiating 19 research projects in the same year, MOFCOM enforced comprehensive evaluations of China's aid delivered since the first pledges made in 2006. Throughout these evaluations, not only were the aid management institutions and delivery enterprises sent to seminars to study China's foreign aid policies but after inspecting the planning and implementation standards of each project and program, MOFCOM rescinded the qualifications of enterprises that had delivered substandard outcomes, and rewarded those who had achieved excellences.[15]

Moreover, besides these efforts in improving China's aid capacity, MOFCOM released an official publication in April revealing how China's aid works. Mainly concerned with obtaining domestic and international support, demonstrating China's determinations in global poverty reduction and comprehensive development, and sharing China's foreign aid experience with the international community, *The White Paper on China's Foreign Aid* systematically explained China's foreign aid policies, key areas of focus, financial resources, and funding and implementation approaches. This may be considered the first attempt by Beijing to make China's foreign aid transparent.

After emphasising improving foreign aid quality in 2011, noted in the document *Open Up New Prospects for A New Type of China-Africa Strategic Partnership* (继往开来, 开创中非新型战略伙伴关系新局面), the 5th Ministerial Conference of FOCAC convened in Beijing in 2012. On the basis of celebrating the progress of China-Africa cooperation since 2006 and the realisation of both the old and new Eight-Point Plans (FOCAC, 2012c), Hu pointed out the tremendous changes that had taken place in the world in the past six years. Not only was the impact of the global financial crisis still affecting developing countries, but uncertainties and destabilising factors in international developments increased (FOCAC, 2012a). Given such a situation, he proposed five priority areas for foreign aid to be used to advance the China-Africa strategic partnership:

> To expand cooperation in investment and financing, to increase development assistance and deliver the benefits to the African people, to support African integration and help Africa bring up overall development capacity, to carry out people-to-people friendship tying actions, and to promote peace and stability in Africa to create a secure developing environment.
>
> (FOCAC, 2012b)

In the interests of furthering the China-Africa strategic partnership, this proposal inherited the principles of China's previous international commitments; and with concerns to open up new prospects for development, it pointed out additional needs for promoting cultural exchanges as well as African integration. Guided by these development prospects, this conference was concluded with a Declaration (中非合作论坛北京宣言) and an Action Plan (中非合作论坛第五届部长级会议 –

北京行动计划) once more to direct China-Africa strategic cooperation in the next three years.

China's foreign aid is currently placing attention on three key areas. First, while continuously focusing on people's livelihoods improvement, in order to enhance African countries' development capacities, 'further assistance is going to be increased in the forms of HRDC instead of the then concentrated *hardware* projects'.[16] Second, to improve the outcomes of China's aid and to accommodate the influence of China's foreign aid across African borders, 'China is going to promote its foreign aid on the sub-regional level, and drive the common bilateral foreign aid towards multilateral cooperation'.[17] Third, to encourage exchanges between governments, enterprises and the peoples, that is, to create a supportive environment for China's enterprises 'going out', 'China is going to extensively boost China-Africa friendship development at the individual level, initiate and support media visits, research activities and other forms of cultural exchange programs'.[18]

Thus from this point on, and following a decade of rising economic interests, Hu's proposal for building a harmonious world brought China's traditional foreign aid back to the diplomatic frontline, being successfully integrated into China's business expansion on the continent. Especially after the 2006 FOCAC meeting, and the successively implemented Plans and Measures, China's traditional foreign aid entered a phase of rapid development. As evidenced by the rapidly elevated bilateral relationships, China's foreign aid became arguably more effective. With regards to China's traditional foreign aid, while putting forward Multilateral Training Programs to link the participating countries, and introducing Bilateral Training Programs to satisfy the specific needs of an individual country,[19] five national institutions were appointed to accommodate China's rapidly expanding HRDC programs from 2008 onwards. These were the Academy for International Business Officials, China Foreign Affairs University, China Executive Leadership Academy in Pudong, Fujian Foreign Economic and Trade Officials Training Centre and the Training Center of Hubei Agricultural Officials. In the interest of improving the efficiencies of Medical Teams, allocation principles were adjusted so as to prioritise regions with established Chinese hospitals, so that the Medical Teams could be better integrated and thus enhance overall outcomes.[20] China also established a Foreign Aid Expert Database (援外专家库) and a Foreign Aid Project Database (援助项目数据库) to further enhance its foreign aid capacity.[21]

Regarding China's commercial interests in its aid, what needs to be particularly clarified is that although the old and new Eight-Point Plans seem to have introduced two new funding methods to China's foreign aid in Africa – the China-Africa Development Fund (CADF, 中非发展基金) and the Special Loan for the Development of African SMEs (非洲中小企业发展专项贷款), neither of these funding methods should be considered as foreign aid. In spite of their specified arrangements aiming to encourage Chinese enterprises to set up cooperation businesses in Africa and to support the development of African small to medium sized businesses, both of these China Development Bank (中国发展银行) managed funding methods are operating on a complete commercial basis.

In sum, as a result of the balance and integration of foreign aid development priorities, along with the deepening strategic relationship of China and Africa, China's traditional foreign aid was taken to the heart of China's African diplomacy once again, and was successfully merged into a modern development plan concerned with both friendship-building and economic benefits. Through the successively settled Declarations and Action Plans, China's foreign aid continued to focus on the development of Africa's hardware, but also began to balance the emphasis towards Africa's social development. In contrast to past foreign aid that was particularly biased towards prompting recipient countries' economic development, and was primarily the result of inter-government cooperation, it can be said that China's current foreign aid is gradually transforming into a more people-focused development assistance agenda.

The current planning and implementation approaches

Having explored the aims and objectives of China's current foreign aid above, this section details the planning and implementation approaches that China has developed as a result. Aimed at improving our understanding of China's foreign aid practices as well as building up the measures required for investigations into China's foreign aid performance, this section is structured in three parts that closely examines China's foreign aid institutions, funding and implementation methods. In accordance with *The White Paper* (2011), MOFCOM is the administrative ministry authorised by the State Council to oversee foreign aid, along with the Executive Bureau of International Economic Cooperation, the China International Centre for Economic and Technical Exchanges and the Academy of International Business Officials in charge of implementation management. Given the earlier findings that China's aid currently employs three primary funding methods and eight implementation methods, this section now explores how each of these institutions and methods relate.

With regards to the planning of China's aid, the authority over decision-making has always resided in the hands of the Central People's Government.[22] Since the first aid China delivered in the 1950s, the State Council has continuously introduced and reformed aid institutions and mechanisms. Today this means that MOFCOM, the MOF and the MFA lead 21 central and provincial institutions in a joint participation planning arrangement. Through the planning process, MOFCOM is primarily concerned with the economic aspects of foreign aid and mainly deals with the establishment of policies, the drafting of country specific plans and the coordination of implementations. The MFA, on the other hand, is responsible for the political aspect of foreign aid such as the foreign aid principles and the decisions on supply. Additionally, the MOF controls the distribution of China's annual foreign aid budget (Huang and Hu, 2009).

Aside from these larger aid planning responsibilities, there are other institutions that take part according to their specialities, and they undertake planning for specific projects and programs. For example, the Ministry of Agriculture arranges agricultural experts to transfer the required technologies to Chinese agricultural sites while the Ministry of Health allocates medical personnel, medicines and medical equipment to dispatch Medical Teams. In addition to these responsibilities, the management of these specialised projects are also passed to these institutions. Furthermore, adhering to the *Notification of Adjustments of Foreign Aid Project Management* (商务部办公厅关于调整援外项目管理工作职能分工的通知) implemented by MOFCOM in 2008, the implementation management of China's primary foreign aid methods (namely Complete Project Aid, Goods and Materials Aid and HRDC), were likewise assigned to subsidiary public institutions of MOFCOM to further enhance administrative efficiency.[23]

However, what needs to be particularly pointed out is that although the participation of specialised institutions have gradually increased in recent years, representing the Chinese government negotiates and signs off foreign aid agreements, MOFCOM remains the most important foreign aid institution (He, 2010). Altogether within MOFCOM, there are seven departments and institutions associated with the policy making, management and liaison of China's foreign aid.

1 Department of Western Asian and African Affairs of the MOFCOM (商务部西亚非洲司)

Liaising with all of the Economic and Commercial Counsellor's Offices stationed in the West Asian and African region, this department collects and researches country specific data and provides policy suggestions. Apart from bringing together information, it also files other reports investigating the recipient country's trade, economic cooperation, and cultural backgrounds.

2 Department of Aid to Foreign Countries of MOFCOM (商务部对外援助司)

The Department of Aid to Foreign Countries is the central administrative division of China's foreign aid. On the basis of planning for China's annual aid, this department negotiates with the recipient country's government in regards to developing agreements. Domestically, it supervises the institutions managing aid and develops and enforces policies and codes of practices.

3 Chinese Academy of International Trade and Economic Cooperation (CAITEC) (商务部国际贸易经济合作研究院)

As a subsidiary academy of MOFCOM, CAITEC only responds to research initiated by the ministry, and it publishes internally circulated journals and statistics. This academy also edits and releases China's official publications on aid. Besides general economic and trade research, it has a dedicated China-Africa Research Centre, established in 2010.

4 *The Executive Bureau of International Economic Cooperation (商务部国际经济合作事务局)*

Established in 2003, this bureau is appointed and commissioned by MOFCOM to manage the implementation of Complete Project Aid, promote aid services and support Chinese enterprises going out. Primarily concerned with the management of Complete Project Aid, it organises the project bidding, tendering enterprises verification, supervision and inspection of contract execution as well as the construction of Complete Project Aid expert teams and databases. In addition, this executive bureau also currently manages the implementation of Technical Aid.

5 *China International Centre for Economic and Technical Exchanges (CICETE) (中国国际经济技术交流中心)*

The CICETE was founded in 1983 as a subsidiary public institution of the then Ministry of Foreign Economic and Trade. It was first assigned to manage cooperative projects between China and United Nations' organisations such as United Nations Development Programme (UNDP) and United Nations Industrial Development Organization (UNIDO) to promote human resources exchanges and to increase economic and trade cooperation to support the modernisation of China. It was later appointed to provide training courses for Chinese foreign aid personnel and to procure China's Humanitarian Aid supplies. In 2008, the CICETE was additionally assigned to the implementation management of Goods and Materials Aid.

6 *Academy for International Business Officials (AIBO) (商务部培训中心)*

Being the only associated training centre of MOFCOM, the AIBO is one of the first State Council approved Foreign Aid Training Centres (援外培训基地). When AIBO began to engage in HRDC programs in 1998, it was initially assigned to provide economic seminars for the commercial officials. Subsequent to the aid management adjustment in 2008, it became the principal coordinator of China's HRDC programs. In addition to preparing training courses for high-level officials, the AIBO was also appointed to arrange specialised training courses and associated training centres.

7 *Economic and Commercial Counsellor's Office (中国驻外使(领)馆)*

Since China established its first Economic and Commercial Counsellor's Office in Vietnam in 1956, these offices have become the frontline communication and management institutions of China's foreign aid. Principally focused on the local environment research, contract negotiation, aid personnel protection and implementation supervision, the offices not only assist in the planning of China's aid but also supervise projects and program deliveries, as well as monitoring effectiveness and sustainability after project completion.

How China processes its foreign aid

In the process of providing foreign aid, the involved institutions closely liaise and cooperate. When MOFCOM draws up country specific foreign aid plans, it seeks advises from the MFA and MOF, along with other participating institutions, to assist and manage. In terms of process, the exercise of Chinese aid usually begins either with a Letter of Intention from the recipient country to the local Economic and Commercial Counsellor's Office or from recommendations from the local Chinese embassy. Upon a feasibility consultation within the Office (normally the request far exceeds China's foreign aid planning), the initially approved requests or accepted recommendations are sent to MOFCOM for a final decision.[24] While most of the proposals are processed within MOFCOM, projects that exceed 100 million Yuan (approximately 12.5 million US dollars) need to be put to the State Council for further approval. Once approved, the Department of Aid to Foreign Countries then assigns responsibilities to the relevant implementation management institutions.

In October 2008, MOFCOM, MFA and MOF established the Foreign Aid Inter-agency Liaison Mechanism (对外援助部际联系机制) to improve collaboration between China's foreign aid institutions.[25] This mechanism was upgraded to the Foreign Aid Inter-agency Coordination Mechanism (对外援助部际协调机制) in February 2011.[26] This latest mechanism is jointly participated in by the International Department of the CCCPC, the Ministry of National Defence, the National Development and Reform Commission, the Ministry of Education, the Ministry of Science and Technology, the Ministry of Industry and Information Technology, the Ministry of Public Security, the Ministry of State Security, the Ministry of Human Resources and Social Security, the Ministry of Land and Resources, the Ministry of Transport, the Ministry of Agriculture, the Ministry of Culture, the Ministry of Health, the People's Bank of China, the China EXIM Bank and the China Export and Credit Insurance Corporation. It is aimed at ensuring the comprehensiveness of China's aid approach and to maximise the contribution aid makes to China's domestic development agenda.

The funding methods of China's foreign aid

Concerning the financial resources underpinning China's aid, Beijing currently utilises two financial resources: China's annual government aid budget and EXIM Bank-raised commercial capital to finance its five primary funding methods (Grant, Interest-free Loan, Low-interest Loan, Concessional Loan and Preferential Buyer's Credit). Despite the concerns raised by Brautigam of the latter two funding methods, 'One is aid, the other is not' (2009: 173), of particular concern to this study is China's traditional foreign aid, which depends on being solely funded by the Chinese government budget and used for the promotion of recipient countries' economic development and welfare. Hence only the Grant, the Interest-free Loan and the Low-interest Loan are considered as foreign aid in this study, provided that the profitability grounded Concessional Loan and Preferential Buyer's Credit are not meeting this criteria. Building from these points, and minus the earlier terminated funding method of the Low-interest Loan, this section elaborates on China's traditional foreign aid funding methods of the Grant and the Interest-free Loan.[27]

Before going further it is important to note that, as an initial step towards drafting country specific foreign aid plans, China first plans its budget by individual country. That is, it has a Country Specific Foreign Aid Budget (国别援款). Despite China's overall foreign aid policy framework, when MOFCOM and other participating government institutions draw up plans, the standard practice is to first calculate and submit an annual budget plan to the State Council per each recipient country. Once approved, the budgets are then distributed by the MOF to each government institution for the building of foreign aid packages. When the recipient countries' request exceeds China's planning for that specific country (usually the mega projects), China disaggregates the funding application and finances the project over successive annual budgets.[28] In extreme situations, for example, when a project demands the budget of several succeeding fiscal years, China will then propose to the recipient country to finance the project with a combination of Grant and Concessional Loan.[29]

The Grant (无偿援助)

Grants are the primary funding method of China's traditional aid. Whilst mainly used for insolvent recipient countries, they focus on projects and programs related to improving people's livelihoods. Besides China's currently favoured HRDC programs, Grants are also utilised to deliver Complete Project Aid such as hospitals, schools, and low-cost housing as per the recipient country's requests. Additionally, Grants are employed to fund Technical Aid as well as other supportive methods, such as Medical Teams and Overseas Volunteer Programs. What needs to be particularly pointed out is that a margin of the budget planned for Grants are also used to finance China's Humanitarian Aid. Upon the delivery of Humanitarian Aid, the expenditures are accounted for in that country's next annual budget plan.[30]

The Interest-free Loan (无息贷款)

Financed in the same way as the Grant, the Interest-free Loans are likewise solely reliant upon China's annual government aid budget and focus on the project and programs related to improving people's livelihoods. Owing to the non-profit nature of such projects and programs, the tenure of Interest-free Loans are usually 20 years, and this period includes: 5 years of use, 5 years of grace and 10 years of repayment (Government of China, 2011: 7). Since the implementation of the Grand Economic Strategy in 1994, China has only kept a minimal amount of Interest-free Loans available for developing countries that have relatively sound economic foundations.[31] In accordance with the principle of 'to lighten the burden on recipient countries as far as possible' (the 3rd principle of the Eight Principles,), these loans are expected to be gradually transformed to Grants.[32]

How China calculates its foreign aid

Since the inauguration of the Concessional Loan in 1995, China's foreign aid expenditures have been closely monitored by the EXIM Bank and the MOF in the categories of Loans and Government Budgets, respectively. Brautigam suggests that to estimate China's foreign aid, three areas need to be assessed: 'Ministry of Finance external assistance expenditure, China EXIM Bank concessional loans, and debt relief' (2009: 168). In contrast, this study believes that in order to learn the extent of China's foreign aid, two references should be primarily considered. First, as Zhou pointed out, 'With concern to China's current calculations, only direct financial transfers between governments are regarded as *aid*, including the proportion of *government subsidised interests* of Concessional Loans, but not the rest of the capital that this subsidised interests has brought' (2008a: 40). Second, according to a senior Chinese official, 'Debt Relief is contributed from China's earlier [i.e. prior to 1993] overdue (write-off) of Interest-free and Low-interest loans'.[33]

Therefore, while China has yet to adopt the DAC introduced foreign aid statistical system, to understand the expenditure of China's traditional foreign aid, the National Bureau of Statistics (国家统计局) published *China Statistical Yearbook* is the best way to collect data on the entire annual government budget of China's foreign aid. This budget includes China's expenditures for infrastructure, agricultural projects, human resources training courses, dispatching medical teams, as well as the subsidised proportion of Concessional Loan interests, with the only exceptions of the rest of the Concessional Loan capital and Debt Relief. To be specific, these annual statistics include the expenditures channelled by the funding methods of Grant and Interest-free Loans, and these two funding methods financed the implementation methods of Complete Project Aid, Technical Aid, Goods and Materials Aid, HRDC, Medical Teams and Overseas Volunteer Programs.

Moreover, whilst this annual government foreign aid budget also includes a margin for Military Aid, Humanitarian Aid, International Multilateral Aid and subsidising the interests of Concessional Loans, it only funds a part of the Fund of Foreign Aid Joint Ventures and Cooperative Projects (援外合资合作项目基金管理办法).[34] To be exact, this particular fund was formed with repayments from China's early Interest-free Loans, Low-interest Loans, and the Fund of Multiple Foreign Aid Forms, with the latter fund collected from the margins of China's aid budget in the 8th Five-Year Plan (1991–1995) period. Under these circumstances, although this fund has been operating on a commercial basis since its establishment, it is not sufficient to argue that 'China has used some of their foreign aid money to support joint ventures between Chinese firms and firms in developing countries' (Brautigam, 2009: 166), without making clear that this fund is both currently individualised and is also the result of China's early attempts in generating financial benefits from its (traditional) foreign aid.

The implementation methods of China's foreign aid

With consideration given to the delivery of China's foreign aid, utilising the funds of Grant and Interest-free Loans, China at present offers six foreign aid implementation methods in accordance with the ODA criteria introduced by the DAC: Complete Project Aid, Technical Aid, Goods and Materials Aid, Human Resource Development Cooperation, Medical Teams and Overseas Volunteer Programs. Whilst China's foreign aid is primarily focused on improving recipient countries' productivity, development foundations and local health and education standards, these implementation methods are comprehensively employed in areas such as industry, agricultural, economic infrastructure, public facilities, education, medicine and public health, as well as clean energy and coping with climate change (Government of China, 2011: 20–26).

1 Complete Project Aid (成套项目援助)

Managed by the Executive Bureau of International Economic Cooperation, Complete Project Aid has always been the primary implementation method of China's aid. It refers to the projects where China is responsible for providing project surveys, design, construction equipment and materials, engineers and technical personnel (sometimes also the marketing of the final product). According to *The White Paper* (2011), China had provided 2,025 Complete Project Aid projects in total in developing countries by 2009 which accounted for 40 per cent of China's foreign aid expenditure (Government of China, 2011: 10). These projects were distributed across a range of sectors including Agriculture (215), Public Facilities (670), Economic Infrastructure (390), Industry (635) and Others (115).

2 Technical Aid (技术合作援助)

As Complete Project Aid, Technical Aid is also currently managed by the Executive Bureau of International Economic Cooperation. Since its inauguration in the 1960s, Technical Aid has focused on transferring technical and management skills after the completion of Complete Project Aid. It was previously integrated with Overseas Training Programs, Medical Teams, and a variety of other Individual Programs as well as Management Cooperation. However, in the 1990s, owing to the failing outcomes of Management Cooperation and the individualisations of HRDC and Medical Teams, China gradually scaled back its Technical Aid and at present only provides short-term onsite training (usually 2 weeks) following the implementations of Complete Project Aid projects.[35]

3 Goods and Materials Aid (物资项目援助)

Under the management of the CICETE, Goods and Materials Aid was one of the earliest introduced implementation methods of China's aid and it was primarily utilised to assist China's neighbouring countries. Currently, Goods and Materials Aid is mainly concerned with the aid that provides recipient country's livelihoods supplies, technical products and individual equipment. Likewise, it supports Complete Project Aid projects in regards to the required construction materials and equipment. After the delivery of goods and materials, the CICETE is also responsible for providing warranty services as well as training courses for the operation of the delivered equipment.

4 Human Resource Development Cooperation (HRDC) (人力资源开发合作)

Initially integrated with Technical Aid, the beginning of China's HRDC programs can be traced back to the 1950s when China offered studentships for North Korean refugee children to study in China. In contrast to the situation in 1998, when only 28 African officials attended the very first African Economic and Management Officer Seminar, by 2008, 10,515 people were training in China in over 150 different subjects.[36] Currently, China's HRDC is organised into two categories: Bilateral and Multilateral Seminars. The courses are offered at three levels: Official, Technician and Student.[37]

5 Medical Teams (援外医疗队)

Also introduced at the beginning of China's foreign aid, Chinese Medical Teams first appeared in Egypt in 1956 during the Suez Crisis. They then became a permanent feature of China's aid in 1963. Since 1985, Medical Teams have been directly

Table 3.1 Chinese Medical Teams to Africa

Country	*Dispatching Province*	*Start Date*	*Changes*
Algeria	Hubei	April 1963	Withdrew in February 1995 due to violence, redispatched in 1997
Zanzibar	Jiangsu	August 1964	
Somalia	Jilin	June 1965	Withdrew in 1991 due to war
Congo-B	Tianjin	February 1967	Withdrew in 1997 due to war; returned in 2000
Mali	Zhejiang	February 1968	
Tanganyika	Shandong	March 1968	
Mauritania	Heilongjiang	April 1968	
Guinea	Beijing	June 1968	
Sudan	Shanxi	April 1971	
Equatorial Guinea	Guangdong	October 1971	
Sierra Leone	Hunan	March 1973	Withdrew in 1993 due to war; redispatched in Dec. 2002
Tunisia	Jiangxi	June 1973	
DR Congo	Hebei	September 1973	Withdrew in 1997 due to war; returned in June 2006.
Ethiopia	Henan	November 1974	Suspended September 1979; returned in December 1984.
Togo	Shanghai	November 1974	

Country	*Dispatching Province*	*Start Date*	*Changes*
Cameroon	Shanghai	June 1975	Interrupted in January1979; dispatched by Shanxi in 1985
Senegal	Fujian	July 1975	Withdrew in 1996; re-dispatched in September 2007
Madagascar	Gansu	August 1975	
Morocco	Shanghai	September 1975	Jiangxi joined in 2000
Niger	Guangxi	January 1976	Withdrew in July 1992; re-dispatched in December 1996
Mozambique	Sichuan	April 1976	
São Tomé and Príncipe	Heilongjiang, Sichuan	June 1976	Withdrew in 1997 after diplomatic relations ended
Burkina Faso	Beijing	June 1976	Withdrew in 1994 after diplomatic relationship ended
Guinea – Bissau	Guizhou	July 1976	Withdrew in 1990 and re-dispatched by Sichuan in 2002
Gabon	Tianjin	May 1977	
Gambia	Tianjin	May 1977	Dispatched by Guangdong instead in 1991; withdrew in 1995
Benin	Ningxia	January 1978	
Zambia	Henan	January 1978	
Central African Republic	Zhejiang	July 1978	Withdrew in July 1991; re-dispatched in August1998.
Chad	Jiangxi	December 1978	Withdrew in 1979 then re-dispatched in 1989. Withdrew in 1997 then re-dispatched in 2006. Withdrew in February 2008 due to war. Re-dispatched in May
Botswana	Fujian	February 1981	
Djibouti	Shanxi	February 1981	
Rwanda	Rwanda	June 1982	
Uganda	Yunnan	January 1983	
Zimbabwe	Hunan	May 1985	
Libya	Jiangsu	December 1983	Contract not renewed in 1994
Cape Verde	Heilongjiang	July 1984	Province changed to Sichuan in February 1998, then to Hunan
Liberia	Heilongjiang	July 1984	Withdrew in 1989; returned in 2005
Seychelles	Guangxi	May 1987	
Burundi	Guangxi	December 1986	Dispatching province was changed to Qinghai
Namibia	Zhejiang	April 1996	
Comoros	Guangxi	1994	
Lesotho	Hubei	June 1997	
Eritrea	Henan	September 1997	
Malawi	Shanxi	June 2008	
Angola	Sichuan	2007	Postponed due to accommodation issues; arrived June 2009
Ghana	Guangdong	2008	Team set off December 2009

Adapted from Li, 2011

managed and dispatched by the Ministry of Health. In addition to medical personnel, the Teams include the supplies of medical equipment, medicines, as well as training courses to local doctors and nurses. Other than emergency situations, Chinese medical teams work in two-year shifts in the recipient country, and since the 1970s, China has implemented the practice which teams up Chinese province with the recipient country to provide sustained medical services.[38]

6 Overseas Volunteer Programs (援外志愿者)

Commissioned by MOFCOM, the Chinese Young Volunteers Association (CYVA) (中国青年志愿者协会) undertakes the recruitment, training and dispatching of Chinese volunteers. Being one of the most recently introduced aid implementation methods, it is aimed at delivering the ostensible benefits of China's aid directly to local people. Offered in programs lasting in duration from six months to two years, the volunteers are dispatched to the recipient countries' education, health or other social development-related sectors. Currently, the majority of these programs are organised in Chinese Language Courses. In spite of a recent government report suggesting that 'demand has yet to be found in most African countries',[39] the scheme is expected to expand into Physical Education and Information Technology.[40]

How China packages its foreign aid

In the pursuit of China's aid objectives, the implementation methods complement one other and are based on collaboration. Besides the specialised works of Medicals Teams, HRDC and Overseas Volunteer Programs which are organised according to China's Plans and Measures promised in the Forum of China-Africa Cooperation (FOCAC) and international meetings, the primary feature of China's aid (Complete Project Aid), is usually determined individually. Provided the importance of Complete Project Aid, which often forms the foundation for other implementation methods (such as Technical Aid and Goods and Materials Aid), as well as China's limited aid capacity and requests that tend to far exceed China's planned country specific budget, Beijing has some guidelines for determining Complete Project Aid projects. This is regardless of its claimed requests-based aid approach.

As a senior Chinese official pointed out, although China has yet to issue official instructions for identifying definitive criteria for accepting proposals, it has preferences which are (in descending order): the project must be within budget allowance; the project at large is in accordance with the needs of the recipient country; the project is mainly concerned with improving people's livelihoods (schools, hospitals, etc.); it is easy to operate and maintain; it is non-productive or technology-based; and/or it involves agricultural development.[41] Hence, on the basis of noting that China has an annual budget for each of its recipient countries and, to some extent, it also has a framework for packaging its foreign aid, this finding contrasts with Davies et al.'s suggestion that 'there is no fixed aid model [from China] and that disbursements are based on the requests received from the recipient country' (2008: 51).

Examining China's current practices, along with the aims and objectives of its aid, the exercising of China's foreign aid has become increasingly proficient and versatile. With consideration given to the planning and implementation management, on the basis of specialised institutions to cope with the expanded scope of its aids, China brought together 24 institutions to jointly participate in the Interagency Coordination Mechanism. With the institutions directly managing projects and programs in their specialities, MOFCOM then established subsidiary public institutions to manage implementation. Concerning implementation, the key aid funding methods were restructured to coordinate with further specified objectives.

As a result of these restructurings, instead of the previous dilemmas caused by rival political and economic interests, the integrated application of Concessional Loans, Preferential Buyer's Credits and the aid budget has improved China's opportunity to realise some of its policy goals. Further, through the utilisation of Complete Project Aid in the assistance given to Africa's infrastructure development and the exercise of Technical Aid, Goods and Materials Aid, HRDC, Medical Teams and Overseas Volunteer Programs, the focus of China's aid has extended to both African people's livelihoods and development capacity. Given these efforts, the development of China's aid in Africa has been advanced.

To accommodate this integrated foreign aid approach, several refinements were made in order to improve capacity. In addition to setting up the EXIM Bank and allocating specific funds to support a more business-orientated approach, China has gradually revised its planning and implementation approaches in response to the return of traditional foreign aid. To be specific, in order to upgrade China's administrative capacity, Beijing first assigned 24 central and provincial institutions to jointly participate in planning and implementation management and then, in the interests of assuring quality, China introduced a number of codes of practices to oversee implementation. To conclude the study of the current development of China's aid in Africa, it may be said that China's aid has evolved from an economic and trade integrated grand economic pursuit to economic and political interests both being considered as part of a comprehensive developmental assistance scheme.

Concluding remarks

By combining traditional foreign aid and a more business-oriented approach, Beijing has employed "friendship building" as a cornerstone of its aid to facilitate enterprises going out. Instead of the previous approaches, which were predominately aimed at promoting economic development, by shifting the emphasis towards recipient countries' people's livelihoods, China's current aid has become notably more insistent on assisting African countries' capacity building. Yet, while identifying Beijing's aid objectives in Africa, the outcomes of China's aid in Africa has been continuously left in the dark by Beijing. In view of the objectives of building African developmental foundations and reducing expenditure while consolidating outcomes and improving people's livelihoods, the question whether China has achieved any of these objectives remains moot. There is very little evidence presented by Beijing to show that China is actually assisting Africa's development. With these questions in mind, the next chapter takes the study to Africa where the exercises and outcomes of China's foreign aid may be plainly demonstrated. On the basis of observing and assessing three foreign aid packages that were implemented according to the aforementioned objectives and approaches, the next chapter attempts to empirically understand the development of China's aid, as well as the effectiveness and sustainability of China's 60 years of so-called friendship commitments.

Notes

1 Unpublished document, *The Loan Regulations of the EXIM Bank.*
2 The countries visited were Kenya, Egypt, Ethiopia, Mali, Namibia and Zimbabwe.
3 Unpublished document, October 2006, *Follow-up Report of the FOCAC 2000*, page 4.
4 See 援外合资合作项目基金管理办法, *Notice of the Ministry of Foreign Trade and Economic Cooperation and the Ministry of Finance on Issuing the Measures for the Management of the Fund of Foreign Aid Joint Ventures and Cooperative Projects*. Ministry of Foreign Trade and Economic Cooperation and the Ministry of Finance, 1998.
5 See *Program for China-Africa Cooperation in Economic and Social Development*, www.MFA.gov.cn/zflt/eng/wjjh/hywj/t157834.htm, accessed 29 June 2012.
6 These codes of practices include but are not limited to: 对外援助支出预算资金管理办法, *Measures for the Financial Administration of General Foreign Aid Provided by the Chinese Government* (1998), 对外援助成套项目施工任务实施企业资格认定办法试行, *Measures for Accreditation of Qualifications of the Enterprises Undertaking the Construction of the Complete Foreign Aid Projects* (2004), 对外援助物资项目实施企业资格认定办法试行, *Measures for Accreditation of Qualifications of the Enterprises Undertaking Foreign Aid Material Projects* (2004).
7 Interview with senior Chinese official, Freetown, Sierra Leone, 2 September 2011.
8 Interview with senior Chinese official, Beijing, China, 1 December 2011.
9 Interview with senior Chinese official, Beijing, China, 16 November 2011.
10 Unpublished document, August 2007, *Bo Xilai Speaks in the National Conference on Foreign Aid*, page 5.
11 Unpublished documents, March 2008, *Wu Speaks at the Conference on Foreign Aid Human Resource Development Cooperation to Africa*, page4.
12 Unpublished document, March 2008, *Increase the Delivery of 'Soft Elements', Boost Our International Influences*, page 39.
13 See *Wen Speaks at the UN High-Level Meeting on the Millennium Development Goals*, (www.un.org/chinese/focus/wen/mdg.shtml)
14 Unpublished document, February 2011, *MOC launches Inter-agency Coordination Mechanism*, page 5.
15 Unpublished document, January 2012, *Report on Foreign Aid in 2011*, p.5.
16 Unpublished document, August 2012, *Chen Instructs After the FOCAC Meeting*, pages 29–39.
17 Ibid.
18 Ibid.
19 Unpublished document, March 2008, *Wu Yi Stress on Human Resources Development Program*, page4.
20 Interview with Chinese official, Freetown, Sierra Leone, 2 September 2011.
21 Unpublished document, June 2008, *Fu Emphasises on Seven Points*, page 4.
22 The original words utilised by this Chinese official were '中央事权, 国家行为', which directly translate as 'central authority, state behaviour'. Interview with senior Chinese official, Freetown, Sierra Leone, 6 August 2011.

23 Unpublished document, January 2009, *MOC Adjusts Its Foreign Aid Management Allocation*, page 42.
24 Interview with senior Chinese official, Freetown, Sierra Leone, 6 August 2011.
25 Unpublished document, November 2008, *MOC launches Inter-agency Liaison Mechanism*, page 4.
26 Unpublished document, February 2011, *MOC launches Inter-agency Coordination Mechanism*, page 5.
27 One Chinese official pointed out that Low-interest Loans were terminated at the end of the 1980s. Interview with Chinese official, Freetown, Sierra Leone, 3 September 2011.
28 Interview with senior Chinese official, Beijing, China, 16 November 2011.
29 Ibid.
30 Interview with senior Chinese official, Freetown, Sierra Leone, 6 August 2011.
31 Ibid.
32 Ibid.
33 Online interview with senior Chinese official, 10 November 2012.
34 See *Notice of the Ministry of Foreign Trade and Economic Cooperation and the Ministry of Finance on Issuing the Measures for the Management of the Fund of Foreign Aid Joint Ventures and Cooperative Projects* Ministry of Foreign Trade and Economic Cooperation and the Ministry of Finance (1998), no. 481.
35 Telephone interview with Chinese official, 30 June 2012.
36 Unpublished document, July 2009, *Fu Speaks at HRDC Experience Exchange*, page 4.
37 Interview with senior Chinese official, Freetown, Sierra Leone, 2 September 2011.
38 Interview with senior Chinese official, Beijing, China, 1 December 2011.
39 Unpublished documents, December 2009, *Dispatch of 300 Overseas Volunteers Completed*, page 7.
40 Unpublished documents, February 2011, *Improve the Management of Overseas Volunteers, Bringing Up Overseas Services*, page 36.
41 Interview with senior Chinese official, Freetown, Sierra Leone, 2 September 2011.

4 China's foreign aid in Africa

Assessments

Having understood both China's aid objectives in Africa and its planning and implementation approaches more broadly, this chapter addresses the next step towards improving our understanding of the topic and the effectiveness and sustainability of China's aid in Africa. In order to survey the performance of China's attempts, as well as the factors that affect performance, the chapter asks two questions: How has China's aid been influencing African development? How have China's foreign aid outcomes been affected? With these aims in mind, this chapter brings the focus to the implementation sites of Chinese aid in Africa. In doing so, it observes and assesses three traditional foreign aid packages that have been implemented according to China's foreign aid objectives as they have developed, namely to build African industrial and agricultural foundations (1958–1978), to reduce expenditure while consolidating outcomes (1982–1993) and to improve people's livelihoods (2005–present).

To maximise the scope of these assessments, besides selecting cases on the basis that each one must coincide with China's distinct aid objectives, in view of extending the assessment in terms of China's implementation methods, the method of Complete Project Aid is duly determined owing to its underlying character of frequently forming the foundation for other implementation methods.[1] It is through this thinking that Chapter 5 understands China's aid in Africa while taking into consideration both its objectives and practices. As a result, the Magbass Sugar Complex in Sierra Leone, the Ghana National Theatre and the Lekma Hospital (also in Ghana) were selected as case studies to represent China's industrial and agricultural projects, landmark projects and people's livelihoods projects, respectively. In addition to each being a Complete Project Aid project, these projects were also in association with other implementation methods including Goods and Materials Aid, Technical Aid, HRDC and Medical Teams.

What needs to be addressed before looking at the case studies is that, while putting forward specific objectives in Africa, China has no restrictions on the projects and programs that are *not* in line with the particular objectives in a given period. According to the Eight Principles, 'In providing aid to other countries, the Chinese government strictly respects the sovereignty of recipient countries, and never attaches any conditions or asks for any privileges'. China's principal request-based aid approach requires its liaising institutions and the Economic and Commercial

Counsellor's Offices only to propose, but not to interfere, and also to respect the final decisions made solely by the recipient governments.[2] Therefore, apart from China's specified objectives, there may also be other projects and programs delivered to the recipient country at the same time. For example, in spite of China's most recent objective of improving people's livelihoods, upon one recipient country's request, China delivered 20 vehicles to that country for its government's use.[3] This is hardly in line with promoting people's livelihoods and much likely to promote gratitude from the recipient state's elites for such expressions of "friendship".

This chapter brings in exclusive observations of China's planning and implementation exercises of its aid and draws upon extensive interviews with Chinese aid officials, workers and academics. In addition to this, at the end of each primary case study, available government data on other similar projects and programs are supplied to supplement the arguments raised.

To "build African industrial and agricultural foundations" (1958–1978)

From the beginning of China's aid enterprise in Africa to the end of the Cultural Revolution, its aid was predominantly influenced by political underpinnings captured in the notion of proletarian internationalism. Whilst its aims in Africa evolved from the desire to support African peoples' liberation movements, to unite African countries against the imperialist world, and then to assist African countries achieve self-reliance, China's aid consistently concentrated on the objective of building African developmental foundations. However, at the early stages, Africa was a completely new continent for China's aid. Thus, in an attempt to identify the most appropriate measures for planning practical and effective aid suited to African conditions, China dispatched a delegation to Africa at the turn of 1964 to explore its economic, cultural and environmental characteristics.

Based on this research visit to Algeria, Mali and Guinea and with a consideration to improving Africa's insufficiencies, in the interests of fulfilling its principal aim of helping African countries achieve self-reliance, China confirmed its long-term foreign aid objective with a Complete Project Aid and Technical Aid combined approach. Abiding by these practical instructions, not only did Chinese aid engage in seeking to contribute to the continent's development but it materially contributed to China's admission into the UN in 1971. Given the rapidly growing number of delivered projects, how to help recipient countries sustain project effectiveness soon became an increasingly prominent issue. Owing to the often advanced technology of China's aid and the insufficiently carried out technology and management transfers, a number of delivered projects failed to achieve planned outcomes. In order to improve this situation, the Ministry of Foreign Economic and Trade rolled out the Technical Aid package with various Management Cooperation methods in 1984. On the basis of this new implementation approach, Chinese experts were encouraged to be more involved in the operation of delivered projects. In effect this meant that while they were providing technical guidance and training, they were also encouraged to participate in actual project management.

However, by the early 1990s, China had gradually reduced its Technical Aid. Based on this evidence as well as China's concern in reducing foreign aid expenditure, what caused the scale back of the arguably essential Technical Aid is a crucial question. Furthermore, considering the achievement of China's political interests, how has the realisation of this objective been effected? This study looks at these concerns through the example of the Magbass Sugar Complex project in Sierra Leone in order to investigate effectiveness and sustainability.

Magbass Sugar Complex,[4] Tonkolili, Sierra Leone, 1982–1995 and 2003–present

The Magbass Sugar Complex (马格巴斯糖联) is a Low-interest Loan funded Complete Project Aid project delivered to Sierra Leone according to an Economic and Technical Cooperation Agreement settled in October 1972.[5] As well as a sugar refinery and adjoining sugar cane fields, the complete packaging of this project also included a fertiliser field and a year of technical cooperation (i.e., Technical Aid). Whilst it was agreed in the first year that China and Sierra Leone established diplomatic relationship, this project is believed to be one of the many foreign aid projects that China has delivered to Africa as appreciation for supporting its admission to the UN. Whether it was the Chinese or Sierra Leonean government who proposed this particular project is untraceable today (Sierra Leonean officials could not advise). A senior Chinese official however suggested that it was 'most likely to be selected from an *achievable* project and program list based on Sierra Leone's foreign aid request'. As further explained by the official, 'At the early stages of China's foreign aid, according to the recipient country's foreign aid requests, China normally proposed a list of project and program offers that it considered to be possible to deliver'.[6]

In February 1973, four months after the initial agreement, the Ministry of Foreign Economic Liaison in China assigned the project's implementation to the Fujian Provincial Foreign Aid Department. This department then immediately dispatched a 13-member team of experts to inspect local conditions. Following a six-month geological survey, the department identified 3 locations (out of 11 proposed areas) in the Northern Province of Sierra Leone, and submitted a report to the Chinese and Sierra Leonean governments for further review as to which location would be best suited to the project. Subsequent to selecting Tonkolili District for the project's implementation in November of that same year, an 11-month project planning process resulted in the drawing up of a contract for the creation of 1,280 hectares of sugar cane fields (including 280 hectares of green manure crops), a 400-ton per day sugar refinery (by-producing 6,000 litres of alcohol), and an estimated annual production time of 150 days.

After the construction began in January 1977, the Fujian Provincial Foreign Aid Department dispatched 779 agricultural experts and professional workers to facilitate the implementation of the project. On the basis of finishing the contract, this department also additionally formatted 1,850 hectares of land, constructed a 460kw water pumping station, a 70.12km cultivation channel, a 98.2km commuting route, and supplied 13 categories of supporting equipment totalling 108 units. By the time the full completion of the Sugar Complex was reached in April 1981, the cost of the project added up to 21.9 million Yuan (approximately 30 million US dollars at the time). After a year of technical cooperation, the running of the project was officially transferred to the Sierra Leonean government in February 1982. Immediately following the transfer, the local government contracted back the Chinese experts and technicians to further participate in the project's operation.

In general, the Magbass Sugar Complex is a comprehensively designed foreign aid project in comparison to modern turnkey projects. 'Particularly in terms of the overall packaging, it is indeed rather considerate', asserted the general manager Li Mao, who has been working in the Sugar Complex for over a decade.[7] But to look more closely at the outcomes, when the Sierra Leonean Civil War broke out in 1991, more than fifty Chinese experts and technicians were still working on site and the whole refinery was in need of an overhaul. The sugar cane fields were largely disintegrating and, as Lai summarised, 'The 14 years of production at Magbass relied heavily on China's continuous financial support, mechanical parts supplies, productive material import tax exemptions, and protective retailing policies' (Lai, 1995: 8). After more than a decade of supplying technical and management support to the Complex, it is not difficult to come to the conclusion that the project was never sustainable without heavy Chinese involvement. Why this was so was summarised by a senior Chinese technician, who pointed out that:

> The location of the project was most definitely inadequate. It is right in the middle of Sierra Leone, hence the transportation costs are high since Sierra Leone produces nothing that is required by the Sugar Complex. Thus everything has to come from China. Although arguably no one would construct such an agricultural-industrial project in the city, this location is far too inland. And regarding the fields, they are not even remotely close to the suitable conditions for growing sugar cane.[8]

Although the location was within a traditional farming region, neither the field conditions nor the transportation links were up to standard for producing sugar at an industrial level. However, did Chinese experts at the beginning survey the location of the project? A senior Chinese official admitted that the reason behind the decision to locate the project where it was, was primarily due to then President Siaka Stevens' attempts to neutralise political tensions in Tonkolili district in the 1970s.[9] Indeed, a report from the Truth and Reconciliation Commission (2004) indicated that 'When Siaka Stevens came to power in 1968, he faced increasing pressure on various issues from prominent natives of Tonkolili District who were in the Army or were members of his APC party. . . Foday Sankoh, the leader of the Revolutionary United Front hailed from the Tonkolili District'.

Setting aside the question of whether utilisation of an aid project to maintain political peace is possible or not, when looking at the nature of the Complex, we must understand that 'all productive projects require a supportive environment in terms of the location and the quality of the local work force'.[10] In this light, 'to implement the project in Tonkolili hardly made any sense' stated a Chinese technician working on the project.[11]

Apart from the problems raised by choosing the location based on Sierra Leonean politics, 'China's feasibility study was also problematic', explained one Chinese manager.[12] 'What China did was a field condition study, but it did not take into consideration the surrounding social environment'. A Chinese technician added that this 'because there are no such employment issues in China'.[13] Various theories were then proffered as to why the project was problematic, including the usual nationalist (if not racist) response: 'Five thousand years of history has taught us basic morality and farming skills', unlike, presumably, the Africans. It is true that Tonkolili District is considered to be a lesser developed region in Sierra Leone, and the local residents are 'more traditionally behaved . . . even our own Sierra Leonean people would not deal with them', stated a former local employee, who resigned after three months of apprenticeship in the Sugar Complex.[14] In view of these comments on the social conditions, and despite China's efforts in supporting the project, the Sugar Complex had a rather challenging beginning.

By 1995, it was already considered to be a 'dated and problematic project' (Lai, 1995: 8). During the period when Chinese experts and technicians were contracted, six institutions from both China and Sierra Leone were either directly or indirectly making decisions on the development of the Complex.[15] In addition to this confusing institutional set up, 'the [decision-making] responsibilities were unevenly distributed. For example, while the Chinese teams were supervising production, the local managers only cared about and fought for the welfare of local workers'.[16] 'Local employees asking for bribes' was also allegedly common.[17] This ranged from 'bags of sugar to bribing. The local workers believe that is what they deserve, and nothing can be achieved without it'.[18] As a result, because everyone was getting a share, the profit margin was slight. However the paradox was that, 'the local government repeatedly accused the Sugar Complex of not contributing enough to the country'.[19]

Aside from the tangled management of the project, and taking into consideration China's limited aid capacity in the 1980s, the execution of Technical Aid was also largely questionable. As a senior Chinese manager pointed out, 'None of the Chinese experts or technicians could speak English or any local language, and there was a lack of appropriately trained translators, so communications were mainly done through body language. Therefore, no one had a clue about what each other was saying'.[20] Although in the end, some of the local employees managed to acquire some basic skills based on Chinese-offered training and through months of work experience, it was impossible for the Chinese experts to establish successful technology and management transfers. As a result of this, less than half of the full-time technical apprentices had learnt the skills needed to work individually.[21] By the early 1990s, growing frustration by locals at the conditions and failure to advance eventually had negative consequences. As Lai highlighted:

> The most confusing issue is the endlessly postponed Major Overhaul Contract. Whilst the Sugar Complex was operating with machineries that broke on

> a daily basis, the Sierra Leonean government decided to enforce import taxes on China's replacement equipment and mechanical parts. It was impossible for the Chinese government to implement such a contract.
>
> (1995: 9)

Thus, a senior COMPLANT official, who was stationed in the Complex during the 1980s, noted that 'even without the civil war, the Sugar Complex was going nowhere and was desperately in need of complete management reform'[22] For 14 years, from the official hand-off of the project in 1982 until the Sierra Leonean Civil War broke out in 1995, the operation of the Sugar Complex was entirely dependent on China's technical and financial support. This ended with the evacuation of the Chinese.

Nevertheless, the story does not end here. In August 2002, encouraged by the Chinese government to resume the production of earlier delivered projects, an expert team formed by COMPLANT and Sichuan Africa-Asia Company (formally a provincial aid department) visited Magbass upon the request of the Sierra Leonean government. Despite the 'near-terminal' damage done to the Sugar Complex during the Civil War (Huang, 2004: 58), COMPLANT found that there was potential in the complex. 'It was still comparatively cheaper to rehabilitate the Sugar Complex rather than build a completely new project', commented the current general manager on this subject.[23] In 2003 a 30-year Lease Contract was thus agreed between the Ministry of Agriculture and Food Security of Sierra Leone and COMPLANT, with concessional terms for import taxes, company income, and work permit exemptions. Upon this agreement, rehabilitation was started and completed in 2005. At this point, the Magbass Sugar Complex came back into production.

As promising as such progress sounds, despite this new lease-based cooperative management approach, which was specifically developed to reduce government influence and to stimulate productivity, an almost identical set of complications subsequently surfaced. 'Besides the usual bribes collected by the local government, the quality of the local work force is even worse than before', complained one Chinese employee. 'Most of the local workers are former rebels and they are very hard to work with', he continued.[24] Because the Sugar Complex is still a SOE, COMPLANT was required to employ a large number of ex-rebels by the local government. Although no official figures were disclosed, sources suggest that a minimum of 40 per cent of current local employees are former Revolutionary United Front rebels.

Given such social conditions, a worrying scene developed for the Chinese, namely labour militancy. 'Since we came back in 2002, strikes have become the biggest problem here', pointed out the general manager Li, occurring at least twice a year. The reason is simple and consistent: pay.[25] Interestingly, the Chinese management claim (no doubt correctly) that the Sugar Complex provides the same salary levels as European industries operating in the capital and that for a small village like Magbass, such pay is considerably more than the regional average.

Clearly, there are high local expectations being placed on the Chinese. As the general manager maintained:

> None of the strikes were legitimate. We were supposed to be given twenty-one days prior notice, but all of the strikes happened without warning and during the busiest harvest season. In such a situation, the strike needed to be resolved in their favour. If not, they would stop other people from working too and the strike leaders would close all the routes in and out of the premises, so nobody can come to replace them, and no one can leave unless they [the striking workers] get a pay rise. In fact, we have just raised their salary again.[26]

The manner in which Sierra Leonean workers exercise their rights is certainly not what the Chinese employees were prepared for. However, there are always two sides of every story and two groups of local employees who were interviewed argued: 'We should be paid more for working here. It is a very hard job. We have to fight for ourselves or we will not get what we want'.[27] This is a logic that coincides with Brautigam's findings regarding the stealing issue at Magbass, where her interviewee argued that 'If you don't want us to thieve, pay us better. That was the whole problem' (2009: 261). Concerning the whole problem, a senior Chinese investor in Sierra Leone pointed out what could arguably be the real issue. 'The lack of language skills made [the Chinese] blind to the local laws'.[28] Indeed, prior to the first official *Investment Guide Series* (中国对外投资和经济合作国别(地区)指南) published by MOFCOM in 2009,[29] the Chinese management barely understood any local legislation, especially in terms of protecting their own rights as employers.[30]

With concerns relating to the language issues that have troubled the project from the very beginning, local employees shared their opinions on this everlasting obstacle. 'Most managers and technicians here don't speak any English at all, and they don't want to talk to us', one worker said, while another pointed out: 'We can't learn anything from waving hands'.[31] A Chinese technician however argued:

> Even with our translator, the difficulties in training local people are beyond your imagination. They don't have any knowledge of basic chemistry and machinery. It is easy to tell them when to open a valve, but why open this valve at this particular time? You cannot explain this question to someone who doesn't even know the character of alcohol.[32]

There is thus clear dissonance going on. The Chinese blame problems on the lack of education and technical prowess of the local staff; whilst the local employees blame the Chinese for not speaking the language where they have invested. Remarkably, this resonates with the same arguments raised more than two decades ago, and it is quite apparent that the Chinese are still struggling with local conditions, conditions that include language (local or English) and the lack thereof.

Moreover, besides the strikes and miscommunication, frequent resignations of local employees has also become an increasingly significant issue. With the discovery of iron mines in Tonkolili in 2008 and the subsequent entrance of a European mining company (African Minerals Limited), the Sugar Complex lost almost a quarter of its local employees in the following year.[33] The general manager lamented: 'Although in Magbass we are paying as much as the Europeans, we are still falling short in terms of working conditions and welfare benefits'. He went on to blame the fact that 'the government [in Freetown] restricted 40% of our products to local market. There is thus not much room for welfare improvement based on our current pay rate'.[34] In addition, regular desertion by trained local workers has compounded problems. Apparently it is common for local employees to leave immediately after training courses have been provided by the Magbass Complex, taking with them the jump suit, boots, and other safety equipment the Complex had provided. Because of the boom in employment in the town, 'not only Magbass, but other Chinese companies too are losing employees to the European companies'.[35]

In addition to the complications grounded in social and institutional behaviours, two years into COMPLANT's management and operation, the 2007 Sierra Leonean presidential election had a significant impact on the Sugar Complex as it became involved in the rivalry between the People's Party (SLPP) and the All People's Congress (APC). As a result, the Lease Contract of the Magbass Sugar Complex, which was agreed by the SLPP, was repeatedly described by the APC as 'a humiliation to Sierra Leone and a forfeit of the country's sovereignty. This contract has cost significant benefits to the Sierra Leonean people'.[36] With the defeat of the SLPP, the APC immediately repealed most of the concessional terms so that 'the tax exemptions and work permit exemptions were all gone'.[37] Thus, the Magbass Sugar Complex operates within a number of serious obstacles both inside and outside of the premises. Despite the general manager's optimism that 'the Sugar Complex is still running, and we are going to hire a lawyer to defend ourselves', the future of the project remains challenging.[38]

Local residents in the seven villages surrounding the Sugar Complex have expressed their dissatisfaction about the project's operations in their different communities. This has been based on allegations that 'workers for the company are dismissed unlawfully' *and* that 'the Chinese have never helped [locals] in terms of scholarships for their children or even building schools' (Sierra Leone Newshunter, 2012). Whether a sugar factory should provide scholarships and build schools is a moot point. It is, however, true that the Complex was charged by the Labour Committee over non-compliance with environmental concerns (*New Citizen*, 2014).

To assess the Magbass Sugar Complex project, during the Technical Aid and Management Cooperation periods, the project achieved its objective of building an industrial and agricultural foundation. To some extent it also fulfilled China's principal aim of helping African countries achieve self-reliance in that prior to the Civil War, the Complex managed to produce 6,000 tons of sugar annually, which equalled 25 per cent of Sierra Leone's sugar imports. It also produced as a by-product 500,000 litres of spirit. Furthermore, during the lease period of COMPLANT (since 2005), production reached 8,000 tons of sugar annually (Corkin and Burke, 2006: 39). Not only did the Magbass Complex end Sierra Leone's dependency on imported sugar, it has also provided permanent employment for more than 300 local people, and seasonal employment for an additional 1,500 people. At the time of writing, the Magbass Sugar Complex remained the only sugar-producing enterprise in Sierra Leone.[39]

However, alongside these achievements, there are clearly a number of shortcomings. Concerning the effectiveness of the project, because the feasibility study only considered the geological conditions of the recipient country, this oversimplified aid allocation approach meant that when the Chinese arrived, they had to deal with unknown local conditions. Then, due to the influences of local decision-makers who favoured the political impacts of the Sugar Complex instead of its practical purposes, the project was further put into a more complicated situation. Moreover, in addition to the multi-pronged management approach which created conflicts between the Sugar Complex's need for production and local employees' demand for social welfare, as a result of China's restrictive policy of non-interference, the operation of the Complex was forced to tolerate regular bribes collected by local government officials. These conditions brought forth significant financial loss, and further worsened the local institutional environment.

In consideration of the sustainability of the Sugar Complex project, there is no current possibility of sustaining production without technical and financial support from China and aid dependency is clearly an issue. As the general manager noted, 'In addition to China's continual provision of production materials and equipment, there was a minimum of 78 Chinese experts and technicians working on site at any given time between 1982 and 1995, fully responsible for the operation of Sugar Complex'.[40] It was China's incompetent Technical Aid and the shortage of foreign aid professionals that primarily caused this outcome. Furthermore, apart from the issue of unsuccessful technology and management transfers to the recipient country, the domestic political competition in Sierra Leone and the excessive local brain-drain to better-paid jobs also contributed to the untenable operation of the project.

All in all, in spite of the seemingly satisfactory outcomes delivered by the Magbass Sugar Complex at first glance, there were various major factors that have affected its effectiveness and sustainability. These were, firstly, the recipient government's repeated interference, which first saw the project introduced into a domestic conflict zone and then later led it into an awkward political rivalry. Secondly, there was China's restrictive aid policy based on The Eight Principles. Although these principles to some extent guarantee implementation standards, given the dominant political emphasis of such guidelines, it also prohibited China from seriously enforcing positive solutions. Thirdly, the incompetent project planning caused major complications. Apart from the incomprehensible project planning which failed to consider local conditions at the beginning, there were also issues with the project's complicated management structures and the shortages of appropriately skilled aid workers. Finally, owing to the extremely limited number of skilled local employees, the lack of control over employment migration has caused high turnover of staff. As a consequence, the project's outcomes were further worsened.[41]

To conclude, the project in Sierra Leone fulfilled only partly China's first foreign aid objective. As estimated by a senior Chinese official:

> The survival rate of the early industrial and agricultural projects is less than 5% . . . not only have these projects generally failed in the sustainability aspect, extreme cases such as the Rice Processing Factory in Sierra Leone (which has not operated at all due to the non-existence of rice grain) are no rarity to China's foreign aid from this period.[42]

Although there is an absence of detailed official statistics on China's industrial and agricultural projects in Africa, with concern to the general outcomes of these projects, Shi has pointed out that 'by the end of 1985, most of the effective and sustained industrial projects survived on China's continuing support' (1989). Whereas with regards to the scale of these projects, the *White Paper* recorded 635 Industrial Projects and 215 Agricultural Projects, making up 41.9 per cent of Complete Project Aid projects that China has delivered globally up until 2009 (2011: 10).

Based on available statistics, the majority of sustained projects have seen similar situations as the Magbass Sugar Complex project. For example: the Mulungushi Textile Factory in Zambia only survived with Chinese Management Cooperation from 1984 onwards (Lin, 1997: 6). Similarly, the Conakry Match and Tobacco Factory (delivered to Guinea in 1964) needed an overhaul and an additional Tobacco Cultivation Centre in 1972, then a complete upgrade in 1976. Even considering some exceptional examples, such as the Rwanda Cement Factory (transferred in 1984 with Management Cooperation until 2006) (MOFCAM, 2004) and the Burundi Bujumbura Textile Factory (opened in 1980, equipment was first upgraded in 1997, and then again in 2006), (Lin, 1997: 7), the result of foreign aid dependencies of China's industrial and agricultural projects in Africa are plainly obvious. Without continuous Chinese support, these projects would all have failed.

Given these almost identical results, it can be seen that China's incompetent foreign aid planning and implementation practices undermined results. To be specific, in addition to the inept allocation approaches which often overlooked local conditions and the restrictive foreign aid principles that rigidly prohibited China's involvement in local affairs, China's lack of adequate aid professionals and a skilled management approach have directly led to insufficient project operations and a lack of success in technology and management transfers. Although after China's domestic reform, the newly founded cooperative foreign aid approaches improved the project sustainability in the short-term, given that the politically-tied foreign aid principles remained and Technical Aid was unimproved, China's industrial and agricultural foundation projects have generally led to disappointing results.

Nevertheless, as pointed out by Liu, 'With the deepest belief in proletarian internationalism, China's attempt in building African industrial and agricultural foundations was sincerely minded in assisting Africa's development'.[43] Albeit it at large failed to deliver the promised assistance, the exercise of this aid objective significantly improved China's aid capacity. By the early 1990s, China stopped this aid implementation method and directed further foreign aid requests to the newly inaugurated Concessional Loan. While adopting commercial funding to improve the outcomes of productive projects as well as to fulfil China's economic interests, in consideration to China's budget-funded traditional foreign aid, it has continued with the delivery of less technical and less financially demanding landmark projects.

To "reduce expenditure while consolidating foreign aid outcomes" (1982–1993)

Following the rapid development of China's diplomatic relationships in the early 1970s, the excessive amount of delivered industrial and agricultural projects induced tremendous challenges for China. In view of this situation, China implemented reform policies and adjustments to its aid. These changes saw the newly awakened economic interests swiftly evolve into The Four Principles used to guide China's aid implementation. The Four Principles continued to build on the concept of non-interference with each other's internal affairs and mutual respect but on the basis of abiding by terms introduced by the Eight Principles, it placed additional emphasis on the realisations of mutual benefit, practical results and diversified implementation forms. In line with this revised guidance, and acting on the newly introduced aid objective of reducing expenditure while consolidating outcomes, the Chinese government immediately reinstated limits to its foreign aid budget and requested that further aid be based on improved feasibility studies, with specific attention to be paid to the appropriateness of the recipient country's local conditions.

Further, in order to improve the planning and implementation approaches, China first upgraded its Technical Aid with Management Cooperation to promote project sustainability and then, in the interest of reducing aid expenditure China introduced the less financially demanding landmark projects. In addition to concern for African countries' shortages in management and human resources capacity, this landmark project planning was also proposed in consideration of maintaining African countries' confidence in China's aid. As pointed out by a Chinese official, 'Given the overall reduction of the foreign aid budget in the 1980s, landmark projects made up the 'friendly' relationship aspect pursued by the Chinese government. That is the reason why most of China's landmark projects were named with *friendship* in their title'.[44]

Owing to the conservative nature of landmark projects, this new planning approach allowed for China's financial shortages and African countries' disadvantages in development capacities. However, it had fundamental limitations in providing adequate development assistance, let alone providing for the need to 'increase income and accumulate capital', the fifth principle of The Eight Principles. While landmark projects remain the second choice of China's aid planning, the effectiveness and sustainability of these projects are still largely unknown.[45] Therefore, given the significant number of landmark projects that China has delivered (and is still delivering to Africa), the question arises whether these projects have contributed positively to Africa's development. Should China carry on delivering such landmark projects as part of its development assistance? This study brings these queries to one of the most iconic Chinese landmark projects in Africa, the Ghana National Theatre.

National Theatre, Accra, Ghana, 1992–present

The Ghana National Theatre (加纳国家剧院) is an Interest-free Loan Complete Project Aid project agreed during President Jerry Rawlings' visit to Beijing in September 1985.[46] Located in downtown Accra, this multi-functional theatre is fitted with a 1,500-seat drama hall, rehearsal rooms, office buildings and a range of other facilities. The project was contracted to Hangzhou Architectural Design Institute for design and allocated to China Guangzhou International Economic Technical Cooperation Company (GIETC) and China Radio and TV (CRTV) for construction. GIETC is a subsidiary provincial enterprise established by the Ministry of Foreign Economic and Trade. The total cost was 60 million Yuan (approximately 15 million US dollar at the time). Upon completion in 1992, the theatre was immediately transferred to the Ghanaian government and went into operation.

However, after more than a decade of service, in 2005 the Ghanaian government approached China for aid regarding the rehabilitation of the theatre. Considering the significance of the project and the historical ties between China and Ghana, China granted 2 million US dollars for the request and repaired equipment and upgraded the theatre to modern standards (MFA, 2005). To mark the opening of the renovated theatre, not only did the Ghanaian government adopt the theatre's image for its newly released 20,000 cedi currency note, but during the visit of Chairman of the National Committee of the Chinese People's Political Consultative Conference, Jia Qinglin, in 2007, the initial Interest-free Loan provided for the project was waived along with other debts that had been due before 2005 (MOFCOM, 2007). Currently, the National Theatre houses three resident companies: the National Dance Ensemble, the National Symphony Orchestra and the National Drama Company.

With all the possible projects available using China's request-based aid planning approach, why would Ghana have requested in 1985 to help build a National Theatre while still being rated by the UN as a Least Developed Country? According to one of the theatre's senior employees:

> We are trying to develop, and we have the people to develop performing arts, that includes music, singing, dancing and comedy. All of these subjects are being studied in schools and universities, and when all these people graduate, where are they going to have the place to practice, to bring up the young ones? There was no such place at that time.[47]

Regardless of the importance of performing arts in Ghana (indeed in Africa as a whole), in the 1980s, 60 million Yuan would have built hospitals, schools, or other non-productive but development-based projects. But apparently a theatre was even more important for Ghana. A senior manager who has been with the theatre since the construction stated: 'Before the theatre there was only a small drama studio in Accra with less than 100 seats. Ghana needed something big, a theatre for everybody. So Ghana asked China for help, and then China made two offers: a stadium or a theatre. At that time, planning for a new theatre had already begun, so it was the obvious choice'.[48]

Although arguably a straightforward reason, whether Ghanaian planning or the Chinese offers really serve as adequate development solutions for a Least Developed Country remains controversial. However, in the particular case of Ghana, as further explained by the theatre's employees, 'Even though Ghana had other problems at that time, Ghana also needed a theatre. If the Chinese hadn't given us the theatre, we don't know who will give us one. Maybe it would take another fifty years'.[49] In contrast to the perspectives of the theatre employees and artists, politicians saw the project in another light. A senior government official who was at the negotiation table in Beijing in 1985 noted that:

> Relationships usually develop informally, it builds without frames or structures, and the theatre project is how it started . . . At that time, China and Ghana had just begin rebuilding our relationship and looking for cultural cooperation, so it was natural to settle the aspirations on a National Theatre. Besides, the Ghanaian government also recognised the expertise of China in cultural development and building construction . . . After the theatre, we have done a few projects, and China and Ghana are now known to each other much better. So in recent times, especially after President Mills' visit to Beijing in 2010 in regards to a framework agreement with the Chinese government, we have decided that China and Ghana should do it within a more comprehensive package.[50]

It is clear that from a political standpoint, the National Theatre project was regarded as a gift or, in political terms, a sign of commitment to Sino-Ghanaian friendship. Whether it was going to be a theatre or a stadium was to a large extent irrelevant. As long as there was a project that demonstrated friendly intentions for bilateral relations. In this particular instance, the National Theatre definitely made a contribution to improving the relationship between China and Ghana. However, as a foreign aid project that was framed in terms of development assistance, neither cultural needs nor relationship building seems to be the adequate answer. As Brautigam plainly pointed out in a case study of building the Bo City Stadium in Sierra Leone, 'They don't meet *our* [i.e. the West's] definition of what a poor country "should" do with pledges of aid' (2009: 138).

Accepting that the theatre was a theatrical gesture by China to demonstrate friendship, there nevertheless remains serious problems with the National Theatre's effectiveness as a symbol. As part of a wider plan for the arts in Ghana, the National Theatre is supposed to promote arts across Ghana and help develop small regional theatres. This has not happened.[51] One theatre employee notes that 'due to financial constraints, it has been impossible for the theatre to achieve that goal':

> And now the government has stopped funding us from last year. We don't know how long this theatre will stay open. It is true that the theatre has to be self-sufficient, but it takes time, and we have not been very lucky. Chairman Mao led China to development, but in Ghana, we have not been able to do so. There is always some other decision made for something else.[52]

Whilst the interviewees were unable to outline the "unlucky" details of the claimed government constraints, a question that goes to the heart of the point of the project is raised: Why has a ticket-selling theatre required two decades of government support (and Chinese intervention)? The nature of the theatrical arts in Ghana seems to hold some answers. As one management employee explained, 'The resident companies hardly stage any shows, and sponsorship is also very difficult to find in Ghana. Since each of the companies have their own directors, sources of funds and bank accounts, they prefer to play and earn elsewhere'.[53] Another informant pointed out another factor however: 'Only some of the internally-generated funds were used to support the actual theatre; most of them were used for the end of year party'.[54] Meanwhile, as one senior theatre employee put it, 'It is common for the staff to not show up for work until 11 a.m.'[55]

With limited government support and poor management, the reason why the theatre still struggles to sustain itself is clear. Touring the theatre, one informant pointed out the lack of maintenance, stating that the air conditioning had not worked for over two years at that point. Whilst the Ghanaian used this to suggest that 'Chinese products are not very good',[56] Chinese officials rebutted this and pointed to a lack of skills and commitment by the Ghanaian side:

> Nothing lasts forever, particularly when you are not servicing things as you should. When China rehabilitated the theatre in 2005, one of the primary reasons why we updated the equipment was because they were beyond repair. Ghana does not have the technicians to maintain the equipment, nor the funds.[57]

This general concern highlights one of the major issues facing China's foreign aid in Africa. In terms of packaging, what technical standards should China adopt: local standards or, according to The Eight Principles, 'The best-quality equipment and materials manufactured by China'?

The initial plan was to build a theatre for local people to enjoy and for arts graduates to perform in, based on income from ticket sales. However, the resident companies have not staged sufficient programs that might earn finances to sustain the theatre. Equally, the initial plan was supposed to consider China's capacity at the time. However, China has had to come back to maintain the project. When all these issues are added up, it is obvious that even today, Ghana is still unable (30 years after the project was initiated) to cope with managing a state-owned theatre. Thus the end-result of a financially burdensome theatre was not really a sound gift for Ghana from the Chinese at all, which raises broader questions over China's landmark projects.

To assess the National Theatre project, in spite of the immediate benefit of showcasing the fact that Ghana has a status symbol such as a National Theatre, there are a number of factors that undermine the theatre's purpose. Regarding project effectiveness in particular, even though there was continuous support granted by the local government and successive financial assistance packages delivered by China, this never solved the problem of a lack of an appropriate management approach. The absence of the resident companies has clearly had an effect on the ability of the theatre to showcase Ghanaian culture. It has also driven the project into the ground. As for the sustainability of the project, the continuation of the National Theatre's existence is in doubt. Because of China's limited aid capacity at the time, the project's outcomes were undermined by its inadequate project planning, which did not evaluate Ghana's technical and management conditions, nor the capacity of Ghana to actually sustain a state-funded national theatre. This has materially restricted the long-term effectiveness of the project.

Aside from the claimed government constraints on the Ghanaian side, which according to the interviewees, to some extent sabotaged the outcome of the project, based on the available project details, the lack of policy enforcement from Accra has substantially harmed the project. In spite of Ghana's efforts in introducing legislation related to the running of the project, the unsatisfactory execution of such legislation and an uncontrolled budget allocation, combined with corruption, has driven the project to complete financial meltdown. The behaviour of the theatre's employees in the meanwhile also made major contributions to its failure.

To summarise, the National Theatre in Accra was gifted to Ghana at a time in the history of China's aid to Africa when reducing expenditure whilst consolidating outcomes in the implementation of landmark projects was central. This has not occurred. This is troubling given that the *White Paper* listed the building of 85 Conference Buildings, 85 Sports Facilities, 12 Theatres and Cinemas, 143 Civil Buildings and 37 Municipal Facilities, making up 17.9 per cent of China's Complete Project Aid projects delivered globally prior to 2009 (2011: 10). Obviously, not all of these landmark projects have been failures. However, the rationale behind many and their effectiveness as aid initiatives is clearly doubtful. Research conducted in the region found out that the following projects are all evident failures: the National Stadium delivered to Sierra Leone in 1979 subsequently required two Chinese Grants for rehabilitation in 1992 and 2002 (MOFCOM, 2003b); the Benin Cotonou Friendship Stadium delivered in 1982 first required the repair of its tennis courts in 1988, and then maintenance of its Light Tower in 1993, and finally a major rehabilitation in 2002 (MOFCOM, 2003a); and the Uganda Stadium delivered in 1994 required Chinese maintenance in 2011 (MOFCOM, 2010b).

In light of these almost identical results, taking into account China's already problematic Technical Aid scheme, which was purposed to transfer the required technical and management skills to recipient countries, China's landmark projects have been substantially undermined by inadequate aid planning. As summarised by one Chinese analyst:

> When the foreign aid package does not match the recipient country's development conditions, it is not going to have sustainable outcomes. Take for example the National Stadium delivered to Tanzania in 2004. It is closed most of the time due to its massive running costs. However, the smaller sports centre next door is as busy as a Sunday market. Although these projects provided some assistance to the recipient country, the practical value was extremely low.[58]

Moreover, as a result of inadequate planning, 'China has to protect its landmarks, and a significant amount of the foreign aid budget has been wasted on maintenance rather than providing further assistances'.[59] This seems indeed to be the legacy of the Chinese-constructed National Theatre in Ghana.

To "improve people's livelihoods" (2005–present)

China has trialled a variety of management cooperation methods to reduce expenditure and consolidate its aid outcomes. It has introduced Foreign Aid Joint Ventures and Cooperative Projects to attempt to create greater financial benefits and, since the move to a greater market economy, launched the funding method of Concessional Loans to take over further aid requests. As a result of these changes, China's aid developed into two divergent paths in the 1990s that aimed to accomplish both of political and economic goals. However, given the significant success of Concessional Loans, China's traditional foreign aid approach was to a large extent unattended.

After being overshadowed by Concessional Loans for almost an entire decade, however, the government began, from about 2002 onwards, to bring its attention back to the traditional aid model. This was in line with the wider foreign policy goals that developed under Hu Jintao. To implement this new objective, rather than solely relying on government budgets to fund traditional aid as previously practiced, China introduced a mixed methodology of traditional aid, Concessional Loans, Zero Duty Treatment and Debt Relief, combined with the ubiquitous Eight-Point Plans that sprung from FOCAC ministerial meetings. Meanwhile, additional measures were presented within the UN system.

According to these new approaches, China's aid began to focus on the long-term impacts of Chinese assistance. As the Minister of MOFCOM emphasised, 'Let the recipient countries share China's development experience. Future foreign aid has to be planned with a minimum of five-year consideration'.[60] While continuously developing planning and implementation approaches, China has also put forward a number of supplementary adjustments. In particular, on the basis of focusing on medical and health, Chinese aid has sought to improve African human capital resources. To drive common bilateral aid towards integrated multilateral cooperation, China has also pushed for aid collaboration across African sub-regions.

In sum, whilst pursuing financial benefits through more business-orientated loan approaches, and improving people's livelihoods with the HRDC, Medical Teams and Overseas Volunteer Programs supplemented traditional foreign aid, China's current foreign aid in Africa is purposed to accomplish both specific political and economic pursuits.[61] However, particular to recipient country's development and in view of the adjusted and improved objectives, planning and implementation approaches of China's traditional aid, a question arises in evaluating the period from 2005 to the present whether Chinese aid has enhanced African countries' self-reliance capacities. With this concern in mind, the study now examines the last case study, the recently transferred Lekma Hospital project in Ghana.

Lekma Hospital, Teshie, Ghana, 2010–present

The Lekma Hospital (also known as the China-Ghana Friendship Hospital, 中国-加纳友好医院) is a Grant funded, Complete Project Aid project that was implemented according to China's first Eight-Point Plan. With a budget of 51 million Yuan (approximately 7.7 million US dollars at the time), it is comprised of an out-patient building, a medical technology building, a ward with 100 beds, an auxiliary building, an anti-malaria clinic and a range of supplementary medical equipment and medicines. The tendering contract was won by China GEO-Engineering Corporation (CGC), while the provisioning of medical supplies was sub-contracted to China National Pharmaceutical Foreign Trade Corporation (SINOPHARM Foreign Trade).

Located in Teshie, a suburban district of Accra, the construction of the hospital was started in April 2009 and finished over a 15-month period, which included the installation and testing of all medical equipment. Upon completion in December 2010, it was transferred to the Ghanaian government and immediately was put under total Ghanaian ownership. Currently, the hospital employs 20 doctors, 128 nurses and 34 maintenance workers.[62] What is worth noting is that, since the Lekma Hospital was the first hospital delivered of the 30 promised new hospitals in Africa by China, its successful transfer to the local government has been in line with the realisation of China's 2006 FOCAC pledges (MOFCOM, 2009a).

Medical Aid mainly refers to the dispatching of medical teams, the provisioning of equipment and medicines, the building of hospitals, and the training of medical professionals. Since China sent its first Medical Teams to Egypt in 1956, according to the *White Paper*, it has dispatched 21,000 medical personnel overseas up to the end of 2009. In 2009 alone, '60 Chinese medical teams composed of 1,324 members provided medical services at 130 medical institutions in 57 developing countries' (2011: 15). Although in the particular case of Ghana, China's first medical team only arrived in 2009, Ghana welcomed its first Chinese hospital as early as 2000 (i.e., Dangme East Hospital). Given the previous aid and hospital building experiences in Ghana, the Lekma Hospital seemed to be a rather straightforward project on paper. However, problems with this hospital appeared even before it opened in December 2010.

To begin with, while the construction of the hospital was fully completed in July 2010, it actually opened five months later.[63] Explanations for this anomaly vary. The managing director of CGC, Feng Nian, claimed that 'the training was already done, it only took a month. The delay was due to the schedule of the president who insisted on being present and announcing the opening of the hospital'.[64] However, another Chinese informant asserted that 'the reason for the delay was because the local government wanted China to operate the hospital as well. Ghana has a National Health Insurance Scheme where the government is responsible for the cost of medical services and medicines. If China had taken over the hospital, then the local government would be seen to be providing medical services at no further expense to themselves'.[65] Reluctance to commit to such a scenario is thus put forward as an alternative explanation. As a side note, the Ghanaian hospital director, Dr. Yaw Antwi Boasiako, claimed that he was initially assigned to direct another hospital but was then unexpectedly allocated to Lekma Hospital and that this complicated matters.[66]

As with the issue of the National Theatre in Accra, the question whether Ghana actually needed this Chinese project needs to be asked. Or, more strictly speaking, did Ghana have the capacity to operate another hospital and were the proper facilities put in place? Firstly, the hospital's own director has stated that a hospital of 300 beds was required for the area, rather than what was delivered. Additionally, the director claims he was told that China would be delivering an anti-malaria centre at Ridge Hospital, a considerably larger hospital in Accra, but then the Chinese decided to build a general hospital instead. This point was later clarified by a senior Chinese official, who stated that 'building an additional sector of a hospital is a lot less recognisable than building a hospital on its own'.[67] This is of course fitting with the wider logic of landmark projects.

The Lekma Hospital was opened successfully by the then Vice President John Mahama on 23 December 2010. However, identified issues are many. In giving a wide evaluation of the project thus far, Dr. Boasiako commented as follows:

> The construction of the building is generally OK, although there are some defects, such as half of the door locks not working. The immediate problem is the equipment. Some are malfunctioning, some are not working at all, and some are not here. For instance, the X-Ray, the CSSD (Central Sterile Supply Department) and the CT are not powered. These machines require a built-in power supply in their construction and that has not been properly done. The X-Ray machine came without the back plate, film, and the chemical analyser in the laboratory is missing cables. The gas plant that supplies oxygen to the ward and theatres is not working. Besides the limited capacity of only eight corpses, the mortuary has never worked. An ambulance-like vehicle was provided, but it is only an ordinary van with flat seats and oxygen cylinders. That broke down after 2 months.[68]

As the examples rapidly piled up, the interview, initially agreed for only 30 minutes, quickly turned into a half-day discussion. We were soon joined by a radiologist, who approached us hastily with relief in his voice and asked, 'Are you the engineer?' After initial disappointment that this was not the case, upon hearing that the research was studying China's foreign aid, he continued with Boasiako's complaints:

> The hospital is not doing well at the moment. If I want to take an X-ray of a patient, I have to ask him to go to another hospital. Apart from the unleaded doors of the X-ray room and the seriously outdated CT equipment, both of the operating boards and the unconnected power distribution cabinets are labelled in Chinese. It requires a lot more than a medical degree to get this equipment into operation.[69]

On realising that there were no specialist engineers suitable for the hospital (nor in Ghana), SINOPHARM Foreign Trade attempted to unsuccessfully teach the radiologist to connect the power cables to the machines through the medium of webcam. Picking up from the radiologist, Dr. Boasiako tried to switch the topic to possible solutions:

> It would be much better if China could send some experienced doctors to help us, not only with the equipment, but also for the herbal treatment department. Although we do have some local specialists, they are not experienced. We also need acupuncturists and people who can teach proper massage. These departments are all still closed.[70]

But then he further pointed out that 'Ghana is short of medical staff. A lot of the doctors have gone to developed countries. Consequently, the staff at Lekma have been drawn from other hospitals, which have of course denuded the capacity of those other facilities'. In addition to the notable shortage of medical staff, the many unopened departments and an anti-malaria centre remaining an empty room with unpacked equipment, the immediate way out for the hospital points to China's HRDC programs.

Aimed at 'helping recipient countries build up their self-development capacity' as stated in the *White Paper* (2011: 5), China's HRDC offers around 200 training programs to Ghana annually. Seven of these programs are medical related, with a total of 19 places.[71] After highlighting problems with Lekma, 15 places in all seven training programs were secured for the hospital. Yet even then, problems abounded. It turned out that some of the programs were relevant and useful, but others were seen as irrelevant. One of the doctors who was enrolled in the Training Course on Malaria Diagnosis Technique and Equipment Usage for Anti-malaria Centres in Africa complained that 'the title [of the course] suggests that it is for the diagnosis of malaria, but it is actually laboratory training and that besides the title, there were no details whatsoever provided about the course before enrolment'.[72] Another doctor added that 'I am happy that China is trying to do something here, but I am also so frustrated because it could just have been better'.[73]

So again, inadequate project planning, sub-standard construction and uncoordinated HRDC programs combine to undermine the efficacy of Chinese aid. Despite the reforms in China's aid planning and implementation approaches, in the Lekma case at least, hardly any improvements have been made. As a senior Ghanaian development planning official commented:

> I am sure somebody will eventually realise that there is only a particular amount of money available. From the Ghanaian point of view, they were saying, 'Let's get as much as we can, let us add to it overtime', and then you really depend on the best project, but it is never going to be. On the other hand, the Chinese are also saying 'you did not plan ahead. We have this money, you want a hospital, and we built it for you'. For China . . . when they go into any country, they must sit down and discuss comprehensively with the recipient country's planning authority, not only by name, but by scope, so that it can have the maximum impact on the people.[74]

With concern to the issues of implementation, the Lekma Hospital was the first hospital that CGC ever constructed.[75] Thus it is not hard to realise why the hospital was constructed in such a way that it was literally disconnected from its equipment. Additionally, there definitely were drawbacks in MOFCOM's process of qualifying aid implementation contractors. Considering the quality and standard of the medical equipment (outdated and broken down machines), problems clearly exist. A senior Chinese official explained that as the project was Grant Aid, 'all materials have to be imported from China. Although it is common for donor countries to restrict grant foreign aid purchases to its own products, in the particular case of China's pharmaceutical equipment that is where the problem lies, as much of the current Chinese machinery manufactured in China is sub-standard.[76]

Since the opening of the hospital, Dr. Boasiako has repeatedly been in contact with the Chinese embassy to raise numerous issues. However, when meeting with Chinese officials, Dr. Boasiako revealed that the 'last time when I was invited [to the embassy] the only problem the Chinese brought up was that they were not happy that the China-Ghana Friendship Hospital plaque at the main gate was missing the Malaria Centre quote!'[77] Based on this conversation, an additional sign was installed at the main gate stating that a China-Ghana Malaria Prevention and Treatment Centre was located at the hospital. Though the actual Centre was standing vacant, no doubt the Chinese embassy was happy with the plaque.

This has been damaging to China's reputation. Recent concerns raised include 'inadequate doctors and senior nurses at the hospital . . . unavailability of mosquito nets, inappropriate mortuary facilities as well as water and electricity supplies' (Ghana Health Nest). In addition to this, on World Malaria Day in 2013, the magazine *Modern Ghana* ran an exposé revealing that not only was the hospital 'decaying and a far cry from the original vision and project dreamed of and initialled by Ghana', but also that the facility had 'not responded to basic health care contingencies' (2013). As a result, the report concluded, 'Most residents in the outlying communities prefer visiting other nearby facilities, some of which are not as esteemed or reputable as the State facility, but which can be relied upon to deliver basic services'.

To assess the Lekma Hospital project, it can be said that it has failed to attain its intended outcomes. On the ground and after only eight months in operation, a number of drawbacks became starkly apparent. Regarding project effectiveness, China's inappropriate planning which first established an overly broad-concerned project unsuited to Ghana's domestic conditions, can be pinpointed. Bearing in mind the recipient country's unsettled plans for project acceptance, the project's operation was then significantly postponed. Given Ghana's limited foreign aid capacity, not only did its underdeveloped technology fail to meet current requirements, but its problematic implementation supervising mechanisms led to sub-standard project constructions, as well as fragmentary delivery *and* the delivery of deficient equipment.

Considering the sustainability of the project, there is a minimal possibility to sustain its operations with the only partly delivered equipment (much of which doesn't work). In addition to this, inadequately coordinated Technical Aid and HRDC programs have compounded the problem, exacerbated by the brain drain of Ghanaian doctors and nurses. The shortage of human resources remains a critical issue for the continuation of the project. Provided China's limited aid capacity, both its inadequate planning and incompetent implementation systems have led to disappointing project outcomes. Aside from the underlying deficiencies of the project primarily caused by planning failures, China's lack of appropriate supervisory mechanisms and supportive measures directly brought about a sub-standard project in its implementation phase and an absence of project operating personnel.

To sum up, outcomes at Lekma are similar to other Chinese aid projects in the health sector. With regard to the hospital project in Sierra Leone, though it was officially transferred on 13 May 2011, it was unable to open due to a lack of medical personnel and utility supplies. As a Chinese informant noted, 'Let alone the shortages of water and electricity, the whole country only has less than eighty doctors. How can it then operate a general hospital?'[78] Given the uncoordinated support of Chinese Medical Teams, the project was renegotiated in March 2012 and a co-management between Shandong Qushan Hospital and the Ministry of Health of Sierra Leone was agreed to. On the basis of adopting a fully commercialised operating approach, this hospital eventually came into operation on 13 November 2012, 18 months after the official transfer.[79]

Regarding a China-Guinea Friendship Hospital project, while it was completed in July 2010, it was only transferred to the local government nine months later, owing to an unsettled management agreement. After the transfer and in spite of the hospital benefiting from the assistance of a Chinese Medical Team in installing and operating Chinese labelled equipment, it was still unable to come into full operation due to the 'absence of initial capital and electricity'.[80] In the end, the hospital ended up depending on a power generator and medicines provided by China. It was only after receiving these that the hospital actually opened, one year later.[81] A Chinese informant explained some factors for this delay, namely that the intense domestic demand for medical professionals in Guinea meant that local doctors 'only care about China's next donation of equipment and medicine', and showed up to work at the hospital only a part-time basis as they were simultaneously taking up positions elsewhere.[82]

Taking into account these virtually identical outcomes in Ghana, Sierra Leone and Guinea, despite China's efforts in adjusting its aid objectives to further accommodate recipient countries' needs, China's current aid is substantially undermined by incompetent planning and implementation as well as local deficiencies. The lack of appropriate implementation supervising mechanisms and effective supporting aid methods, as well as poor standards and uncoordinated HRDC programs have all led to China's goal of improving people's livelihoods being severely compromised. Aid dependency meanwhile has clearly increased in these recipient nations.

In general, since China decided to focus on traditional foreign aid once again, and since it decided to further promote its relationships with Africa, China's aid has emphasised improving people's livelihoods. However, despite this, it has at large not been able to improve on this. At present, China's still limited aid planning and implementation capacities means that promoting African self-reliance is unlikely to be met.

Concluding remarks

Whilst the case studies all demonstrated recipient countries' influences on China's aid to some degree, the actual outcomes of the aid projects were substantially affected by limited aid capacity. For instance, with regards to China's inadequate planning, the insufficient understanding of African countries' diverse domestic conditions has obviously resulted in a number of problems. Besides the oversimplified allocation approach which at first overlooked the political, social and institutional culture of recipient countries (and thus placed China's aid in complicated situations), the improperly arranged packages then further undermined circumstances given that technology-based projects were only able to deliver short-term benefits, whilst the non-technology based projects struggled to be effective at all. In the end, the majority of the projects were only able to continue operating with additional inputs of foreign aid and continual Chinese help.

In addition to the consequences caused by inadequate planning, with reference to China's incompetent implementation, an ineffective administration also led to project outcomes characterised by aid dependency. As a result, as well as the previously provided technical cooperation and China-based training programs, which declined due to the lack of suitable aid professionals, the recent HRDC programs have also failed to sustain outcomes for the delivered projects. Although arguably the HRDC programs to some extent addressed concerns over China's shortage of aid human resources, it was yet another example of inadequate planning. Likewise, the integration of HRDC and the coordination of all of China's implementation methods were found to be disorganised. Furthermore, since China has been delegating implementation and promoting traditional aid as a way to encourage its enterprises "going out", given the unequally developed supervisory mechanisms, the quality of China's aid has become an increasing concern.

To conclude the assessment of China's aid performance, as much as China has sought to improve its aid effectiveness and sustainability, it has in general not been able to improve its aid outcomes, nor deliver the proposed development assistance to Africa. Given that China's development agenda continues to lean heavily towards promoting Concessional Loans, as illustrated in the case studies, there remain many unresolved concerns. Such concerns include a lack of understanding of African countries' diverse domestic conditions and an absence of adequate aid administration systems. These concerns have hampered the continuous efforts that China has made in promoting its aid outcomes. As a result of this weak capacity, China's foreign aid continues to face many challenges.

After investigating the outcomes of some of China's aid projects in Africa and identifying the factors that have affected this, attention is drawn back to the overall development of China's aid. After more than six decades, why have the effectiveness and sustainability of China's aid in Africa barely improved? What reasons are there for China's aid to still be struggling to cope with Africa's domestic conditions? In order to find the answers to these questions, the next chapter brings this study back to the making of China's foreign aid. Along with looking at China's successes and failures, it reveals the underlying characteristics of China's foreign aid, which is a – if not *the* – source of the problems identified.

Notes

1 Interview with senior Chinese official, Freetown, Sierra Leone, 6 August 2011.
2 Interview with senior Chinese official, Freetown, Sierra Leone, 6 August 2011.
3 This example was provided by a Chinese official. Interview with Chinese official, Freetown, Sierra Leone, 6 August 2011.
4 Unless otherwise noted, all figures presented in this case study have been collected from the Fujian Provincial Chronicle (www.fjsq.gov.cn/showtext.asp?ToBook=217&index=134).
5 Interview with senior Chinese official, Freetown, Sierra Leone, 2 September 2011.
6 Interview with senior Chinese official, Freetown, Sierra Leone, 6 August 2011.
7 Interview with Li Mao, General Manager of Magbass Sugar Complex (1991–1995 and 2003–2012), Freetown, Sierra Leone, 3 September 2011.
8 Interview with Chinese technician, Freetown, Sierra Leone, 3 September 2011.
9 Interview with senior Chinese official, Freetown, Sierra Leone, 2 September 2011.
10 Interview with Li Mao, Freetown, Sierra Leone, 3 September 2011.
11 Interview with Chinese technician, Freetown, Sierra Leone, 3 September 2011.
12 Interview with Chinese manager, Freetown, Sierra Leone, 3 September 2011.
13 Interview with a group of Chinese technicians, Freetown, Sierra Leone, 3 September 2011.
14 Interview with former local employee, Freetown, Sierra Leone, 5 September 2011.
15 Three of these institutions were from China: the Ministry of Foreign Economic Liaison, the Fujian Light Industrial Department, and the Fujian Agriculture Department.
16 Interview with Li Mao, Freetown, Sierra Leone, 3 September 2011.
17 The original words said in the interviews were '吃拿卡要', which directly translate as 'eat, take, extort and demand'.
18 Interview with a group of Chinese employees, Freetown, Sierra Leone, 4 September 2011.
19 Ibid.
20 Interview with senior Chinese manager, Freetown, Sierra Leone, 3 September 2011.

21 Ibid.
22 Interview with senior COMPLANT official, who was stationed in the Complex during the 1980s, Beijing, China, 15 November 2011.
23 Interview with Li Mao, Freetown, Sierra Leone, 3 September 2011.
24 Interview with Chinese employee, Freetown, Sierra Leone, 3 September 2011.
25 Interview with Li Mao, Freetown, Sierra Leone, 3 September 2011.
26 Ibid.
27 Interview with two groups of local employees, Tonkolili, Sierra Leone, 4 September 2011.
28 Interview with senior Chinese investor, Ma, Tema, Ghana, 16 August 2011.
29 Available online at http://fec.mofcom.gov.cn/gbzn/gobiezhinan.shtml.
30 Admitted all interviewed Chinese companies, including: Yan Tai International, Economic Counsellor's office rehabilitation, Ghana; BUCG, Bintumani Hotel, Sierra Leone; COMPLANT, Magbass Sugar Complex, Sierra Leone; Shenzhen Energy, Sunon Asogli Power Plant, Ghana; SINOHYDRO, Bui Dam, Ghana.
31 Interview with two groups of local employees, Tonkolili, Sierra Leone, 4 September 2011.
32 Interview with Chinese technician, Freetown, Sierra Leone, 3 September 2011.
33 Interview with Chinese informant, Freetown, Sierra Leone, 2 September 2011.
34 Interview with Li Mao, Freetown, Sierra Leone, 3 September 2011.
35 Interview with Chinese technician, Freetown, Sierra Leone, 3 September 2011.
36 Quoted by Li Mao. Interview with Li Mao, Freetown, Sierra Leone, 3 September 2011.
37 Interview with senior Chinese official, Freetown, Sierra Leone, 2 September 2011.
38 Interview with Li Mao, Freetown, Sierra Leone, 3 September 2011.
39 Ibid.
40 Ibid.
41 Two senior Chinese officials interviewed in Sierra on 1 September 2011.
42 Interview with senior Chinese official, Freetown, Sierra Leone, 6 August 2011.
43 Interview with Professor Liu Liyun, Renmin University, Beijing, China, 27 November 2011.
44 Interview with Chinese official, Freetown, Sierra Leone, 29 August 2011.
45 Interview with senior Chinese official, Accra, Ghana, 20 August 2011.
46 Jerry Rawlings was the first President of Ghana, and he was in office in between 1993 and 2001.
47 Interview with Public Relations Officer, Francis Aklie, Accra, Ghana, 19 August 2011.
48 Interview with Estate Manager, Kwesi Wilson, Accra, Ghana, 19 August 2011.
49 Interview with General Management Officer, Accra, Ghana, 24 August 2011.
50 Interview with senior Ghanaian official, Accra, Ghana, 18 August 2011.
51 Interview with Public Relations Officer, Accra, Ghana, 19 August 2011.
52 Interview with senior National Theatre employee, Accra, Ghana, 24 August 2011.
53 Interview with General Management Officer, Accra, Ghana, 24 August 2011.
54 Interview with National Theatre employee, Accra, Ghana, 24 August 2011.
55 Interview with senior employee, Accra, Ghana, 19 August 2011.
56 Ibid.
57 Telephone interview with the project leader of the National Theatre Rehabilitation, Beijing, China, 2 November 2011.
58 Interview with Chinese scholar, Zhejiang Normal University, Zhejiang, China, 14 October 2011.
59 Ibid.
60 Unpublished document, August 2008, *Fu Ziying Speaks in Regional Economic Counsellors' Training*, p.4.
61 Unpublished document, August 2007, *Wu Yi Stresses the Obligations of Foreign aid in Serving China's Foreign Policy*, p.4.
62 Interview with Hospital Director, Dr. Yaw Antwi Boasiako, Accra, Ghana, 23 August 2011.

63 Interview with China Geo-Engineering Corporation Managing Director, Feng Nian, Accra, Ghana, 26 August 2011.
64 Ibid.
65 Interview with Chinese informant, Accra, Ghana, 24 August 2011.
66 Interview with Dr. Yaw Antwi Boasiako, Accra, Ghana, 23 August 2011.
67 Telephone interview with senior Chinese official, Accra, Ghana, 24 August 2011.
68 Interview with Dr. Yaw Antwi Boasiako, Accra, Ghana, 23 August 2011.
69 Interview with resident Radiologist, Dr. Jaren N. Oblitey, Accra, Ghana, 23 August 2011.
70 Interview with Dr. Yaw Antwi Boasiako, Accra, Ghana, 23 August 2011.
71 Data base on 2011 Medical Training Programs (Ghana).
72 Interview with resident doctor, Accra, Ghana, 23 August 2011.
73 Interview with resident doctor, Accra, Ghana, 23 August 2011.
74 Interview with senior Ghanaian development planning official, Accra, Ghana, 18 August 2011.
75 Interview with Chinese informant, Accra, Ghana, 24 August 2011.
76 Interview with senior Chinese official, Accra, Ghana, 26 August 2011.
77 Ibid.
78 Interview with Chinese informant, Freetown, Sierra Leone, 2 September 2011.
79 Online interview with senior Chinese official, St Andrews, Scotland, 10 November 2012.
80 Online interview with Chinese informant, St Andrews, Scotland, 24 November 2012.
81 Ibid.
82 Ibid.

5 China's foreign aid in Africa

Efforts and concerns

Having traced the development of China's aid in Africa and examining some factors that have affected its performance, this chapter seeks to understand the successes and failures of China's aid with regard to the factors that have affected its outcomes. Given the considerable reforms in China's aid planning and implementation approaches, it is perhaps intriguing that Beijing's aid still often struggles to maximise benefits for its intended recipients. This has occurred during the three periodisations of China's aid trajectory: building African development foundations (1958–1978), reducing expenditure while consolidating outcomes (1982–1993), and improving people's livelihoods (2005–present)).With the purpose of investigating the underlying characteristics of China's aid, as well as exploring plausible solutions, this chapter looks at some key topics namely, decision-making, planning and implementation. After understanding the underpinning of its objectives, other sections will investigate China's aid in practice. The allocation approach and packaging of aid is examined, with a finding that "friendship" appears to be a key explanatory factor in where the aid goes but that China's own considerations – rather than the recipient countries' actual needs and conditions – often trump matters.

Of course, what needs to be pointed out is that while this study is attempting to break down and differentiate the process of China's aid, the decision-making, planning and implementation of China's foreign aid are indeed interconnected. After the decision-maker plans for aid objectives, the participating institutions implement the planning (and the projects and programs) accordingly. However, whilst these processes are very similar to each other (the decision-making of aid objectives and the planning of packages according to set objectives) and interact throughout (both the planning of aid packages and their implementation are managed by the same institution), they all have their individual impacts on the eventual outcomes of China's aid in Africa.

How China decides its foreign aid objectives in Africa

In the period from 1955 to 1976, when the Mao Zedong–led state was striving to consolidate its regime and break out of the diplomatic isolation created by the capitalist world, China utilised aid as a stepping stone to expand its relationships with African countries. Set against an international background in which both China and African countries were trying to pursue independence and self-reliance, China focused its first objective in Africa on helping build industrial and agricultural foundations. This objective was established subsequent to a research visit led by the State Planning Commission to three African countries in 1964 (Algeria, Mali and Guinea). However, during its execution, not only did African countries' divergent local conditions exceed China's expectations, but Chinese capacity was weak. As a result, the objective was generally not met and undermined many aid outcomes.

In the interests of revising this situation, during the period from 1979 to 1993, the inauguration of the reform policy drove China's aid to the objectives of reducing expenditure while consolidating outcomes. Aimed at both preserving China's development capacity and coping with African countries' divergent local conditions, objectives were primarily implemented in the forms of less financially-demanding and less-technical landmark projects, as well as Management Cooperation. To a broader extent, this objective achieved some of its purposes but neither managed to bring financial benefits to China nor sustained generally positive outcomes in Africa. The number of non-maintained and underperforming landmark projects built by the Chinese and which litters the African vista, stands as a testament to this reality. As a result, China terminated its Management Cooperation in the early 1990s and focused most of its attention on the creation of the Concessional Loan.

Since Concessional Loans only require relatively limited financial inputs from Beijing, landmark projects remained the primary choice of China's foreign aid in Africa until the new century, when the contemporary take-off of Sino-Africa relationship drove events. By this time, a growing interest in Africa as a major partner, as well as promoting the idea of China fulfilling its international responsibility, led Beijing's aid program to embrace a new and third objective, i.e., to improve people's livelihoods. However, despite this reform, the outcomes for China's aid in Africa have stayed largely the same, at least thus far. According to evidence garnered from the case studies, Chinese aid still creates aid dependencies while only marginally benefiting Africa's development.

The foundation of China's foreign aid

Where aid is focused is one of the most important decisions that any government with foreign aid aspirations must make. Although it seems a more technical process, perhaps mainly involving feasibility research, the considerations and criteria that determine the focus are far-reaching. As Lancaster pointed out in a study of eight bilateral and multilateral donors (the United States, France, the United Kingdom, Japan, Sweden, Italy, the World Bank and the European Union), 'Promoting economic development in recipient countries is typically only one of the objectives for which aid is given and not always the predominant one. Others include advancing political and security concerns . . . Domestic and bureaucratic politics also frequently play a role in aid decisions' (1999: 74). However, in the particular case of China, its foreign aid decision-making process is completely different from those of "traditional" donors. For the most part, it is *only* the domestic politics that account for determining aid objectives. Hence, as an initial step towards understanding the decision-making process of China's objectives, its underlying considerations are first discussed.

As an initial statement on this matter, the words of one senior Chinese official are quoted:

> Friendship (友好) and assistance (帮助) – these are the foundations of China's foreign aid. China's aid is provided, insisting on maintaining friendly foreign relationships. Regardless of the recently emerged economic interests of our aid, these must *not* interfere with the political interests of aid at any time.[1]

To elaborate on this point, one Chinese government report notes that 'China's foreign aid is a state behaviour. Its projects and programs are the substance of cooperation between the Chinese government and recipient countries' governments. China's foreign aid is not a business activity, nor is it poverty alleviation. Further, it is not a commercial program for enterprises to make profits'.[2] Indeed, China's aid 'is concerned about maintaining national interests and national security'. In the main, in the words of the Chinese government 'The goal of aid is to, through implementing foreign aid projects and programs, to build, consolidate and to develop our [China's] friendly cooperative relationship (友好合作关系) with developing countries'.[3]

It is on this friendship-emphasised foundation that China's foreign aid put forward three distinct foreign aid objectives in Africa. At the beginning, when this friendship was exercised through the belief in proletarian internationalism, it was materialised in the building of African industrial and agricultural foundations. With the purpose of boosting their capacities to stand against imperialism and hegemonism, as well as assisting 'brotherhood countries' (CCCPC, 1958) to acquire economic independence and ultimately achieve self-reliance, this friendship quickly evolved into claims regarding the mutual nature of Chinese aid-giving.[4] Even when China was suffering from the Cultural Revolution, it continued with friendship-building through foreign aid.[5]

With the reform policy, primarily inaugurated to resuscitate China's economy, given the financial circumstances that China was in and the pressing domestic demands, friendship was transformed into an alignment with the established foreign aid budget (Liu, 2009: 51). At this stage, within the context of financial shortages and the experiences gathered from the previous period, friendship was realised in landmark projects across Africa. Most of these projects were notable for including in their official titles the word Friendship. These were funded so as to maintain friendly relationships with China and to aid social infrastructure development. In addition to this, China also introduced Management Cooperation to enhance aid efforts. Meanwhile, although China began to explore financial benefits from its aid, with the view to reduce expenditure, fundamentally it nevertheless intended to 'actively develop equal and mutually beneficial relationships with all foreign countries' (CCCPC Party Literature Research Office, 1982a: 5).

Moving towards the end of the twentieth century, the continuous failings in China's aid frustrated China's friendship-building goals. Given the demands of domestic economic development, China searched for mutual benefits. Nonetheless, whilst promoting the Concessional Loan, this friendship-building was still carried out primarily through the delivery of landmark projects. By the early 2000s, and with a much increased financial capacity, this friendship was then ostensibly directed to improving people's livelihoods. Aimed at raising their development capacities, this friendship emerged via health and educational projects and programs promised through FOCAC and other international meetings. Alongside this came a stress on 'the particularities of African human resources development in strengthening the China-Africa friendship'.[6] This manifested itself through a rapidly expanded HRDC program.

Although it can be seen that the underpinnings of China's foreign aid have evolved and progressed, it is nevertheless driven by the underlying political consideration of building friendly foreign relationships. As one senior Chinese researcher has affirmed, 'In substance, the economic interests are nonetheless attached to the political interests of China's foreign aid rather than dictating its making'.[7] 'It is owing to this friendship emphasis and the equality and mutually beneficial stresses thereby embodied, that the non-conditionalities underpinning China's aid are welcomed by all African recipient countries'.[8] Be that as it may, despite these objectives, the emphasis on "friendship" has also resulted in complications both domestically and abroad. In particular, because of the insistence on friendship, the initial economic development of the People's Republic of China was arguably delayed. Some Chinese scholars in particular have argued that the expenditure on aid to some extent affected the livelihoods of China's own people (e.g., Xue, 2013a). It was only after the inauguration of the reform policy in 1978, that the repeated stress to 'act according to one's capability' (量力而行) (Shi, 1989) finally calmed this out-of-control expenditure level.

Given that neither China nor most African countries placed sufficient attention on exploring appropriate aid objectives for Africa, rather relying on aspirations based on friendship building, the objectives that China implemented did not sufficiently address the immediate development concerns of recipient countries. As admitted by an African development planning official, 'China doesn't seem to have a firm idea of what we [Africans] really need. But that said, nor does Africa. So while China's foreign aid is generally beneficial to our development, we just pick what China has got on offer'.[9] In addition to this lack of insistency from the recipient countries, with consideration to the responsibilities of the donor country, a senior Chinese official indicated that the current objective of improving people's livelihoods (and indeed all of China's foreign aid objectives), were primarily determined by principal decision-makers' personal visits to recipient countries and were predominately considered as *only* "friendship" building.[10]

More to the point, considering that China has always regarded African countries as a whole in determining foreign aid objectives (Li, 2008), as one senior Chinese official pointed out, 'Whilst all of our [China's] foreign aid objectives were extensively concerned for Africa's development difficulties, they were clearly lacking pertinences to each African recipient country'.[11] In this situation, with both donor and recipient countries being indifferent to immediate development concerns, the overly broad settlement on friendship has directly limited China's aid efforts. In a word, despite China's objectives all being duly determined according to the 'observable development concerns' of Africa,[12] given they were at the same time focused almost solely on friendship and for the greater part influenced by decision-makers' personal preferences, not only did most objectives fail to adapt to the immediate development concerns of each African recipient country, but they were also only to some extent relevant to the general development concerns of recipients.

To take account of these fundamental pitfalls in determining foreign aid objectives, China needs to place specific emphasis on pushing forward its aid from friendly help to practical development assistance. Equally, 'the decision-making of China's foreign aid objectives should be further allowed for scientific research' (Huang, 2007: 10). All projects should be adjusted to each recipient country's immediate development concerns rather than the general needs of the African continent as a whole.[13] An African development planning official strongly argues this point, stating that 'China and Africa need to work a lot more closely together, to help us [Africa] strengthen our process and planning arrangements to make us better able to program our national development structures, and to identify priority development areas where China can help'.[14]

All in all, despite more than 60 years of aid experience in Africa, China is still unable to come up with adequate approaches for identifying appropriate aid objectives, nor to help its African recipient countries set up priority development areas. Not only are the decision-making goals of China's objectives overwhelmingly focussed on "friendship", but they are also disproportionately influenced by decision-makers' personal preferences. As a result of this fundamental lack of scientific research and relevance, the objectives that China has introduced over the years have to an extent undermined China's foreign aid outcomes in Africa. Given this emphasis on "friendship", China and Africa need to work much more closely together to find which areas one recipient country should focus the most on, and for China to assist.

Although the decision-making processes of China's aid are heavily influenced by its domestic political consideration, this friendship emphasis does not interfere with the 'aid-for-development' norm (Lancaster, 2006: 7). To a large extent, the objectives that China has put forward actually correspond to the general development concerns of African recipient countries. The next two sections investigate the practices of China's aid. Given that the objectives that China has implemented until now have all generally been unsuccessful, how China's underdeveloped aid planning and implementation methods have failed to deliver these intended development goals will be discussed.

How China plans its foreign aid in Africa

With regards to the planning of China's aid in Africa, while China has been continuously increasing its aid and adjusting its implementation methods, there still remain many drawbacks with its planning approaches. In particular, this study has found that the oversimplified aid allocation approach and improperly arranged aid packages are the main weaknesses in China's aid planning in Africa. Not only have such issues led China's aid into unknown local conditions, but they have also brought inappropriate technical and management standards to the recipient countries' development conditions, as well as an inadequate coordination of implementation methods. Even though China has been attempting to overcome these drawbacks for years, it is still unable to provide suitable solutions. In view of this situation, and given that planning of China's foreign aid in Africa has undergone significant evolution, how does China make progress on its aid allocation and packaging?

To reiterate, the distribution of China's aid was at the beginning fully dependent on the recipient countries' relationships with the Soviet Union and the United States. During the middle of the twentieth century when the political confrontation between communism and capitalism was at its peak, China's aid was prioritised to neighbouring communist and Asian countries and African nationalist countries. Aside from this greater planning arrangement, the amount of aid to each recipient country, as well as its packaging, were mainly settled according to China's principal decision-makers' political considerations. With political interests dominating China's foreign aid planning, subsequent to the research visit in 1964, the initial packaging of China's aid in Africa was focused on industrial and agricultural projects, with a combined approach of Complete Project Aid and Technical Aid to help them make use of their natural resources, master technologies and ultimately achieve self-reliance.

Following the change of principal leadership in 1978, China's growing demand for economic development and a stabilising international environment directed the planning of China's aid to prioritising domestic development. Along with the inauguration of the reform policy, China adjusted its objectives to reducing expenditure while consolidating outcomes. In line with this adjustment, during the 1980s and early 1990s, the less financially demanding and less technical landmark projects became the primary choice of China's aid packaging in Africa. This was collaborated with the Management Cooperation integrated Technical Aid, paying attention to the earlier delivered industrial and agricultural projects. At this stage, on the basis of China beginning to accept development assistance from traditional foreign aid donors, its political bias towards communist and nationalist countries was also duly dropped. This extended the reach of China's aid to include a wider range of African countries.

By the mid-1990s, China's aid planning was first steered to promote economic cooperation with the introduction of the Concessional Loan. Following substantial economic development in the early 2000s, China's planning then shifted to improving people's livelihoods, with prospects set for advancing both Africa's social and infrastructure development. Today, while being directed by the 24 government institutions jointly participating in the Inter-agency Coordination Mechanism, the planning of China's aid is focused on the development sectors including industry, agricultural, economic infrastructure, medicine and public health, education, public facilities, and clean energy and coping with climate change. Further, it is employing two funding methods of Grant and Interest-free Loan, and six implementation methods of Complete Project Aid, Technical Aid, Goods and Materials Aid, HRDC, Medical Teams and Overseas Volunteer Programs in the assistance of Africa's development.

Nevertheless, in spite of this progress China's insufficient understanding of African countries' diverse domestic conditions still undermines China's foreign aid outcomes. To be specific, regarding China's first foreign aid objective, it was commonly planned only considering the political interests and natural environments of the recipient countries. Because of this oversimplified approach which fundamentally disregarded the political, social and institutional conditions of the recipient countries, not only did the unknown conditions of the local work force and management behaviours affect the operations of China's projects immediately after transfers, but this problematic planning also put the continuation of these projects in a further complicated situation given the restrictiveness of China's aid principles. As a result, whilst Chinese involvements were largely prohibited from local affairs, many of these projects ended in continuous dilemmas.

Subsequent to confronting this situation in the implementation of industrial and agricultural projects, by the time China proposed its second foreign aid objective centred on delivering landmark projects, Beijing began specifically asking for attention to be paid to local conditions. It thus introduced Management Cooperation to promote outcomes. However, due to the largely neglected conditions of the recipient countries, these landmark projects (which were often packaged with advanced technologies) only benefited the recipient countries' in the short-term and quickly fell into abeyance. Concerning their long-term impact, the Chinese government was required to repeatedly provide additional aid inputs just to sustain the projects. Reputationally, this was damaging whilst clearly relationships of dependencies developed on the Chinese.

Entering the new century, increased Chinese aid and adjusted implementation methods to some extent improved this situation. China began to aim for comprehensively assisting Africa's development and additional implementation methods and a plethora of institutions jointly participated in the mechanism process. However, despite these significant improvements, not only did the problematic allocation approach still produce complications but the improperly arranged aid packages also undermined the efforts that China has made in advancing other areas of its foreign aid. As a result, as well as often being involved in complex local situations, China's foreign aid projects and programs often currently fail to match the recipient countries' development conditions and coordinate with each other. In response to these unsatisfactory outcomes, this section now examines the allocation approach and the packaging of China's foreign aid in Africa to find out what problems are there buried in its planning processes.

The allocation approach of China's foreign aid

At the beginning, when China's foreign aid was primarily utilised for political purposes, its allocation was heavily influenced by its principal decision-makers' political considerations and to a large extent lacked financial assessments, feasibility studies, and other necessary processes of adequate planning. After the Cultural Revolution, the allocation of China's foreign aid was then asked to be 'planned comprehensively, with particular attention drawn to match the local conditions' (Shi, 1989). Particularly after the inauguration of the reform policy (as well as China opting for landmark projects in an attempt to minimise local influences), Management Cooperation was promoted with a view to overcoming the setbacks brought about by the differences between local conditions and China's understandings.

However, regardless of these early attempts to cope with the recipient countries' divergent political, social and institutional conditions, by the time China returned its attention back to Africa in the new century with newly adjusted foreign aid objectives and a focus on 'feasibility research', a number of these people's livelihoods-related projects are again found to be suffering from the recipient countries' local conditions.[15] Not only have their effectiveness been fundamentally restricted, but as pointed out by both Chinese aid experts and African officials, these projects face substantial difficulties in terms of prospective development.[16] In the light of this situation, and given that China now has greater capacities for foreign aid than ever before, what reasons are there for its aid problems?

With regard to the allocation principles of China's foreign aid, "Traditional friendly countries" (传统友好国家) is the most commonly adopted concept by the Chinese officials interviewed for this study when asked how China allocates aid.[17] As one of the most fundamental decisions that the Chinese government must make before drafting aid plans, indeed even prior to reviewing aid requests, Chinese officials determines the input of aid to each of its recipient countries (i.e., the Country Specific Foreign Aid Budget) according to the perceived "level of friendliness".[18] As a senior Chinese official indicated, 'Even though the allocation of foreign aid was repeatedly requested to take into consideration the recipient countries' local conditions, the changes applied to the shares of foreign aid input to each recipient country over the years are only marginal' and "friendship" remains the determining criteria.[19] As specified by another official, 'Except in extreme situations, such as civil wars or diplomatic breakdown, whilst the amount of foreign aid to each recipient country is raised by a certain proportion every year, the percentage to each of them has remained almost exactly the same as Prime Minister Zhou outlined in the 1970s'.[20] In other words, what countries deemed "friendly" by Beijing can rely on a steady supply of aid, irrespective of developments within the country. As long as they are considered friendly to China, that is enough. This rather remarkable situation was elaborated on by two more senior Chinese officials:

> Although traditionally friendly countries almost always have better creditability in terms of responding to our [China's] political interests and economic cooperation, frankly speaking, the allocation of our foreign aid is neither dependent on the recipient countries' strategic importance to China nor their economic potential. It is solely rested on how traditionally friendly they are to China.[21]

In short, whether the recipient country is politically stable, or institutionally suitable for a certain amount of foreign aid input or in fact whether the recipient country actually needs Chinese aid, these factors are not a part of the consideration for providing foreign aid by Beijing. 'It is simply only friendship that matters'.[22]

Not only is there thus still a lack of any rational approach to the allocation of China's foreign aid, but even allowing for the continuously changing international situation, as another Chinese official pointed out:

> Carry on (沿袭) is practically what we [China] have been doing, and are doing at the moment. After Prime Minister Zhou sketched the foreign aid allocation framework, no one has dared to make adjustments. . .[aid] is still largely provided on the friendship emphasis.[23]

Another senior Chinese official admitted about the current situation that:

> Even if we [China] have encountered so many problems with some of the African recipient countries' divergent local conditions, such as changes of governing parties and local behaviours, it is not that we are not attaching importance to these conditions. However on the one hand we are strictly prohibited by The Eight Principles in participating in local affairs and on the other hand, we are tied by the friendship-determined foreign aid approach i.e. where you have to spend it all.[24]

In spite of the potential challenging outcomes, 'If the allocated budget isn't fully turned into aid agreements by the third quarter, we [China] have to actively look for additional projects to fulfil it'.[25] It is owing to this friendship underlying consideration, that concerns over local conditions are only secondary (if not ignored outright). Long ago it was decided which countries were "friendly", a budget is calculated and then officials in each individual recipient country are required to spend this budget. No wonder that China's foreign aid experiences various complications.

Specifically, China's oversimplified foreign aid allocation approach undermines its efforts in building coherent relationships or successfully implementing aid that actually works. These shortcomings have caused a substantial wastage of China's resources. Equally, the over-simplified and rigid approach has meant that China's aid projects have often been dragged into local political situations in the recipient countries. As a senior Chinese official pointed out, 'One of the biggest challenges that our [China's] foreign aid is facing in Africa is actually their presidential electoral system. When the political leader of the recipient country is suddenly changed, the friendship that we have been building can be ruined as quickly as overnight'.[26]

In attempts to 'bypass the increasingly proficient democratic systems of the African recipient countries', the planning of China's aid has gradually led to include more turnkey projects, instead of the earlier prioritised BOT approach (Build, Operation and Transfer) which required considerable more involvement by the recipient countries.[27] As a senior Chinese official indicated, 'Apart from opting for turnkey projects at every opportunity, we [China] are also looking with favour on short-term projects and programs. Particularly when there is only one year ahead of the next presidential election in the recipient country, all of our new foreign aid agreements are most likely to be set up to be complete before then'.[28] This will obviously have an impact on their relevance and usefulness to the recipient country.

With regard to the complications created by ignoring local conditions, a Chinese official noted that 'Most of the African recipient countries have difficulties in reading the foreign aid contract'.[29] By this it is meant that the long-term implications and commitments implied by Chinese aid contracts are often misunderstood (or ignored) by local African officials. This then causes complications, frustrations and often, recriminations. For example, one of the most common requirements in a contract is that the recipient countries prepare for the arrival of the aid projects by providing 'the supply of water, electricity, roads and levelled ground (三通一平)'.[30] However,

> Not only do most of the African recipient countries tend to make unexpected demands half way through the project implementation, such as additional roads or an extension of the number of floors [of a building project], but they are also often unable to fulfil their part of the contract responsibilities. This then causes significant delays that require much additional aid input.[31]

The packaging of China's foreign aid

Improperly arranged aid packages have also undermined the effectiveness and sustainability of China's foreign aid. Not only has this been a result of the absence of supportive implementation methods, which broadly restricted the outcomes of China's aid, but due to the inappropriately identified technical and management standards, its landmark projects have only been able to deliver short-term effects – or struggled to be effective at all. Moreover, even the effective projects have been unsustainable without continual additional inputs from Beijing.

At present, the packaging of China's foreign aid is put together by MOFCOM, MFA and MOF and twenty-four institutions jointly participating in the Inter-agency Coordination Mechanism. Aside from being supported by the specialised institutions in planning specific projects and programs, the method has benefited from the expanded aid focus and the specifically refined implementation methods. However, in spite of these improvements, with regards to China's recent focus on people's livelihoods-related projects and programs, as demonstrated in the case studies they are still largely unsuited to the recipient countries' conditions. Equally, these projects and programs have also failed to be coordinated with each other.

With regard to project identification in China's aid, 'To deliver what kind of aid projects and programs and utilising which method, this decision is still being made largely according to the Eight Principles'.[32]This senior Chinese official has been in the seat of reviewing foreign aid requests for more than two decades. 'In short, it is basically what China has, and what the recipient country needs'.[33] After the State Council approves the planning for a Country Specific Foreign Aid Budget and allocates them to corresponding government institutions, the Economic and Commercial Counsellor's Offices situated in the recipient countries are then tasked to begin to review aid requests. If the requests are 'either too big or unrealistic', the Counsellor is required to make proposals for reasonable adjustments.[34] In practice, the packaging of China's foreign aid is principally organised on the basis of 'Keep in mind the primary principles, respond creatively to the practical situations'. Even though the input of China's aid is specifically allocated to each of its recipient countries, the packaging of this is exceptionally flexible. As one senior Chinese official indicated, 'As long as the projects and programs to some degree correspond to the primary emphasis on building friendly foreign relationships, and the budget in the application is within the allowance of that particular country, it will most likely be approved without any further investigations'.[35]

Whilst neither China nor Africa are especially clear on what is really needed, nor have either side been able to propose an adequate approach to identifying priority development areas for African recipient countries. Thus the packaging of China's aid is consequently 'referred back to the friendship emphasis'.[36] Whether or not the aid package is appropriate to the recipient country's current development capacities, it is (again) 'not a part of our [China's] consideration'.[37] In general, 'We [China] only take into account the natural environments of the recipient countries'.[38] Given that the allocated budget is set up on a must-spend basis, the packaging of China's aid can be sometimes based on pure conjecture. For example, the packaging of contemporary people's livelihoods related projects and programs. As one Chinese official explained, 'With consideration to the current objective, most of the African recipient countries were actually requesting food supplies. But we have been providing food for many years, so we changed it to schools'.[39] Additionally, 'Even if there is no one in the recipient countries to operate the schools, it cannot always be food'.[40] This is one typical logic of China's aid packaging at present and one that is clearly irrational. Moreover, looking at the other side of the situation, 'In spite of some of the projects not quite suiting the development capacities of the recipient countries, every single project that we [China] delivered is agreed to by them if not proposed by them in the first place'.[41]

The coordination of China's aid then is problematic. Although some efforts at reform have been made, for example the launching of the Inter-agency Liaison Mechanism in 2008 (and subsequently upgrading this to the Inter-agency Coordination Mechanism in 2011), these mechanisms only convene all of the participating institutions on an annual basis.[42] Further, as asserted by Guo, 'Whilst there is no legislation laid down to govern this mechanism, and its administrating division is not an individual government institution, the orders enacted by one institution are very difficult to coordinate other participating institutions' (2014). The fact that there is only one Secretary Office established in the Department of Aid to Foreign Countries of MOFCOM to operate this mechanism speaks volumes. It is thus not hard to explain why 'when a British official asked the Ministry of Health's International Cooperation Department where China was building the hospitals and malaria centres promised in the 2006 Beijing Summit, they replied that they had no clue, they were waiting for the Ministry of Commerce to inform them' (Brautigam, 2009: 109). Even when a similar question was asked of the Department of Aid to Foreign Countries of MOFCOM itself, the reply was likewise unsettling: 'We are waiting for higher-level instructions'.[43]

With an eye to this situation, seeing the reliance on projects and programs that agree with the primary emphasis on building friendly foreign relationships, it is once more this friendship underlying consideration that has disoriented the packaging of China's foreign aid. As a result, due to the largely assumed development needs of the recipient countries, the general feasibility of China's aid is called into question. As one senior Chinese official pointed out with regards to the recent tendency towards making international pledges (i.e. the Eight-Point plan[s] and the Six Measures):

> Given the pre-determined projects and programs, as well as the allocated foreign aid budget, the usual planning practice of "looking for projects with money in hand" has caused a number of our [China's] hospitals and schools delivered to Africa of late, if not all of them, to be unable to open or immediately falling into foreign aid dependencies.[44]

Grounded on falsely identified project standards, the overall outcomes of China's foreign aid is currently fundamentally limited. Besides the case studies noted in this work, a tendency to add additional landmark projects for friendship demonstration purposes is a major temptation. Like the earlier landmark projects, which were frequently found to have only short-term effectiveness (at best), a similar pattern is quickly beginning to appear with the recent people's livelihoods related projects.[45]

Even considering the aid projects that have to some extent reflected the immediate development needs of the recipient countries and suited their technical and management development capacities, the misleading positioning of the project sometimes also leads to further concerns. As a senior Chinese official pointed out, 'Under the implication of "foreign aid should be superior than the current standard of living in the recipient countries", the project is largely appropriate to the recipient country's development capacity, or relatively comprehensively packaged. Yet it can still end up in dilemmas'.[46] According to an example given by another Chinese official with regards to China's preference for building rice projects in Africa instead of supporting their cassava cultivation, while rice is generally considered to be a classy food in Africa, in contrast to cassava which is considered to be a traditional and low-cost food, 'given the significantly higher production cost of rice, it neither makes economic sense nor is acceptable to the general public of African recipient countries'.[47] Yet it goes ahead. As one official admitted, 'We [China] have to emphasis friendship, which has made our foreign aid unique and possibly of benefit to African recipient countries' development. However, if everything is referred back to the friendship emphasis and is blind to the practical situation, it is not going to work for both China and Africa'.[48]

Having in mind this friendship consideration, something which has fundamentally frustrated the coherent planning of China's aid in Africa, it can be said that similar to the decision-making process of China's objectives, while following after the primary emphasis on building friendly foreign relationships, China only has very vague ideas about how to allocate its aid inputs and arrange its aid packages. To practically improve its outcomes in Africa, China would need to attach particular importance to the adaptations of its projects and programs to the recipient countries' diverse domestic conditions. Specifically speaking, with regards to the allocation of China's aid, the input to each recipient country would have to be adequately and promptly adjusted according to local conditions. While it is not possible at the moment to make major alterations to the allocation framework per se, 'attempts should be considered in the long-term country specific foreign aid planning so that the allocated budget can be preserved in the meantime and utilised in relatively suitable circumstances of the recipient countries'.[49]

Furthermore, regarding the coordination of projects, apart from the additional efforts needed to improve the current Inter-agency Coordination Mechanism, one senior Chinese official has suggested, that 'The universal packaging of China's foreign aid should take note of the agricultural projects and programs that we [China] delivered to Africa' and use them as a guide to best practice.[50] Given that each of the Agricultural Demonstration Centres came packaged with equipment and training programs, and all of the agricultural expert teams were integrated with local language interpreters in the initial planning, 'they have a much better chance of achieving the intended outcomes'.[51] To elaborate on the importance of arranging self-sufficient aid packages, as another senior Chinese official asserted:

> The planning of China's foreign aid should be paying a lot more attention to long-term effects. Instead of continuing to build new projects, priorities should be given to the continuation of existing projects. Indeed, that is the emphasis on integrating supportive measures to ensure existing projects are able to make the most and sustainable impacts on Africa's development.[52]

In short, after decades of attempting to promote its aid outcomes, the underlying tendency of "friendship" above all other factors stands as one of the most dominant drawbacks that is negatively influencing China's aid outcomes in Africa. It has made the planning of China's foreign aid neglect the local conditions of the recipient countries and led to China's aid often being unsuited to the recipient countries' needs and conditions. China needs to take the initiative to act upon this situation. Not only should research play a role in the planning of China's aid in Africa, but particular attention should be given to project and program coordination. Self-sufficient aid packages in the meantime should also see materially improved end results.

How China implements its foreign aid in Africa

With concerns given to the implementation of China's aid in Africa, on the basis of knowing that China has been continuously developing its capacities in terms of both governing institutions and operating mechanisms, the outcomes of China's aid have arguably scarcely achieved any significant improvements. Although as surveyed in the previous sections, the outcomes of China's foreign aid in Africa are seriously affected by the friendship-emphasised objectives and largely inconsiderate planning, in addition to these concerns the implementation approaches of China's foreign aid are problematic. This study has found that the lack of foreign aid professionals and undeveloped supervisory mechanisms are the principal deficiencies in China's aid implementation. Not only have these issues caused failings in technology and management transfers ever since the establishment of China's foreign aid, but they have also led to the recent decline in implementation quality.

To review the development of the implementation approaches of China's foreign aid, initially China's aid was solely administrated by the Central People's Government and coordinated by the State Planning Commission. After the establishment of the specialised ministries in the 1950s, aid administration was taken over by them while the project and program implementation was delegated to their subsidiary institutions. In 1961, the administration of China's aid was fully unified under the Bureau of Foreign Economic Liaison, and the Delivery Ministry In-chief Mechanism was set up. In 1964 China's foreign aid gained its first upgrade as the bureau was elevated to the Foreign Economic Liaison Commission. In 1970, this was elevated again with the Ministry of Foreign Economic Liaison being established. At the same time, the Complete Plant Export Company was also founded to manage the implementation of China's aid, whilst the Contract Ministry In-Chief Mechanism was introduced to organise the process.

In the 1980s and in accordance with the reform policy, the Ministry of Foreign Trade, Ministry of Foreign Economic Liaison, State Planning Committee and Foreign Investment Managing Committee merged into the Ministry of Foreign Economic and Trade. In this merger, the management of aid implementation was delegated to the Complete Plant Export Company, while SOEs were established to replace government subsidiary institutions for project and program implementation. At this stage, the Investment Responsibility Mechanism and the Contract Responsibility Mechanism were duly introduced. By the beginning of 1993, in order to further boost capacity, the existing ministry was promoted to the Ministry of Foreign Trade and Economic Cooperation, and the Complete Plant Export Company was transformed into the Complete Plant Import and Export Cooperation Group as an enterprise implementing China's foreign aid. This new setup was conducted by the Enterprise Contract Responsibility Mechanism.

Moving into the contemporary era, and with rapidly growing international responsibilities, China's foreign aid first concentrated on organising integral mechanisms to encourage the participation of SOEs and introducing codes of practices to govern the amplified aid process. In 2003 and in the interest of integrating its domestic economic growth into overseas economic cooperation, China converted the Ministry of Foreign Trade and Economic Cooperation into MOFCOM and charged it with the complete administration of China's internal and external economic and trade affairs. After laying this foundation for current foreign aid implementation, not only has China's aid further benefited with a number of dedicated databases coordinating aid experts and projects and programs, but by fully delegating the implementation management to the subsidiary public institutions of MOFCOM and other specialised institutions, the administrative capacity and overall implementation arrangement of China's aid is supposed to be able to better cope with the large increase in foreign aid.

However, despite these continuous improvements to implementation capacity, China's ineffective aid administration nevertheless delivers disappointing outcomes. To begin with, considering the first objective of China's aid (the building of African industrial and agricultural foundations) has actually resulted in foreign aid dependencies. Apart from some of the projects *eventually* making profits and becoming sustainable, the majority of China's aid delivered between the 1950s and 1970s suffered from unsuccessful technology and management transfers, mostly due to a lack of human resources. Hence, when the second foreign aid objective was proposed in the 1980s, China specifically called for less technical landmark projects. Still, while the human resources of China's foreign aid remained largely unimproved, this fundamental issue went on affecting outcomes so much so that China had to scale back its Technical Aid and terminate its Management Cooperation by the beginning of the 1990s.

After focusing on delivering the less technical landmark projects for almost two decades, the introduction of the HRDC programs at the turn of the century to some extent improved this situation by providing technology and management training in China. Particularly after the inauguration of the third foreign aid objective in 2005 (Africa's social development), the rapidly expanded HRDC schemes significantly improved the diversity and capacity of China's foreign aid training programs. However, at this stage, due to China's incompetent aid planning, the aid packages caused these HRDC programs to be largely uncoordinated with African people's livelihoods. At present, China only offers short-term onsite training following the transfers of Complete Project Aid projects. These usually last only two weeks and the HRDC programs nor the extremely compressed onsite training meets the current demands of the recipient countries. It also does not make up for the difficulties brought about by the underlying deficiency of Chinese aid workers.

Moreover, apart from this human resources capacity-based drawback to China's aid implementation, the supervision of this is problematic. Regardless of what the Four Principles promised and the continuous efforts that China has made in putting forward mechanisms and codes of practices to guide its aid implementation, since the introduction of the market economic system, the competition that has developed among and between aid implementation parties have to a great degree further threatened the quality of China's aid. As a result of the shortage of aid professionals and the unequally developed supervisory mechanisms, as a senior Chinese aid worker noted, 'While the projects that we [China] built in the 1960s are still up and running, the maintenance team has already come back twice on a recently transferred project'.[53] In reference to these complications, this section now delves into the handling and supervisory mechanisms of China's aid to explore the shortcomings that are hidden within its foreign aid implementation.

The handling of China's foreign aid

As learnt in previous chapters, in the course of delivering aid, the related departments of the Chinese government closely liaise and cooperate with each other. From the planning of aid to the eventual transfer, each project is at the least processed through three institutions within the Chinese government, namely the Economic and Commercial Counsellor's Office, the Department of Aid to Foreign Countries of MOFCOM, and the relevant implementation management institutions. The Department of Western Asian and African Affairs of MOFCOM and the Chinese Academy of International Trade and Economic Cooperation also supplies research whilst a number of specialised government institutions provide planning suggestions. The State Council of course oversees the whole process.

However, given all of these institutions collectively processing China's aid, it still turns out to be insufficient in assisting Africa's development. As explained by Brautigam earlier, 'The Department of Foreign Aid is unbelievably small, with a staff of only about 100 (seventy professionals) in thirteen divisions' (2009: 109). This "Department of Foreign Aid" is currently titled the Department of Aid to Foreign Countries of MOFCOM. According to Brautigam the thirteen divisions were made up of eight regional divisions (including five for Africa), and five administrative divisions i.e. human resources, financial management and planning, laws and regulations, information systems, and overall coordination. At the time of writing, there are now 15 divisions, with only four divisions for Africa. There is also now a division (the Division of International Exchange and Cooperation) which organises international collaboration.

With regard to the front line of China's aid, Brautigam notes that the 'Chinese Economic and Commercial Counsellor's office attached to China's embassy will designate one or more staff to oversee the aid program, trouble-shooting, monitoring, and checking up at their completion. These officials are not expected to be experts in development' (2009). As much as this is problematic, the human resources foundation of China's foreign aid is even more hard pressed. Indeed, where located in the Economic and Commercial Counsellor's Offices attached to the Chinese embassies, there is generally only *one* person who is assigned to take charge of aid full-time, and this person is not even expected to be experienced in foreign aid.[54] Apart from the Counsellor, who is primarily involved in the negotiations of aid items with the recipient country, this one person deals with the contract drafting, liaison with MOFCOM, and the supervision of the implementation of the project. In the particular case of Africa, where the staffing of the Economic and Commercial Counsellor's Offices are also arranged according to the concept of traditional friendly countries, a minimum of seventy per cent of these offices are staffed with less than eight people in total.[55]

After sending the aid proposal back to China for further review, the first department it reaches is the Department of Aid to Foreign Countries of MOFCOM and there is a general office taking charge of internal works. As the central administrative department of China's foreign aid, as well as the largest department of MOFCOM, the staffing of the Department of Aid to Foreign Countries has 96 people, plus an additional 80 people (mainly coordinated from other central and provincial economic departments).[56] With particular attention on Africa, the 4 regional divisions on average have one person dealing with three recipient countries at a time.[57] Taking account of the person who is assigned to handle foreign aid in the Economic and Commercial Counsellor's Office, as one senior Chinese official described the current situation, 'There is an average of 1.3 people looking after each African recipient country'.[58]

After aid requests are approved, these are then passed on to the appropriate implementation management institutions for contract bidding, preparation and implementation of the agreed terms. Aside from the specific Medical Teams and Youth Volunteer Programs, which are assigned to specialised government institutions (each of these specialised institutions have one dedicated office for organising aid-related tasks), the primary features of China's aid i.e. Complete Project Aid, Goods and Materials Aid, and HRDC, are processed by the subsidiary public institutions of MOFCOM. Of these, the Executive Bureau of International Economic Cooperation is set up with 96 staff spread between 17 divisions arranging Complete Project Aid and Technical Aid.[59] The China International Centre for Economic and Technical Exchanges, on the other hand, has 18 divisions and employs 140 people in the management of Goods and Materials Aid.[60] Finally, executing and coordinating China's HRDC programs, the Academy for International Business Officials has 190 staff across 18 divisions.[61]

As for the research departments, the Department of Western Asian and African Affairs of MOFCOM only has 30 staff, who process information gathered from the Economic and Commercial Counsellor's Offices abroad i.e. an average of 5 countries per person.[62] The Chinese Academy of International Trade and Economic Cooperation in the meanwhile has only four people focusing on research related to development assistance (including managing the statistics of China's foreign aid). In addition to this, the China-Africa Research Centre housed within this academy has ten researchers.[63] With regard to the databases constructed in support of China's aid implementation, in spite of information that indicated that the Foreign Aid Expert Database had already registered 4,373 experts by the end of 2008,[64] the problem is that (as pointed out by one Chinese researcher), these individuals are all 'experts in technical fields, such as construction and water exploration'.[65] None of them are experts in development.

In view of this significant shortage of foreign aid professionals, it is not hard to realise how the implementation of China's foreign aid in Africa encounters substantial difficulties. It is indeed curious why the human resource capacities of the aid institutions have not improved. It is, after all, now sixty years since China began involvement in disbursing aid. In answering this question, one senior Chinese researcher notes that 'It is because of the staffing plan (人员编制) set for these ministries'.[66] Due to the staffing arrangement of the Chinese government, the number of staff recruited in each government institutions is strictly controlled. Whilst it is not possible to increase the human resources capacity of one government institution over another, the Adjustments of Foreign Aid Project Management implemented by MOFCOM in 2008 (which devolved its aid implementation management to subsidiary public institutions) was particularly purposed to cope with this situation.[67] 'Of course this is much behind the rapid development of our [China's] foreign aid'.[68]

Considering the possibility of establishing a dedicated institution administrating foreign aid (as with the traditional aid donor countries), another Chinese researcher has stated that this was 'Highly unlikely to happen within the next two decades'.[69] As a consequence, not only is 'the lack of expertise of the seconding staff troubling the process of our [China's] foreign aid implementations', but 'we [MOFCOM] are at the moment unable to provide any foreign aid planning suggestions longer than a one-year period. With regard to foreign aid research, evaluation, projects and programs coordination, these institutional functions are all extremely limited.[70]

Furthermore, with particular concerns to the technical experts of China's aid, whilst there seems to be many located in the Foreign Aid Expert Database, in fact 'the current foreign aid expert teams, including teachers, engineers, doctors and so forth, despite being competent in terms of their own specialities, are helpless in terms of language skills'.[71] Even though China is now organising language training courses for all of its so-called aid expert teams before their overseas duties, and is continuously focused on improving the capacity of its HRDC programs, neither of these attempts are delivering the intended result at present. The lack of human resources with appropriate language skills is an additional (and considerable) drawback affecting China's foreign aid implementation in Africa.[72] Not only does this shortage repeatedly cause China's to fail in technology and management transfers, it also drives foreign aid dependency amongst recipient countries.

The supervision of China's foreign aid

The undeveloped supervisory mechanisms have also resulted in a number of difficulties in recent years. Particularly after the introduction of the market economic system in the early 1990s, the implementation quality of China's foreign aid has progressively declined. Although there are no official figures recording unsatisfactory projects and programs, as asserted by several Chinese foreign aid officials and workers, and as assessed by this study, a notable proportion of the projects delivered to Africa of late are 'found to be sub-standard'.[73] Leaving aside inadequately planned technological standards of the equipment, the installation of such equipment and the construction of projects, the supervision of delivered aid is disappointing.

At present, the supervision of China's foreign aid is mainly carried out by the Department of Aid to Foreign Countries of MOFCOM. Besides administrating the entire foreign aid process, it is responsible for both the development and enforcement of China's aid polices and codes of practices. Working in conjunction with this department, there is also the Economic and Commercial Counsellor's Office onsite overseeing the implementation of China's aid as well as monitoring operations after transfers. In addition to this basic arrangement, following the lead of the Central Committee (which designated 2011 as the Year of Foreign Aid Quality), MOFCOM executed a comprehensive inspection of the projects and programs that China had delivered since its first modern pledges made in 2006. However, there still remain many drawbacks regarding the auditing and legislation setup of China's foreign aid.

With concerns to the calculation of China's foreign aid, it is currently dealt with by the Chinese Academy of International Trade and Economic Cooperation, and is published by the National Bureau of Statistics in the *China Statistical Yearbook*. Although the figures are aggregates rather than the result of in-depth audits, as a senior Chinese official asserted, 'It is the only calculation of China's foreign aid at the moment'.[74] Note that this only refers to China's traditional foreign aid which depends on being solely funded by the Chinese government budget. The Concessional Loans are separately administrated by the EXIM Bank. Since China's aid has always been implemented as a state behaviour, that is, it has no relevance to the Chinese people, there has never been an auditing mechanism or department established. As for the need to keep a detailed record for the Chinese government itself, aid officials dismiss this basic idea: 'Foreign aid is our [China's] gift to our friendly countries, what is the reason for an audit?'[75]

In fact, it was only in 2010 that the need for auditing foreign aid was first suggested.[76] While progress on this is unknown, the Chinese Academy of International Trade and Economic Cooperation is only now putting together two sets of figures which calculate China's total aid expenditures and which specific countries this goes to. Whereas with regards to the other part of auditing, the evaluation of implementation, the Financial Management and Planning Division of the Department of Aid to Foreign Countries of MOFCOM has only ten staff monitoring the execution of the *whole* of China's foreign aid.[77] Even though they are informed by the one person based in the individual Economic and Commercial Counsellor's Offices abroad, this remains a profoundly weak link in China's aid implementation.[78] In fact, MOFCOM in reality only cares about the completion of China's foreign aid projects and programs. Whether they are actually serving their intended purposes or not, stays only with the ones who are receiving them.[79]

Regarding the construction of rules and regulations for China's foreign aid, subsequent to the inauguration of the Eight Principles in 1964, this became the *only* norm for China's foreign aid (Huang, 2007). Aside from the Four Principles which were later brought in as an addition to the Eight Principles, China has been continuously setting up internal mechanisms and codes of practices to conduct aid implementation. For example, following allowing enterprises to take part in foreign aid in 1983, China implemented the Contract Responsibility Mechanism to administrate the process. After the launch of the Fund of Foreign Aid Joint Ventures and Cooperative Projects in 1998, China installed the Measures for the Management of the Fund of Foreign Aid Joint Ventures and Cooperative Projects to supervise its application. However, despite these attempts in regulating the implementation of China's foreign aid, none of them has the restraining force of law.[80] At present, similar to the much-needed auditing mechanisms, there has not been any legislation laid down to *legally* govern China's foreign aid implementation.

Given the deficiency of both adequate auditing mechanisms and effective legislation, supervision of China's aid is lamentable. As one senior Chinese official pointed out, this 'is because we [MOFCOM] are significantly short of hands'.[81] MOFCOM may be asked to improve on evaluations and take the current rules and regulations up to a legislation level, 'but with less than 20 people put together (the Financial Management and Planning Division and the Laws and Regulations Division of the Department of Aid to Foreign Countries of MOFCOM), even the ongoing tasks are demanding'.[82] Once again, as a result of the substantial shortage of human resources, the implementation capacity of China's foreign aid is materially undermined. Not only has the consequent lack of adequate auditing caused China's foreign aid to be wasted, but due to the underdeveloped legislation, the existing rules and regulations cannot be effectively enforced to govern the implementation of China's aid.[83]

With both of these drawbacks brought together, given that China's policy agenda continues to lean heavily towards promoting economic interests and supporting its enterprises going out, the undeveloped supervisory mechanisms have immediately pushed the implementation of China's foreign aid into 'dangerous zones'.[84] On the basis that the criteria for qualifying aid implementation parties are now 'overwhelmingly stressed on their business competitive capacities, and specifically laid upon their ability of staying out rather than their practical project implementation quality',"[85] the efficiency of China's foreign aid is not guaranteed. As a senior Chinese official noted, 'Whilst our [China's] foreign aid subtly progressed from strictly a political mission to additionally considering establishing businesses in recipient countries, the uneven implementation quality confuses the primary emphasis on building friendly foreign relationships'.[86] Given that China's foreign aid in Africa is at present not being supervised at either end, nor concerned with the workmanship of the implementation parties nor the outcome after transfers, the implementation quality of China's foreign aid continues to decline.

Concluding remarks

In summary, after delivering aid to Africa for more than half a century, the shortage of foreign aid human resources is still one of the most fundamental shortcomings that is undermining China's aid outcomes in Africa. Not only has it led to China's foreign aid to fail in technology and management transfers, but it also led to a continuous decline in implementation quality. While it is not possible to rectify this shortcoming with a simple increase in administration capacity, China clearly needs to seek other ways to boost its foreign aid human resources. Viable solutions may include an expanded participation of other professional institutions, advanced training for foreign aid human resource, and improved coordination of human resources and HRDC training programs. Nevertheless, in spite of the possibilities for improvement provided by these solutions, in the end, it is still the concern over human resources capacity that dominates. Indeed, the staffing arrangement of the Chinese government needs to be addressed. Before successful measures can be taken and this problem seriously addressed, the outcomes of China's aid in Africa is likely to be continuously challenged.

Notes

1 Interview with senior Chinese official, Freetown, Sierra Leone, 2 September 2011.
2 Unpublished document, October 2006, *Discussions with Foreign Aid Participating Enterprises*, page 4.
3 Unpublished document, October 2006, *Discussions with Foreign Aid Participating Enterprises*, page 4.
4 The first principle of the Eight Principles.
5 The issue of how foreign aid affected China's economic development during the 1970s is discussed in detail in Chapter 3 in the 'The Outrageous' section.
6 Unpublished documents, March 2008, *Wu Speaks at the Conference on Foreign Aid Human Resource Development Cooperation to Africa*, page 4.
7 Interview with senior Chinese researcher, Beijing, China, 22 November 2011.
8 Interview with senior Chinese official, Beijing, China, 2 November 2011.
9 Interview with African development planning official, Accra, Ghana, 21 August 2011.
10 Interview with senior Chinese official, Freetown, Sierra Leone, 2 September 2011.
11 Interview with senior Chinese official, Beijing, China, 15 November 2011.
12 Ibid.
13 Unpublished document, April 2007, *Discussion With Foreign Aid Experts And Academics*, page 8.
14 Interview with development planning official, Accra, Ghana, 21 August 2011.
15 A stress on feasibility research was made by Prime Minister Wen Jiabao again during the 9th National Conference on Foreign Aid convened in August 2010 (*Xinhua*, 2010).
16 Interviews with Chinese foreign aid officials, workers and African officials, Freetown, Sierra Leone; Accra and Tema, Ghana; Beijing, China, 2011 and 2012.
17 Interviews with Chinese foreign aid officials and researchers, Freetown, Sierra Leone; Accra, Ghana; Beijing, China, 2011 and 2012 and online interview with a senior Chinese official, St Andrews, Scotland, 10 November 2012.
18 Interview with senior Chinese researcher, Beijing, China, 22 November 2011.
19 Interview with senior Chinese official, Freetown, Sierra Leone, 6 August 2011.
20 Interview with senior Chinese official, Freetown, Sierra Leone, 2 September 2011.
21 Discussion with senior Chinese officials, Beijing, China, 19 November 2011.
22 Ibid.
23 Interview with senior Chinese official, Freetown, Sierra Leone, 2 September 2011.
24 Discussion with senior Chinese officials, Beijing, China, 19 November 2011.
25 Ibid.
26 Ibid.
27 Interview with senior Chinese official, Freetown, Sierra Leone, 2 September 2011.
28 Interview with senior Chinese official, Beijing, China, 16 November 2011.
29 Interview with senior Chinese official, Freetown, Sierra Leone, 2 September 2011. Interview with senior Chinese official, Beijing, China, 10 November 2011. Discussion with senior Chinese officials, Beijing, China, 19 November 2011.
30 Interview with senior Chinese official, Freetown, Sierra Leone, 2 September 2011.
31 Interview with senior Chinese official, Beijing, China, 16 November 2011. See also "商务部关于进一步加快对外援助项目实施进度的意见", *Notice of the Department of Aid to Foreign Countries of the Ministry of Commerce on Further Promote the Implementation Process of Foreign Aid Projects and Programs*. Ministry of Commerce [2005], no. 623.
32 Interview with senior Chinese official, Freetown, Sierra Leone, 5 August 2011.
33 Ibid.
34 Interview with senior Chinese official, Freetown, Sierra Leone, 6 August 2011.
35 Interview with senior Chinese official, Beijing, China, 16 November 2011.
36 Ibid.
37 Interview with senior Chinese official, Beijing, China, 16 November 2011.

38 Ibid.
39 Interview with Chinese official, Beijing, China, 15 November 2011.
40 Ibid.
41 Discussion with Chinese officials, Beijing, China, 17 November 2011.
42 Unpublished document, November 2008, *The Official Launch of The Foreign Aid Inter-agency Liaison Mechanism*, page 5.
43 Interview with senior Chinese official, Beijing, China, 16 November 2011.
44 Interview with senior Chinese official, Beijing, China, 15 November 2011.
45 Interviews with Chinese foreign aid officials, workers and African officials, Freetown, Sierra Leone; Accra, Tema, Ghana; Beijing, China, 2011 and 2012.
46 Interview with senior Chinese official, Freetown, Sierra Leone, 2 September 2011.
47 Interview with Chinese official, Freetown, Sierra Leone, 3 September 2011.
48 Interview with senior Chinese official, Beijing, China, 16 November 2011.
49 Interview with senior Chinese official, Freetown, Sierra Leone, 2 September 2011.
50 Interview with senior Chinese official, Freetown, Sierra Leone, 2 September 2011.
51 Interview with senior Chinese official, Freetown, Sierra Leone, 2 September 2011.
52 Interview with senior Chinese official, Beijing, China, 19 November 2011.
53 Interview with senior Chinese foreign aid worker, Freetown, Sierra Leone, 4 September 2011.
54 As this official further pointed out, this person is 'almost always on secondment from provincial economic departments'. Interview with senior Chinese official, Freetown, Sierra Leone, 6 August 2011.
55 Interview with senior Chinese official, Freetown, Sierra Leone, 2 September 2011.
56 Interview with senior Chinese official, Beijing, China, 10 November 2011.
57 Ibid.
58 Ibid.
59 Interview with senior Chinese official, Beijing, China, 16 November 2011.
60 Interview with Chinese official, Beijing, China, 12 November 2011.
61 Ibid.
62 "Exclusive of the administrative staff and so forth", as this official added. Interview with senior Chinese official, Beijing, China, 16 November 2011.
63 Interview with senior Chinese researcher, Beijing, China, 22 November 2011.
64 Unpublished document, January 2009, *Strive for the Advancement of Both Foreign Aid Management and Promotion*, page 14.
65 Interview with Chinese researcher, Beijing, China, 28 November 2011.
66 Discussion with Chinese researchers, Beijing, China, 22 November 2011.
67 Ibid.
68 Ibid.
69 Interview with senior Chinese official, Freetown, Sierra Leone, 3 September 2011.
70 Discussion with Chinese officials, Beijing, China, 17 November 2011.
71 Interview with Chinese official, Freetown, Sierra Leone, 2 September 2011.
72 Discussion with senior Chinese officials, Beijing, China, 19 November 2011.
73 Interviews with Chinese foreign aid officials and workers, Freetown, Sierra Leone; Accra and Tema, Ghana; Beijing, China, 2011 and 2012.
74 Interview with senior Chinese official, Freetown, Sierra Leone, 2 September 2011.
75 Ibid.
76 This was first brought forward by Prime Minister Wen Jiabao during the 9th National Conference on Foreign Aid, convened in August 2010. See *Xinhua* (2010). National Conference on Foreign Aid Convened in Beijing, Wen Delivers an Important Speech. *People's Daily*, 15 August.
77 Interview with senior Chinese official, Beijing, China, 10 November 2011.
78 Discussion with Chinese officials, Beijing, China, 17 November 2011.
79 As one of the Chinese officials further pointed out during this discussion, 'Whether the projects and programs worked or not is not a part of the evaluation, at least it is not one of the main purpose'. Ibid.

80 Interview with senior Chinese researcher, Beijing, China, 22 November 2011.
81 Interview with senior Chinese official, Beijing, China, 16 November 2011.
82 Discussion with Chinese officials, Beijing, China, 17 November 2011.
83 Discussion with senior Chinese officials, Beijing, China, 19 November 2011.
84 Interview with senior Chinese official, Freetown, Sierra Leone, 2 September 2011.
85 Online interview with senior Chinese official, St Andrews, Scotland, 10 November 2012.
86 Interview with senior Chinese official, Freetown, Sierra Leone, 2 September 2011.

6 Concluding remarks

With the aim of improving our understanding of China's foreign aid in Africa, and promoting China's foreign aid outcomes, this study has surveyed one of the fastest expanding but least explored aid practices in the contemporary world, China's foreign aid in Africa. Whilst previous studies have made much of China's massive concessional loan deals and the generous investments in natural resources, very little is known with regard to how China actually delivers its foreign aid, and even less is known about how this aid works in African recipient countries. With a view to addressing this gap in our prior knowledge, and to shed light on its development in the near future, this study has delved into the development, performance and shortcomings of China's foreign aid.

At the beginning of China's foreign aid in Africa (1955–1978), it was found that with the purpose of breaking out of the diplomatic isolation created by the capitalist countries, and consolidating China's newly-founded regime, China's aid aimed at a desire to build friendship with African countries. Thus China's foreign aid settled on the principal aim of helping African countries achieve self-reliance. The goals then quickly began with an objective of building African industrial and agricultural foundations to help them achieve economic independence. During the implementation of this objective, not only did China continuously reform its aid administration and operating mechanisms, but along with the increase in recipient countries, it also expanded its foreign aid implementation approaches to include three funding methods (Grant, Interest-free Loan and Low-interest Loan), and four implementation methods (Complete Project Aid, Technical Aid, Goods and Materials Aid and Cash Aid).

However, whilst this early development of China's foreign aid in Africa helped extend China's diplomatic relationships to forty-one countries on the continent by the end of 1978 (and successfully brought it back to the UN in 1971), the majority of the industrial and agricultural foundations that China delivered to Africa during this period were mired in continued dilemmas. As a result of the decision-makers' personal preferences, a naive friendship-determined allocation policy and underdeveloped aid capacity combined with the neglected political, social and institutional conditions of the African recipient countries essentially led to classic foreign aid dependency situations. Additionally, on the basis that China's aid was primarily carried out as part of the obligation to proletarian internationalism (and ignored

China's domestic economic situation), Chinese aid during the Maoist period was criticised within China as having hampered China's own development.

During the initial reform of China's aid in Africa (1979–1993), despite the frustrating outcomes from the previous period and the domestic demand for economic development, China still came up with a necessary budget for aid. Built on an underlying consideration of consolidating friendship with African countries, China's aid was now driven by a second objective i.e. reducing expenditure while consolidating aid outcomes. China's foreign aid at this stage was primarily focused on delivering landmark projects that were less demanding both financially and technically. Apart from further reforming the administration and operating, Beijing also integrated Technical Aid with Management Cooperation to assist those industrial and agricultural projects that had been delivered earlier.

Nevertheless, even though the initial reform of China's aid in Africa helped diplomatic relationships (expanding by an additional seven African countries), and to some extent balanced the political emphasis and economic considerations of China's aid, it only minimally impacted African recipient countries' development. Owing to the friendship-emphasised planning approaches, which essentially disregarded the divergent development conditions of recipient countries, the landmark projects China delivered during this period were commonly only of short-term benefit at best. Further, given the persistent emphasis that the Chinese government would strictly respect the sovereignty of recipient countries and the largely unimproved aid capacity levels, despite the immediate contributions made by the Management Cooperation, it was also unable to sustain China's aid outcomes in the long-term.

Moving into the contemporary period, China's aid was first directed to search for mutual benefits via the implementation of the Concessional Loan. As a result of substantial economic development at the turn of the century and growing international responsibility, and following an intention to continuously develop friendships with African countries, China's foreign aid was then led to embrace a third objective i.e. to improve people's livelihoods. By this time, China sought to integrate its domestic economic activities and trade into overseas economic cooperation. China thus adjusted its aid implementation approaches and inaugurated the twenty-four government institutions jointly participating in the Inter-agency Coordination Mechanism whilst establishing a number of dedicated databases to improve planning capacity. In the meantime, China also delegated implementation management to the subsidiary public institutions of MOFCOM and other specialised institutions.

However, China's foreign aid currently is still struggling to materially benefit African recipient countries' development. On account of the problematic planning approaches which continuously emphasise "friendship", many of China's livelihood-related projects delivered to Africa of late have been unsuited to the recipient countries' domestic conditions. Although the recent Human Resource Development Cooperation significantly improved China's capacity in transferring the required technical and management skills to recipient countries (in comparison to the late terminated Management Cooperation and the greatly scaled back

Technical Aid), because of inept planning they have been mostly uncoordinated with China's foreign aid projects. Furthermore, due to limited capacity, the implementation of China's aid has declined in terms of quality.

On the whole, after learning about the development of China's foreign aid and discovering its disappointing outcomes, this study comes to the conclusion that, whilst meeting China's national interests, China's foreign aid has only worked in African recipient countries to some extent and quite unevenly (if not accidentally). Despite the underlying consideration of building "friendly" foreign relationships, this commitment has in general not been able to improve African recipient countries' abilities in achieving self-reliance. In the interest of really improving China's foreign aid so that it can benefit African recipient countries' development, this study has identified two factors that demand China's immediate attention.

Firstly, "friendship" (a factor that is frequently overlooked by Western scholars and one that is often patriotically interpreted by Chinese scholars) sits at the top of China's national priorities in guiding China's aid and influencing outcomes. Even though the emphasis on friendship has brought China's foreign aid an uniqueness that is welcomed by many African recipient countries (or at least their elites), it also substantially simplifies the decision-making process of China's objectives and confuses China's aid planning. The emphasis on "friendship" has made China's aid objectives unaligned to the immediate development concerns of the African recipient countries and has also made many projects and programs largely unsuited to the recipient countries' development conditions.

China needs to prioritise scientific research in the decision-making processes. After identifying the priority development areas for each African recipient countries (rather than regarding African countries as a monolithic entity), research needs to be taken into account in the allocation and packaging of aid projects and programs so that they accommodate the recipient countries' diverse domestic conditions. This is basic stuff. Particularly regarding the packaging of projects and programs, apart from focusing on generating standards that the recipient countries are in a position to implement, and improving the efficiency of the current Inter-agency Coordination Mechanism to properly bring into play the advantages of the HRDC programs, the planning of self-sufficient foreign aid packages should also benefit the effectiveness and sustainability of China's aid.

The lack of human resources is the other key issue facing the future success of Chinese aid. Whilst it may be too basic to draw attention to in an examination of one of the most complex contemporary relations between states, it is nevertheless responsible for many shortcomings in China's foreign aid implementation. Not only has the shortage of appropriate and sufficient human resources made China's aid continuously incompetent in carrying out successful technology and management transfers, it has also impaired China's capacity to conduct research, supervision, coordinate projects and programs and undermined the implementation process. Although China has been attempting to overcome this basic weakness by reforming its foreign aid administration (introducing provincial institutions to take part in foreign aid implementation (1970s), allowing SOEs to implement aid projects (1980s), and delegating foreign aid implementation management (2000s), Beijing to date has not been able to improve upon this difficult situation.

In order to materially boost China's foreign aid capacity, this study suggests that efforts should be made to further devolve its foreign aid management to public institutions. Since a dedicated foreign aid institution is apparently unlikely to be established in the near future (even though this would be the most logical step), China could alternatively pass on its aid management to other government institutions, so as to concentrate MOFCOM's capacity in planning and the construction and enforcement of rules and regulations. Moreover, China could sub-contract specific tasks (such as auditing and research) to specialised institutions to promote transparency and greater empirical knowledge. While expanding the foreign aid databases has been positive, the fact that most of the identified experts do not speak any languages used widely in Africa makes their contributions moot. China should thus focus on advancing language training courses for existing aid experts (or at least boost the number of interpreters as integral parts of the expert teams). In the meantime, an improved coordination of HRDC programs could also benefit outcomes.

To conclude this study on China's foreign aid in Africa, "friendship", a factor that, for the most part, is meaningless in the Western study of China's foreign aid as a moral pursuit that is deeply rooted in Chinese culture, drives the development of China's foreign aid in Africa and irrationally influences outcomes. If China could rationalise this "friendship" in a more considerate way in its planning and implementation processes, and of course, improve capacity, China's foreign aid might make more of a positive impact upon recipient countries' development. It is important to remember that, as Mao Zedong emphasised, 'It was our African friends who brought us back to the UN. We shouldn't forget the helping hand lent by the Third World countries in any way'. Additionally, 'As long as the line is correct, the future is bright'.[1]

Note

1 This is a widely quoted public interpretation of Mao's '路线是个纲, 纲举目张' during the Cultural Revolution, which translate as 'once the key link is grasped, everything else falls into place'. The original quote was made by Chairman Mao during his visit to the southern provinces in August 1971 (see Xue, 2013b).

Bibliography

Anderson, M. 2014. *African Presidents "Use China Aid for Patronage Politics"*, www.theguardian.com/global-development/2014/nov/19/african-presidents-china-aid-patronage-politics [Accessed: 3 January 2016].

Anon. 1988a. 'Bu Qiong Bu La Lian He Fang Zhi Chang Lian Nian Ying Li' (Complexe Textile de Bujumbura Kept on Making Profit). *Guo Ji Jing Ji He Zuo (International Economic Cooperation)*, (12), 12–13.

Anon. 1988b. 'Sai Gu Fang Zhi Chang Guan Li He Zuo Yi Nian Mian Mao Gai Guan' (The Improvement of the Segou Textile Combine following One Year of Management Cooperation). *Guo Ji Jing Ji He Zuo (International Economic Cooperation)*, (12), 22–24.

Anon. 1988c. 'Tan Zan Tie Lu Shou Yi Ke Guan Chu Xian Liang Xing Xun Huan' (The Improving Outcomes of the Tanzam Railway). *Guo Ji Jing Ji He Zuo (International Economic Cooperation)*, (12), 7–9.

Asian-African Conference. 1955. 'Final Communique of the Asian-African Conference', Asian-African Conference, Bandung, April 18–24.

Askouri, A. 2007. 'China's Investment in Sudan: Displacing Villages and Destroying Communities'. In Manji, F. and Marks, S. (eds.) *African Perspectives on China in Africa*, Oxford: Fahamu, pp. 71–86.

Bailey, M. 1976. *Freedom Railway: China and the Tanzania-Zambia Link*, London: Rex Collings.

Bin, K. 2008. '"Yi" "Li" Xuan Ze Yu Zhong Guo Dui Wai Yuan Zhu De Bian Hua' (The Balance of "Righteousness" and "Interests" and the Evolution of China's Foreign Aid). *Xiang Chao*, (8), 36–38.

Bobiash, D. 1992. *South-South Aid: How Developing Countries Help Each Other*, London: Macmillan.

Brautigam, D. 1998. *Chinese Aid and African Development: Exporting Green Revolution*, Basingstoke: Macmillan.

Brautigam, D. 2008. 'China's Foreign Aid in Africa: What Do We Know?'. In Rotberg, R. I. (ed.) *China into Africa: Trade, Aid, and Influence*, Washington, DC: Brookings Institution Press, pp. 197–216.

Brautigam, D. 2009. *The Dragon's Gift: The Real Story of China in Africa*, New York: Oxford University Press.

Buckley, L. 2011. 'Eating Bitter to Taste Sweet: An Ethnographic Sketch of A Chinese Agriculture Project in Senegal', International Conference on Global Land Grabbing, Universiyt of Sussex.

Cao, J. 2014. 'Zhong Guo Dui Wai Yuan Zhu Li Fa De Jia Zhi Ding Wei Ji Li Fa Zong Zhi' (Legislating China's Foreign Aid). *Guo Ji Jing Ji He Zuo (International Economic Cooperation)*, (9), 77–82.

Cao, Q. 2013. 'Zhong Guo Xiang Fei Zhou Pai Qian Qing Nian Zhi Yuan Zhe Xiang Mu Yan Jiu' (Probing into China's Policy of Sending Young Volunteers to Africa). *He Nan Gong Ye Da Xue Xue Bao: She Hui Ke Xue Ban (Journal of Henan University of Technology: Social Science)*, (3), 46–48.

CCCPC. 1958. 'Zhong Gong Zhong Yang Pi Zhuan Chen Yi, Li Fuchun "Guan Yu Jia Qiang Dui Wai Jing Ji, Ji Shu Yuan Zhu Gong Zuo Ling Dao De Qing Shi Bao Gao"' (Report on Strengthening Foreign Economic and Technical Cooperation by Chen Yi and Li Fuchun). In CCCPC Party Literature Research Office (ed.) *Jian Guo Yi Lai Zhong Yao Wen Xian Xuan Bian Di Shi Yi Ce (Important File Selection Since the Establishment of the People's Republic of China, 11)*, Beijing: Central Committee Literature Press, pp. 27–39.

CCCPC Party Literature Research Office (ed.). 1982a. *San Zhong Quan Hui Yi Lai Zhong Yao Wen Xian Hui Bian (Important File Collection Since the 3rd Plenary Session of the Eleventh CPC Central Committee)*, Beijing: People's Press.

CCCPC Party Literature Research Office (ed.). 1982b. *San Zhong Quan Hui Yi Lai Zhong Yao Wen Xian Xuan Bian (Important File Selection Since the 3rd Plenary Session of the Eleventh CPC Central Committee)*, Beijing: People's Press.

CCCPC Party Literature Research Office (ed.). 1990. *Zhou En Lai Wai Jiao Wen Xuan (Anthology of Zhou Enlai's Diplomacy)*, Beijing: CCCPC Party Literature Press.

CDB. 2009. *Special Loan for the Development of African SMEs*, Beijing: China Development Bank.

Chaponniere, J.-R. 2009. 'Chinese Aid to Africa, Origins, Forms and Issues'. In Dijk, M. P. V. (ed.) *The New Presence of China in Africa*, Amsterdam: Amsterdam University Press, pp. 55–82.

Chen, C.-C. and Lee, Y.-T. (eds.). 2008. *Leadership and Management in China: Philosophies, Theories, and Practices*, New York: Cambridge University Press.

Chen, D. 2007. *Tan Lu Zai 1964: Zhou En Lai Fei Wang Fei Zhou (Exploring in 1964: Zhou Enlai Flies to Africa)*, Beijing: PLA Literature and Art Publishing House.

Chen, X. 2012. 'Zhong Guo, Na Tan Zan Tie Lu Zen Me Ban' (China, What Can You Do About the Tanzam Railway). *Shi Jie Zhi Shi (World Affairs)*, (21), 50–58.

Chen, Y. 2008. *Jiang Zemin "Zou Chu Qu" Zhan Lue De Xing Cheng Ji Qi Zhong Yao Yi Yi (The Formation and Importance of Jiang Zemin's "Going Out" Strategy)*, http://theory.people.com.cn/GB/40557/138172/138202/8311431.html [Accessed: 22 June 2012].

Cheng, W., Liu, A. and Dong, W. 2015. 'Zhong Guo Jiao Yu Yuan Zhu Fei Zhou Xiang Mu You Xiao Xing Yan Jiu' (Assessment on China's Foreign Aid Educational Programs in Africa). *Gao Deng Nong Ye Jiao Yu (Higher Agricultural Education)*, (3), 29–32.

Chin, G. and Frolic, B. 2007. *Emerging Donors in International Development Assistance: The China Case*, Ottawa: IDRC/CRDI.

Cooke, J. (ed.) 2008. *U.S. and Chinese Engagement in Africa*, Washington, DC: Center for Strategic and International Studies.

Condon, M. 2012. 'China in Africa: What the Policy of Nonintervention Adds to the Western Development Dilemma'. *PRAXIS: The Fletcher Journal of Human Security*, 27, 5–25.

Corkin, L. and Burke, C. 2006. *China's Interest and Activity in Africa's Construction and Infrastructure Sectors*, Stellenbosch: Centre for Chinese Studies.

Cotula, L., Vermeulen, S., Leonard, R. and Keeley, J. 2009. *Land Grab or Development Opportunity? Agricultural Investment and International Land Deals in Africa*, London/Rome: International Institute for Environment and Development/Food and Agriculture Organization.

Dasgupta, S. 2015. 'UN Fears Rights Violations in China-backed Projects'. *Voice of America*, July 6.

Davies, M., Edinger, H., Tay, N. and Naidu, S. 2008. *How China Delivers Development Assistance to Africa*, Stellenbosch: Centre for Chinese Studies.

De Bary, W. T. (ed.). 2008. *Sources of East Asian Tradition: Premodern Asia*, New York: Columbia University Press.

Deng, X. 1994. *Selected Works 1982–1992*, vol. III, Beijing: Foreign Languages.

Ding, S. 2010. *Da Guo Dui Wai Yuan Zhu: She Hui Jiao Huan Lun De Shi Jiao (Major Power's Foreign Aid: An Insight from Social Exchange Theory)*, Beijing: Social Sciences Academic Press.

Donnan, S. 2015. 'China's Aid Splurge Fails to Bridge Credibility Gap in Africa'. *Financial Times*, October 28.

Dreher, A. and Fuchs, A. 2012. 'Rogue Aid? The Determinants of China's Aid Allocation'. *Courant Research Centre: Poverty, Equity and Growth – Discussion Papers, No. 93*, Gottingen: University of Gottingen.

Feng, H. 2007. *Chinese Strategic Culture and Foreign Policy Decision-making: Confucianism, Leadership and War*, New York: Routledge.

Feng, Z. 1987. 'Lu Wang Da De Gong Chang Zhong Guo Ren De Xin' (Factory in Rwanda, Chinese People's Heart). *Guo Ji Jing Ji He Zuo (International Economic Cooperation)*, (12), 39–40.

FOCAC. 2012a. 'Open Up New Prospects for A New Type of China-Africa Strategic Partnership'. The 5th Ministerial Conference of Forum on China-Africa Cooperation, July 19–20.

FOCAC. 2012b. 'President Hu Proposes Measures in Five Priority Areas to Boost China-Africa Ties', The 5th Ministerial Conference of Forum on China-Africa Coopeartion, July 19–20.

FOCAC. 2012c. 'President Hu: Important Progress Made in Realizing China-Africa New Strategic Partnership', The 5th Ministerial Conference of Forum on China-Africa Coopeartion, July 19–20.

Ghana Health Nest. 2013. *Health Minister Moves to Solve Problems Facing Lekma Hospital*, http://ghanahealthnest.com/2013/02/01/health-minister-moves-to-solve-problems-facing-lekma-hospital/ [Accessed: 8 December 2014].

GIETC. *Jia Na Guo Jia Da Ju Yuan Xiang Mu (Ghana National Theatre Project)* China Guangzhou International Economic and Technical Cooperation Company, www.gzietcot.com/023.html [Accessed: 11 November 2010].

Government of China. 2011. *China's Foreign Aid*, Beijing: People's Press.

Government of China. *Fu Jian Sheng Qing Zi Liao Ku (Chronicle of Fujian Provincial Foreign Trade)*, www.fjsq.gov.cn/showtext.asp?ToBook=217andindex=134 [Accessed: 3 March 2012].

Grimm, S. 2014. 'China-Africa Cooperation: Promises, Practice and Prospects'. *Journal of Contemporary China*, 23(90), 993–1011.

Grimm, S., Hob, H., Knappe, K., Siebold, M., Sperrfechter, J. and Vogler, I. 2010. *Coordinating China and DAC Development Partners: Challenges to the Aid Architecture in Rwanda*, Bonn: German Development Institute.

Grimm, S., Rank, R., Schickerling, E. and McDonald, M. 2011. *Transparency of Chinese Aid: An Analysis of the Published Information on Chinese External Financial Flows*, Stellenbosch: Centre for Chinese Studies.

Gu, W. 1995. *Conflicts of Divided Nations: The Case of China and Korea*, Westport, CT: Praeger.

Guloba, M., Kilimani, N. and Nabiddo, W. 2010. 'The Impact of China-Africa Aid Relations: The Case of Uganda'. *AERC Collaborative Research China-Africa Project*, African Economic Research Consortium.

Guo, H. 1965. 'Ji Nei Ya Juan Yan Huo Chai Chang Jian Chang Ji' (A Story About the Guinea Cigarette and Match Factory). *Shi Jie Zhi Shi (World Affairs)*, (12), 28–29.

Guo, Y. 2014. *Zhong Guo Dui Wai Yuan Zhu Yi Zhao De Shi Na Xie Fa Gui (What Legislation Do China's Foreign Aid Currently Have?)*, www.thepaper.cn/newsDetail_forward_1284956 [Accessed: 16 January 2015].

He, D. 2013. '"Fu Bu Qi De" You Yi Fang Zhi Chang' ("The Failing" Friendship Textile Mill). *Zhong Guo Fang Zhi (China Textile)*, (5), 35.

He, W. 2010. 'Zhong Guo Yuan Zhu Fei Zhou: Fa Zhan Te Dian, Zuo Yong Ji Mian Lin De Tiao Zhan' (China's Aid to Africa Development Feature, Functions and Challenges). *Xi Ya Fei Zhou (West Asia and Africa)*, (7), 12–19.

Hee, Y. 2011. 'Zhong Guo Dui Wai Yuan Zhu Guan Li Mo Shi De Jian Li He Wan Shan' (The Establishment and Improvement of China's Foreign Aid Administration). *Hu Xiang Lun Tan (Huxiang Forum)*, (4), 74–78.

Hess, S. and Aidoo, R. 2010. 'Beyond the Rhetoric: Noninterference in China's African Policy'. *African and Asian Studies*, 9(3), 356–383.

Hu, J. and Huang, M. 2012. 'Zhong Guo Dui Wai Yuan Zhu Guan Li Ti Xi De Xian Zhuang Yu Gai Ge' (The Status and Reform of China's Foreign Aid Management System). *Guo Ji Jing Ji He Zuo (International Economic Cooperation)*, (10), 55–58.

Hu, Z. 2000. 'Tan Zan Tie Lu De Guo Qu, Xian Zai He Wei Lai' (The Past, Present and Future of the Tanzam Railway). *Tie Dao Jing Ji Yan Jiu (Railway Economics Research)*, (2), 47–48.

Huang, J. 2004. 'Ma Ge Ba Si Tang Lian Gan Zhe Nong Chang Kao Cha Bao Gao' (Report of Magbass Sugar Complex). *Gan Zhe (Saccharum)*, 11(1), 58–60.

Huang, M. 2007. 'Zhong Guo Dui Wai Yuan Zhu Ji Zhi: Xian Zhuang He Qu Shi' (China's Foreign Aid: The Current Model and Trends). *Guo Ji Jing Ji He Zuo (International Economic Cooperation)*, (6), 4–11.

Huang, M. 2010. 'Zhong Guo Zheng Fu Dui Wai You Hui Dai Kuan De Fa Zhan Li Cheng Yu Qian Jing' (Introduction to the Development of China's Foreign Preferential Loan and Its Prospects). *Guo Ji Jing Ji He Zuo (International Economic Cooperation)*, (11), 47–53.

Huang, M. and Hu, J. 2009. 'Zhong Guo Dui Wai Yuan Zhu Guan Li Ti Xi De Xing Cheng He Fa Zhan' (The Formation and Development of Chinese Foreign Aid Management). *Guo Ji Jing Ji He Zuo (International Economic Cooperation)*, (5), 33–40.

Huang, M. and Lang, J. 2010. 'Zhong Guo De Dui Fei Yuan Zhu Ji Qi Mian Lin De Tiao Zhan' (An Analysis on Chinese Economic Aid to African Countries and Corresponding Challenges). *Guo Ji Jing Ji He Zuo (International Economic Cooperation)*, (6), 34–40.

Huang, M. and Xie, Q. 2013. 'Zhong Guo Dui Wai Yuan Zhu Xiang Mu De Zu Zhi Yu Guan Li' (The Arrangement and Management of China's Foreign Aid Projects). *Guo Ji Jing Ji He Zuo (International Economic Cooperation)*, (3), 63–66.

Jiang, X. 2014. 'Zhong Fei Wei Sheng He Zuo De Te Dian: Ji Yu Gang Guo Min Zhu Gong He Guo De An Li Yan Jiu' (Characteristics of China-Africa Health Collaboration: The Case of Democratic Republic of Congo). *Zhong Guo Wei Sheng Zheng Ce Yan Jiu (Chinese Journal of Health Policy)*, 7(3), 64–68.

Jin, D. 1987. 'Can Yu Guan Li Xiao Yi Xian Zhu Tan Zan Tie Lu Niu Kui Zeng Ying' (Management Cooperation Succeeded the Tanzam Railway Is in Profit). *Guo Ji Jing Ji He Zuo (International Economic Cooperation)*, (12), 11–12, 15.

Jin, H. (ed.). 1996. *Dang Dai Zhong Guo Tie Lu Dui Wai Jing Ji Ji Shu Yuan Zhu (China's Railway Foreign Aid)*, Beijing: China Railway Publishing House.

Kaplinsky, R. and Morris, M. 2006. 'Dangling by A Thread: How Sharp Are the Chinese Scissors?', paper prepared for DFID Trade Division. Brighton: Institute of Development Studies. Keller, S. 2009. 'Against Friendship between Countries'. *Journal of International Political Theory*, 5(1), 59–74.

Kishi, R. and Raleigh, C. 2015. 'When China Gives Aid to African Governments, They Become More Violent'. *Washington Post*, December 2.

Kragelund, P. 2008. 'The Return of Non-DAC Donors to Africa: New Prospects for African Development?'. *Development Policy Review*, 26(5), 555–584.

Lai, X. 1995. 'Jing Yuan Xiang Mu Guan Li Ji Dai Gai Ge: Dui Ma Ge Ba Si Nong Tang Lian He Qi Ye De Diao Yan Fen Xi' (Aid Project Waiting for Reform: An Analysis on Magbass Sugar Complex). *Guo Ji Jing Ji He Zuo (International Economic Cooperation)*, (8), 7–9.

Lancaster, C. 1999. *Aid to Africa: So Much to Do, So Little Done*, Chicago: University of Chicago Press.

Lancaster, C. 2006. *Foreign Aid: Diplomacy, Development, Domestic Politics*, London: University of Chicago Press.

Lancaster, C. 2007. *The Chinese Aid System*, Center for Global Development.

Lebow, R. N. 2007. 'Classical Realism'. In Dunne, T., Kurki, M. and Smith, S. (eds.) *International Relations Theories: Discipline and Diversity*, Oxford: Oxford University Press, pp. 52–70.

Lengauer, S. 2011. 'China's Foreign Aid Policy: Motive and Method'. *Culture Mandala: The Bulletin of the Centre for East-West Cultural and Economic Studies*, 9(2), 35–81.

Li, A. 2006. 'Lun Zhong Guo Dui Fei Zhou Zheng Ce De Shi Tiao Yu Zhuan Bian' (The Adjustment and Change of China's African Policy). *Xi Ya Fei Zhou (West Asia and Africa)*, (8), 11–20.

Li, A. 2008. 'Wei Zhong Guo Zheng Ming: Zhong Guo De Fei Zhou Zhan Lue Yu Guo Jia Xing Xiang' (In Defense of China: China's African Strategy and State Image). *Shi Jie Jing Ji Yu Zheng Zhi (World Economics and Politics)*, (4), 6–15.

Li, A. 2009. 'Zhong Guo Yuan Wai Yi Liao Dui De Li Shi, Gui Mo Ji Qi Ying Xiang' (The History, Scale and Impact of Chinese Medical Teams). *Wai Jiao Ping Lun (Foreign Affairs Review)*, (1), 25–45.

Li, A. (2011) Chinese Medical Cooperation In Africa With Special Emphasis on the Medical Teams and Anti-Malaria Campaign Uppsala: Nordic Africa Institute Discussion Paper no. 52.

Li, A. 2012. 'Lun Zhong Fei He Zuo Lun Tan De Qi Yuan' (The Origin of the FOCAC). *Wai Jiao Ping Lun (Foreign Affairs Review)*, (3), 15–32.

Li, B., Dong, X. and Zhu, H. 2010. 'Jia Na Bei Bu Xiang Cun Lu Qiao Jian She Shi Gong Ying Xiang Yin Su Fen Xi' (Investigating the Factors That Affected the Road and Bridge Construction in Northern Rural Ghana). *An Hui Jian Zhu (Anhui Architecture)*, (6), 123–125.

Li, J. 2003. 'Zhong Guo Dui Wai Jing Ji He Zuo De Xin Fa Zhan' (China's Economic Cooperation with Foreign Countries). *Wai Jiao Xue Yuan Xue Bao (Journal of China Foreign Affairs University)*, (2), 80–84.

Li, K. 2014. 'Lun Wo Guo Dui Wai Yuan Zhu Zhuan Men Li Fa De Bi Yao Xing' (The Necessity of Legislating Our Foreign Aid). *Guo Ji Jing Ji He Zuo (International Economic Cooperation)*, (11), 37–40.

Li, L. 2000. 'Zai Jia Na Dang Xiang Mu Jing Li' (Being a Project Manager in Ghana). *Guo Ji Jing Ji He Zuo (International Economic Cooperation)*, (9), 35–38.

Li, L. 2006. 'Zhong Guo Yu Hei Fei Zhou Zheng Dang Jiao Wang De Li Shi Yu Xian Zhuang' (Today and the History of Political Relationship between China and Africa). *Xi Ya Fei Zhou (West Asia and Africa)*, (3), 16–19.

Li, W. 2010. 'Xin Zhong Guo Dui Wai Jing Ji Ji Shu Yuan Zhu Zheng Ce De Yan Jin Ji Ping Xi' (An Analysis of the Evolution of PRC's Policy for the Foreign Economic and Technical Support). *Dang Shi Yan Jiu Yu Jiao Xue (Party History Research and Teaching)*, (2), 19–29.

Li, X., Tang, L. and Wu, J. 2009. *Guo Ji Fa Zhan Yuan Zhu Gai Lun (International Development Assistance: Evolution, Management and Institutions)*, Beijing: Social Sciences Academic Press.

Li, X. and Wu, J. 2009. 'Zhong Guo Dui Fei Yuan Zhu De Shi Jian Jing Yan Yu Mian Lin De Tiao Zhan' (A Study of China's ODA to Africa). *(China Agricultural University Journal of Social Sciences Edition)*, 26(4), 45–54.Lin, M. 1995. 'Xin Xing Shi Xia Yuan Wai Gong Zuo Gai Ge Fang Zhen Chu Tai' (The New Guidance of Foreign Aid). *Guo Ji Jing Ji He Zuo (International Economic Cooperation)*, (7), 23.

Lin, M. 1997. 'Dui Wai Yuan Zhu Fang Shi De Gai Ge Yu Shi Jian' (The Reform and Practice of Foreign Aid Methods). *Guo Ji Jing Ji He Zuo (International Economic Cooperation)*, (11), 4–7.

Liu, H. 2008b. 'Zhong Fei Guan Xi 30 Nian: Qiao Dong Zhong Guo Yu Wai Bu Shi Jie Guan Xi Jie Gou De Zhi Dian' (Thirty Years of Sino-African Relations: A Pivot in Reshaping the Structure of China's Relations with the Outside World). *Shi Jie Jing Ji Yu Zheng Zhi (World Economics and Politics)*, (11), 80–88.

Liu, X. 1998. 'Zhong Guo Dui Wai Yuan Zhu Gai Ge Yu Tiao Zheng Er Shi Nian' (20 Years of Foreign Aid Reform). *Guo Ji Jing Ji He Zuo (International Economic Cooperation)*, (10), 30–31.

Liu, Z. 2009. 'Cong Dan Fang Yuan Zhu Dao Hu Li Gong Ying: Zhong Guo Yu Fa Zhan Zhong Guo Jia Jing Ji Guan Xi Liu Shi Nian' (From Unilateral Aid to Mutual Profit: The Economic Relationship between China and Developing Countries in These 60 Years). *Ning Xia She Hui Ke Xue (Social Science in Ningxia)*, (6), 49–54.

Lu, C. 2009. 'Political Friendship among Peoples'. *Journal of International Political Theory*, 5(1), 41–58.

Lu, C., Zhu, D. and Huang, M. 2014. 'Guo Ji Fa Zhan Yuan Zhu Qu Shi Yu Zhong Guo Yuan Zhu Guan Li Ti Xi Gai Ge' (The Trend of International Development Assistance and the Reform of China's Foreign Aid System). *Guo Ji Jing Ji He Zuo (International Economic Cooperation)*, (11), 41–46.

Lu, M. 2006. 'Mao Ze Dong Zhu Xi Dui Zhong Fei Guan Xi De Li Shi Xing Gong Xian' (Mao's Contribution to China-Africa Relationship). In Lu, M., Huang, S. and Lin, Y. (eds.) *Tong Xin Ruo Jin: Zhong Fei You Hao Guan Xi De Hui Huang Li Cheng (If Concentric Gold: The Glorious History of China-Africa Friendly Relations)*, Beijing: World Affairs Press, pp. 56–72.

Lu, X. 1988. 'Tan Suo Duo Zhong Xing Shi Gong Gu Jing Yuan Cheng Guo' (Exploring Multiple Approach, Strengthening Foreign Aid Effectiveness). *Guo Ji Jing Ji He Zuo (International Economic Cooperation)*, (12), 3–6.

Lum, T., Fischer, H., Gomez-Granger, J. and Leland, A. 2009. *China's Foreign Aid Activities in Africa, Latin America, and Southeast Asia*, Washington: Congressional Research Service.

Luo, J. and Liu, H. 2007. 'Lun Zhong Guo Dui Fei Zhou Yuan Zhu De Jie Duan Xing Yan Bian Ji Yi Yi' (Discussing the Periodical Evolution and Its Meanings of China's Foreign Aid to Africa). *Xi Ya Fei Zhou (West Asia and Africa)*, (11), 25–30.

Malone, A. 2008. 'How China Is Taking over Africa, And Why the West Should Be Very Worried'. *Daily Mail*, July 18.

Manning, R. 2006. 'Will "Emerging Donors" Change the Face of International Cooperation?'. *Development Policy Review*, 24(4), 371–385.

Mao, X. 2012. 'Zhong Guo Dui Wai Yuan Zhu Fang Shi Hui Gu Yu Chuang Xin' (Review and Innovation of China's Foreign Aid Approach). *Guo Ji Jing Ji He Zuo (International Economic Cooperation)*, (3), 89–91.

Marks, S. 2007. 'Introduction'. In Manji, F. and Marks, S. (eds.) *African Perspectives on China in Africa*, Oxford: Fahamu, pp. 1–14.

Marks, S. 2010. *China in Africa: Realism Conquers Myth*, www.pambazuka.net/en/category.php/books/63128 [Accessed: 16 May 2012].

McGreal, C. 2007. 'Chinese Aid to Africa May Do More Harm Than Good, Warns Benn'. *Guardian*, February 8.

Modern Ghana. 2013. *Lekma Hospital Still Losing Focus . . . As Malaria Research Facility Turns Net Distributors*, www.modernghana.com/news/461097/1/lekma-hospital-still-losing-focus.html [Accessed: 8 December 2014].

MOFCOM (ed.). 1995. *Zhong Guo Dui Wai Jing Ji Mao Yi Nian Jian 1994 (Almanac of China's Foreign Economic Relations and Trade 1994)*, Beijing: China Society Press.

MOFCOM. 2003a. *Ke Tuo Nu You Yi Ti Yu Chang Xiu Fu Gong Zuo Yuan Man Wan Cheng (Completion of the Cotonou Friendship Stadium Rehabilitation)*, http://bj.mofcom.gov.cn/aarticle/ddfg/200301/20030100064958.html [Accessed: 11 May 2012].

MOFCOM. 2003b. *Guo Jia Ti Yu Chang Xiu Fu Xiang Mu Jun Gong (Completion of the National Stadium Rehabilitation)*, http://sl.mofcom.gov.cn/sys/print.shtml?/jmjg/law/200304/20030400085526 [Accessed: 10 May 2012].

MOFCOM. 2004. *Yuan Lu Wang Da Shui Ni Chang Yun Ying 20 Nian Cheng Ji Hui Huang (The Achievement of the Rwanda Cement Factory in the Past 20 Years)*, http://rw.mofcom.gov.cn/article/jmxw/200407/20040700250234.shtml [Accessed: 4 April 2012].

MOFCAM. 2006. *China's African Policy Paper*, Beijing: People's Press.

MOFCOM. 2007. *Jia Qinglin Chu Fang Jia Na (Jia Qinglin Visits Ghana)* [Online], http://gh.mofcom.gov.cn/article/zxhz/tzwl/200704/20070404595481.shtml [Accessed: 3 March 2011].

MOFCOM. 2009a. *Wo Yuan Jia Na Zong He Yi Yuan Xiang Mu Shi Gong He Tong Qian Zi Yi Shi Zheng Shi Ju Xing (The Agreement of Foreign Aid Hospital Project)*, http://gh.mofcom.gov.cn/aarticle/slfw/200901/20090105992495.html [Accessed: 28 April 2012].

MOFCOM. 2009b. *Chen De Ming Biao Shi: Zhong Fang Jiang Li Ji Qi Dong Dui Fei 8 Xiang Xin Ju Cuo De Luo Shi Gong Zuo (Chen Deming Promises to Implement the Eight New Measures Immediately)*, www.mofcom.gov.cn/article/ae/ai/200911/20091106608673.shtml [Accessed: 7 August 2012].

MOFCOM. 2010a. *Yuan Ji Ren Min Gong Quan Mian Xiu Fu Xiang Mu She Ji He Tong Zai Ji Qian Shu (The Agreement of the People's Palace Upgrade Program)*, http://dj.mofcom.gov.cn/article/jmxw/201009/20100907168362.shtml [Accessed: 2 June 2012].

MOFCOM. 2010b. *Yuan Wu Gan Da Ti Yu Chang Ti Yu She Bei Wei Xiu Xiang Mu Dui Wai Shi Shi He Tong Qian Shu (The Agreement of Uganda Stadium Rehabilitation)*, http://jjhzj.mofcom.gov.cn/article/ldhd/shaanxi/bx/201002/20100206773485.shtml [Accessed: 10 May 2012].

MOFCOM. 2011. *China's Foreign Aid*, Information Office of the State Council, People's Republic of China, April 2011, Beijing, www.eu-china.net/upload/pdf/nachrichten/2011-04-21Chinas-ForeignAid-WhitePaper.pdf [Accessed: 6 January 2014].

MOFCOM. 2012. *Wo Yuan Gang Guo Jin San Ge Xiang Mu Kao Cha Ji Yao Zai Jin Sha Sa Qian Shu (The Agreement of Three Foreign Aid Projects)*, http://cd.mofcom.gov.cn/article/jmxw/201205/20120508152040.shtml [Accessed: 2 June 2012].

Monson, J. 2009. *Africa's Freedom Railway: How a Chinese Development Project Changed Lives and Livelihoods in Tanzania*, Bloomington: Indiana University Press.

Naim, M. 2007. 'Rogue Aid'. *Foreign Policy*, 159, 95–96.

New Citizen. 2014. 'Over Non-compliance . . . EPA Complains Sierra Fisheries, Others', November 5.

Niu, C. 2011. 'Ji Yu Jiao Yu Yuan Zhu You Xiao Xing Shi Jiao De Zhong Fei Jiao Yu Jiao Liu Yu He Zuo Ping Gu: Ka Mai Long De Ge An' (Evaluation of Sino-Africa Educational Cooperation Based on the Effectiveness of Education Aid: The Case Study of Sino-Cameroonian Cooperation). *Bi Jiao Jiao Yu Yan Jiu (Comparative Education Review)*, (12), 43–47.

Nour, S. M. 2010. 'The Impact of China-Africa Aid Relations: The Case of Sudan'. *Policy Brief*, African Economic Research Consortium.

Paulo, S. and Reisen, H. 2010. 'Eastern Donors and Western Soft Law: Towards A DAC Donor Peer Review of China and India?'. *Development Policy Review*, 28(5), 535–552.

Pehnelt, G. 2007. 'The Political Economy of China's Aid Policy in Africa'. *Jena Economic Research Papers*, (51), 1–18.

Poncet, S. 2012. 'Foreign Aid with Chinese Characteristics'. *Defining the Post-2015 Development Goals*, October 9.

Qi, G. 1995. 'Zai Xin Xing Shi Xia Jin Yi Bu Gai Ge Yuan Wai Gong Zuo' (Further Reform of China's Foreign Aid in New Situation). *Guo Ji Jing Ji He Zuo (International Economic Cooperation)*, (11), 4–5.

Rotberg, R. I. 2008. 'China's Quest for Resources, Opportunities, and Influence in Africa'. In Rotberg, R. I. (ed.) *China into Africa: Trade, Aid, and Influence*, Washington, DC: Brookings Institution Press.

Shi, G. 2000. *Jia Qiang Zhong Fei He Zuo Gong Chuang Mei Hao Wei Lai (To Intensify China-Africa Cooperation for a Brilliant Future – Speech by Minister Shi Guangsheng of MOFTEC in the "Forum on China-Africa Cooperation")*, www.fmprc.gov.cn/eng/wjdt/zyjh/t24974.htm [Accessed: 10 July 2012].

Shi, L. 1989. *Dui Wai Jing Ji He Zuo (Economic Cooperation with Foreign Countries)*, Beijing: China Social Sciences Press.

Shinn, D. H. 2009. 'Comparing Engagement with Africa by China and the United States. China in Africa', Symposium for African Studies Program, East Asian Studies Center and the Center for International Business Education and Research, Bloomington, March 6–7.

Sierra Leone News Hunters. 2012. '7 Villages Disgruntled over Magbass Sugar Project', www.sierraleonenewshunters.com/content/7-villages-disgruntled-over-magbass-sugar-project [Accessed: 8 December 2014].

Sun, L. 2007. 'Cong Guo Jia Li Yi Shi Ye Xia Kan Zhong Guo Jian Guo Yi Lai De Dui Wai Yuan Zhu Zheng Ce' (National Interests and China's Foreign Aid). *Shi Dai Jin Rong (Times Finance)*, (11), 9–10.

Tang, L., Li, X. and Qi, G. 2014. 'Zhong Guo Dui Fei Zhou Nong Ye Yuan Zhu Guan Li Mo Shi De Yan Hua Yu Cheng Xiao' (The Evolution and the Effectiveness of the Management Approach of China's Agricultural Aid to Africa). *Guo Ji Wen Ti Yan Jiu (China International Studies)*, (6), 29–40.

Taylor, I. 2006. *China and Africa: Engagement and Compromise*, London: Routledge.

Taylor, I. 2008. 'Sino-African Relations and the Problem of Human Rights'. *African Affairs*, 107(426), 63–87.

Truth and Reconciliation Commission. 2004. *Witness to Truth: Final Report of the TRC*, Freetown: Truth and Reconciliation Commission.

UN. 1971. *The United Nations General Assembly Session 26 Resolution 2758: Restoration of the Lawful Rights of the People's Republic of China in the United Nations*, www.un.org/ga/search/view_doc.asp?symbol=A/RES/2758(XXVI) [Accessed: 5 November 2010].

Wang, B. N. A. 2010. *Leng Zhan Hou Zhong Fei Zheng Zhi Jing Ji Guan Xi: Zhong Guo Dui Fei Zhou De Xin Xing Can Yu Mo Shi Fen Xi (China-Africa Political and Economic Relations in the 21st Century: An Analysis of China's New Involvement into Africa)*, PhD, Jilin University.

Wang, W. 2014. 'Zhong Guo Dui Wai Yuan Zhu Cheng Tao Xiang Mu Zhong De Fa Lu Guan Xi Tan Xi' (The Legislation Regarding Complete Project Aid). *Fa Zhi Yu She Hui (Legal System and Society)*, (24), 231–232.

Wang, W. and Zhu, H. 2008. 'Jian Xi Gai Ge Kai Fang Yi Lai Zhong Guo De Dui Wai Yuan Zhu' (On China's Aids to Foreign Countries Since the Reform and Opening Up). *Mao Ze Dong Deng Xiao Ping Li Lun Yan Jiu (Studies on Mao Zedong and Deng Xiaoping Theories)*, (8), 45–49.

Woods, N. 2008. 'Whose Aid? Whose Influence? China, Emerging Donors and the Silent Revolution in Development Assistance'. *International Affairs*, 84(6), 1205–1221.

Wu, J. 2008. 'Sui Zhou Zong Li Fang Fei Shang Jian Tan Zan Tie Lu' (With Prime Minister Zhou Negotiating the Construction of the Tanzam Railway). *Bai Nian Chao (Hundred Year Tide)*, (5), 25–29.

Wu, Y. 1994. 'Ji Yu Yu Qian Jing: 90 Nian Dai Zhong Guo Dui Wai Jing Mao Fa Zhan De Ji Ben Gou Xiang' (Opportunities and Prospects: A Framework for Foreign Economic Development Strategy). *Guo Ji Jing Ji He Zuo (International Economic Cooperation)*, (6), 4–8.

Xiao, Z. and Zhang, D. 2002. 'Zhong Guo Wu Shi Duo Nian Lai De Dui Wai Jing Ji Ji Shu Yuan Zhu Ping Xi' (On China's Economical and Technical Assistance to Foreign Countries during 50 Years or More). *Bei Jing Ke Ji Da Xue Xue Bao: She Hui Ke Xue Ban (Journal of University of Science and Technology Beijing: Social Science Edition)*, 18(4), 80–83.

Xinhua. 1956a. 'Zhou En Lai Zong Li Tan Dang Xia De Xing Shi' (Prime Minister Zhou Enlai's Speech on the Current Situation). *People's Daily*, June 29.

Xinhua. 1956b. 'Ji Nian Sun Zhong Shan' (Sun Yat-Sen Memorial). *People's Daily*, November 12.

Xinhua. 1963. 'Mao Zhu Xi Hui Jian Fei Zhou You Ren' (A Conversation between Chairman Mao and African Friends). *People's Daily*, August 9.

Xinhua. 1964. 'Zhou En Lai Zong Li Zai Di San Jie Quan Guo Ren Min Dai Biao Da Hui Yi Ci Hui Yi Shang De Zheng Fu Bao Gao' (Prime Minister Zhou Enlai's Report on the Work of the Government – Delivered at the First Session of the Third National People's Congress). *People's Daily*, December 31.

Xinhua. 1983. 'Zhao Zi Yang Zong Li Chu Fang Fei Zhou Shi Guo' (Prime Minister Zhao Visits Ten Nations in Africa). *People's Daily*, January 15.

Xinhua. 2004. 'Wen Jia Bao Zai Zhong Guo Dui Fa Zhan Zhong Guo Jia Jing Ji Wai Jiao Hui Yi Shang De Jiang Hua' (Wen Speaks at the Conference on China's Economic Diplomacy in Developing Countries). *People's Daily*, September 2.

Xinhua. 2005. 'Hu Jin Tao Zhu Xi Zai Lian He Guo Feng Hui Shang Fa Biao Zhong Yao Jiang Hua' (Chairman Hu Jintao Delivers An Important Speech on the UN Summit). *People's Daily*, September 16.

Xinhua. 2006a. 'Hu Jin Tao Zai Zhong Yang Wai Shi Hui Yi Shang Fa Biao Zhong Yao Jiang Hua' (Hu Jintao Speaks at Central Meeting on Foreign Affairs Work). *People's Daily*, August 23.

Xinhua. 2006b. 'Kai Qi Zhong Fei Guan Xi De Xin Pian Zhang' (The New Beginning of China-African Relationship). *People's Daily*, November 17.

Xinhua. 2008. 'Wen Jia Bao Zai Lian He Guo Qian Nian Fa Zhan Mu Biao Gao Ji Bie Hui Yi Shang De Jiang Hua' (Wen Speaks at the UN High-Level Meeting on the Millennium Development Goals). *People's Daily*, September 26.

Xinhua. 2009. 'Hu Jin Tao Can Jia Ba Ma Ke Di San Da Qiao Kai Gong Yi Shi' (Hu Jintao Attends the Groundbreaking Ceremony for the Bamako No. 3 Bridge). *People's Daily*, February 14.

Xinhua. 2010. 'Quan Guo Yuan Wai Gong Zuo Hui Yi Zai Jing Zhao Kai, Wen Jia Bao Zuo Zhong Yao Jiang Hua' (National Conference on Foreign Aid Convened in Beijing, Wen Delivers an Important Speech). *People's Daily*, August 15.

Xinhua. 2011. 'Yuan Fei Shi Wei Le Zi Yuan? Yi Pai Hu Yan!' (China's Aid to Africa for Friendship, Not Resources: MOFCOM). *People's Daily*, April 26.

Xue, H. 2011. 'Dui Wai Yuan Zhu: Ji Dai Ling Dao Ren De Zhan Lue Jue Ce' (Foreign Aid: The Decisions of Many Leaders). *Shi Jie Zhi Shi (World Affairs)*, (13), 14–16.

Xue, L. 2013a. 'Dui Gai Ge Kai Fang Qian Zhong Guo Yuan Zhu Fei Zhou De Zhan Lue Fan Si' (Rethinking China's Strategy of Foreign Aid to Africa before the Reform). *Dang Dai Shi Jie She Hui Zhu Yi Wen Ti (Issues of Contemporary World Socialism)*, (1), 103–115.

Xue, Q. 2013b. *Mao Ze Dong "Nan Fang Jue Ce" (Mao Tes-tung Southern Decision)*, Beijing: Sino-culture Press.

Yan, H. and Sautman, B. 2013. '"The Beginning of a World Empire"? Contesting the Discourse of Chinese Copper Mining in Zambia'. *Modern China*, 39(2), 131–164.

Yan, X. 1987. 'Jin Yi Bu Fa Zhan Zhong Guo Fei Zhou You Hao Guan Xi' (Improving the Friendship Relations between China and Africa). *Shi Jie Jing Ji Yu Zheng Zhi (World Economics and Politics)*, (9), 52–56.

Yang, H. and Chen, K. 2010. 'Zhong Guo Dui Wai Yuan Zhu: Cheng Jiu, Jiao Xun He Liang Xing Fa Zhan' (China's Foreign Aid: Achievements, Lessons and Benign Development). *Guo Ji Zhan Wang (World Outlook)*, (1), 46–56.

Youde, J. 2010. 'China's Health Diplomacy in Africa'. *China: An International Journal*, 8(1), 151–163.

Yu, D. and Yuan, L. 2010. 'Wo Guo Ti Yu Dui Wai Yuan Zhu De Li Shi Hui Gu' (A Review on China's Sports Foreign Aid History). *Bei Jing Ti Yu Da Xue Xue Bao (Journal of Beijing Soprt Univeristy)*, 33(8), 39–45.

Yu, G. T. 1971. 'Working on the Railroad: China and the Tanzania-Zambia Railway'. *Asian Survey*, 11(11), 1101–1117.

Yu, G. 1978. 'China's Impact'. *Problems of Communism*, 27, 40–50.

Yu, G. 1991. 'Chinese Foreign Policy Since Tiananmen: The Search for Friends and Influence'. In Lee, T. (ed.) *China and World Political Development and International Issues*, Taipei: Cheng Chung Book Company, pp. 83–98.

Yuan, X. and Yang, Y. 2003. 'Zhong Guo Wai Yuan: Zheng Fu Zai Wai Yuan Zhong De Jiao Se Bian Huan' (China's Foreign Aid: The Character Changes of Government in Delivering Foreign Aid). In Xiao, J. and Tang, X. (eds.) *Da Guo Wai Jiao: Li Lun, Jue Ce, Tiao Zhan (Diplomacy of the Great Powers: Theory, Decision-making and Challenge)*, Beijing: Current Affairs Press, pp. 25–39.

Zhang, H. 2006. 'Zhong Guo Dui Fei Yuan Zhu Zheng Ce De Yan Ge Ji Qi Zai Zhong Fei Guan Xi Zhong De Zuo Yong' (History of China's Aid Policies and Its Role in Sino-Africa Relations). *Ya Fei Zong Heng (Asia and Africa Review)*, (4), 44–49.

Zhang, M. 2009. *Zhong Guo Dui Wai Jing Ji Ji Shu Yuan Zhu Tiao Zheng Yu Gai Ge Lun Shu (Research on the Adjustments of China's Foreign Aid)*, www.hprc.org.cn/gsyj/yjjg/

zggsyjxh_1/gsnhlw_1/baguoshixslwj/201110/t20111018_162332.html [Accessed: 6 July 2012].

Zhang, Q. 2001. 'Dui Zhong Duo Bu Tong Guo Jia De Yi Ge Xiang Tong Zheng Ce – Qian Xi Zhong Guo Dui Fa Zhan Zhong Guo Jia De Zheng Ce' (A Common Policy towards Unalike Countries – A Preliminary Analysis of China's Policy towards Developing Countries). *Dang Dai Zhong Guo Shi Yan Jiu (Contemporary China History Studies)*, (1), 36–46.

Zhang, Q. 2010. 'Cong "Guo Ji Zhu Yi" Dao "Ping Deng Hu Li" Zhong Guo Dui Wai Yuan Zhu Zheng Ce De Yan Bian' (From Internationalism to Mutual Benefit: The Evolution of China's Foreign Aid Policy). *Zu Guo (Motherland)*, (9), 24–25.

Zhang, S., Pu, J., Zhao, Y., Yao, G., Yang, M., Xie, J. and Li, D. 2013. 'Wo Guo Dui Wai Yi Liao Yuan Zhu 50 Nian Hui Gu Yu Si Kao' (A Review of the 50 Years of China's Medicine and Public Health Aid). *Ren Min Jun Yi (People's Military Surgeon)*, (12), 1458–1459.

Zhang, X. 2006c. 'Zan Bi Ya Jing Ji Yu Tan Zan Tie Lu Wei Lai De Fa Zhan' (Zambian Economy and the Tanzam Railway). *Guo Ji Jing Ji He Zuo (International Economic Cooperation)*, (3). 63–65.

Zhang, Y. 2011. '"Yi Bian Dao" De Wai Jiao Zhan Lue Yu Zhong Guo Dui Wai Yuan Zhu' (China's "One-Sided" Diplomatic Strategy and Its Foreign Aid). *Guo Ji Guan Xi Xue Yuan Xue Bao (Journal of University of International Relations)*, (3), 18–24.

Zhang, Y. 2012b. *Zhong Guo Dui Wai Yuan Zhu Yan Jiu 1950–2010 (Research of China Foreign Aid 1950–2010)*, Beijing: Jiuzhou Press.

Zhang, Y. and Qin, W. 2012. 'Lun Zhong Guo Zheng Fu Dui Wai Yuan Zhu Li Nian Zhong De Chuan Tong Wen Hua Yin Su' (An Analysis of Foreign Aid by the Chinese Government in the Concept of Traditional Cultural Factors). *Yun Cheng Xue Yuan Xue Bao (Journal of Yuncheng University)*, (3), 55–58.

Zhao, C. and Xue, Y. 2010. 'Xin Xing Shi Xia Zhong Guo Dui Fei Yuan Zhu Tan Xi' (Exploring China's Foreign Aid in the New Situation). *She Hui Zhu Yi Yan Jiu (Socialism Studies)*, (1), 139–143.

Zhao, Z. 1986. 'Zheng Fu Gong Zuo Bao Gao 1984 Nian' (Government Report 1984). In CCCPC Party Literature Research Office (ed.) *Shi Er Da Yi Lai Zhong Yao Wen Xian Xuan Bian (Important File Selection Since the Twelfth CPC Central Committee)*, Beijing: People's Press, pp. 27–41.

Zheng, K. 2000. 'Ba Shi Nian Dai Chu Qi Zhong Guo Dui Fei Zhou Zheng Ce De Tiao Zheng' (The Adjustment of China's African Policy in the Early 80s). In Lu, T. and Ma, R. (eds.) *Zhong Guo Yu Fei Zhou (China and Africa)*, Beijing: Beijing University Press, pp. 63–79.

Zhou, H. 2008a. 'Zhong Guo Dui Wai Yuan Zhu Yu Gai Ge Kai Fang 30 Nian' (China's Foreign Aid and 30 Years of Reform). *Shi Jie Jing Ji Yu Zheng Zhi (World Economics and Politics)*, (11), 33–43.

Zhou, H. 2008b. 'Zhong Guo Xin De Dui Wai Yuan Zhu' (China's New Foreign Aid). In Wang, Y. (ed.) *Zhong Guo Dui Wai Guan Xi Zhuan Xing 30 Nian, 1978–2008 (Transformation of Foreign Affairs and International Relations in China, 1978–2008)*, Beijing: Social Sciences Academic Press, pp. 17–31

Zhou, X. 2007. 'Wo Kan Zhong Su Guan Xi Jin 40 Nian Bian Qian' (40 Years of Sino-Soviet Relationship). *Bai Nian Chao (Hundred Year Tide)*, (12), 12–18.

Zou, C. 1995. 'Wo Guo Jiang Jin Yi Bu Gai Ge Yuan Wai Gong Zuo' (Further Reforming Our Foreign Aid). *People's Daily*, October 18.

Index